PUGIN-LAND

A.W.N. Pugin, Lord Shrewsbury and the Gothic Revival in Staffordshire

Aton Castle c1860, lithograph by Newman & Co., London (Staffordshire County Record Office)

PUGIN-LAND

A.W.N. Pugin, Lord Shrewsbury, and the Gothic Revival in Staffordshire

A.W.N. Pugin, 1812-1852
drawn from recollection by Joseph Nash
(Benjamin Ferrey, *Recollections of A.N. Welby Pugin,* 1861)

MICHAEL FISHER

with Foreword by
ALEXANDRA WEDGWOOD

MICHAEL J. FISHER (PUBLISHING) 2002

To Liam,
and the rising generations who have yet to visit
Pugin-Land

Printed in Great Britain by Counter Print,
3, Tipping Street, Stafford, Staffordshire ST16 2LL

Published by M.J. Fisher
35, Newland Avenue, Stafford, Staffordshire ST16 1NL

British Library Cataloguing in Publication Data
A Catalogue record for this book is available
from the British Library

ISBN 0 9526855 3 1

CONTENTS

Photography by the author, except where indicated otherwise.

List of colour plates (between pages 91 and 92)

List of diagrams, maps and plans

Cover Illustrations

Front: S. Giles' Church, Cheadle; the Chapel of the Blessed Sacrament.

Back: East view of Alton Castle.
Pugin/Warrington glass in the Armoury, Alton Towers.

FOREWORD

'Pugin-Land' was Prof. Sir Nikolaus Pevsner's phrase to describe an area of North Staffordshire which is centred on Cheadle and Alton. He also said: 'Nowhere can one study and understand Pugin better than in Staffordshire - not only his forms and features but his mind, and not only his churches but his secular architecture as well. That his churches and patrons were Catholic needs no saying.' So Pugin-Land is also a Catholic land, and a place in which to ponder the differences between Catholics and Protestants and the whole character of the Gothic Revival in England. A local newspaper correspondent commented on the opening ceremonies of St. Giles' Church, Cheadle, in the late summer of 1846: 'We can scarcely imagine anything more calculated to make men forget that they are living in a Protestant country than the scene and circumstances now presented....... here was enough sight and sound to affect the dullest imagination, and make one almost fancy it as a vision of past ages.' The essential figure to make possible Pugin's vision was John Talbot, 16 h Earl of Shrewsbury, who was prepared to put some of his great wealth into the creation of this Catholic and Gothic Revival. The story of his friendship with Pugin has always been very one-sided, in large part because the Earl kept most of the letters that Pugin wrote to him, whereas few of his to Pugin have survived. The picture emerges of an attractive, gentle and scholarly aristocrat who took his position as the leading Catholic layman of his day very seriously. The end of the Catholic branch of the Shrewsburys led to the impoverishment of church projects in North Staffordshire, but the attraction of the Gothic Revival did not die. The style was taken up in the Anglican church, eventually turning into the Arts and Crafts movement, and had a remarkable late flowering in this locality.

Michael Fisher guides his readers through this complicated story with an expert hand. He has indeed the perfect qualifications for doing so, being both a historian with local and ecclesiological interests and an Anglican priest. He is already the author of an innovative book, *Alton Towers, a Gothic Wonderland*, 1999, and here he sets the magnificent seat of the Shrewsburys into its rich background. His detailed knowledge of medieval church fittings demonstrates why the simple little building of St. Mary's Catholic Church, Uttoxeter, was in reality such a revolutionary one, the first to display 'the true thing', which Pugin was to elaborate to such good effect in St. John's Alton, St. Mary's Brewood, St. Wilfrid's Cotton and above all in the splendid St. Giles' Cheadle. As well as Pugin and Lord Shrewsbury, the leading protagonists, Michael Fisher also describes the fascinating lesser characters who move in and out of the story. His wide reading has worked out all the connecting links, both personal and religious, between the people he introduces, such as the university connections between F.W.Faber and Michael Watts Russell, and he shows this with great skill. Nor does he forget to mention the local craftsmen, the Baileys and John Bunn Denny of Alton and Thomas Roddis and Thomas Harris of Cheadle. This would please 'the Good Earl John', who was always concerned that his charitable works should benefit his own estate workers. The illustrations are the result of much imagination and research, and it is very good to see published for the first time Samuel Rayner's drawings of Alton Towers, c. 1840, especially the one with Edward Jervis, the blind Welsh harper at the entrance door.

Michael Fisher's enthusiasm and knowledge illuminates this episode, which was dealt a heavy blow one hundred and fifty years ago with the premature deaths in the autumn of 1852 of both the Earl and his architect. Since then, though many of their architectural ideals lived on until the end of the nineteenth century, as is shown in this book, there have been long periods when their achievements were neglected or, worse, scorned and destroyed. The end of the twentieth century and the beginning of the twenty-first century, however, have shown a major revival of interest in the ideas, forms and colours of the Gothic Revival - Pugin's 'true principles' - and the architecture and decoration of Alton Towers and St. Giles' Church, Cheadle, are now widely known and appreciated.

There are many reasons to see the beauties of North Staffordshire, but this book will add significantly to the pleasure and understanding of a visit. I strongly recommend it.

Alexandra Wedgwood

March 2002

AUTHOR'S PREFACE

This book has been published to mark the 150th anniversary of the deaths of A.W.N. Pugin and his patron, John Talbot, sixteenth Earl of Shrewsbury, whose contributions to the Gothic Revival figure so prominently and uniquely in the North Staffordshire landscape that the year 2002 almost demands some special tribute to their vision and to their achievements. It has been written from a perspective that is both local and personal. I have lived in the area for most of my life, and the seeds of my affection for Pugin's work were sown in childhood days. My family then lived in Leek, and steam-trains still ran along the Churnet Valley Line, the opening of which in 1849 was greeted by Pugin with great enthusiasm. Summer excursions with the family included visits to Alton, to the Towers, and the delightful Dimmingsdale. Setting foot for the first time in the precincts of Alton Castle was like crossing the threshold of another world: the castle on the edge of a cliff, the coloured tiles of the chapel roof shimmering in the sunlight; S. John's church with its glorious altar and screen; the sixteenth earl's coronet and hatchment still hanging above his memorial, and the statue of S. Joseph where we lit our votive candles. That atmosphere of other-worldliness has never departed. To enter the precincts of S. John's is to enter the minds of Pugin and his noble patron, and the eternal concepts of beauty and truth which they wished to set at the very heart of this village community, accessible to all. As T.S.Eliot wrote of another place,

> ...... Here, the intersection of the timeless moment
> Is England and nowhere. Never and always" *(Little Gidding)*

In those childhood days I knew nothing of Pugin - he was a discovery made during my time as a history undergraduate at Leicester University, when I had the chance to see one of the early fruits of the Pugin-Shrewsbury partnership, Mount Saint Bernard Abbey, and Grace Dieu, the former home of Ambrose Phillipps de Lisle. My principal interest was medieval England, but I also chose the Victorian age as a special study, which is how I encountered Pugin and Newman and others who shaped the nineteenth-century Catholic and Gothic Revivals: an intoxicating mixture.

Returning to Staffordshire, I became re-acquainted with Pugin's buildings at Alton, seeing them now with a better-informed eye; and eventually the opportunities to research and publish came my way, one of which was a commission from Alton Towers in 1998 to carry out a survey of the Towers buildings. Thus I have been brought into ever closer contact with the mind of Pugin through the buildings which I have known since childhood. This has meant delving into theology as well as architectural history; and although I have remained an Anglican, my beliefs and outlook have been shaped by some of the same forces that worked so powerfully upon Pugin: a love of Gothic architecture and an appreciation of the old English Liturgy for which our medieval churches were built. I therefore venture to call myself a "full-faith" Catholic, for despite the woes that the Church of England has heaped upon itself in recent decades, I believe that there survives within it a tradition of English Catholicism continuous with the Church of S. Augustine and S. Chad. It is of course quite possible to view Pugin's buildings purely as works of art, and from no particular religious standpoint, just as it is possible for an agnostic to enjoy listening to Gregorian chant. To understand the reasons why Pugin - and those who followed him - built and decorated as they did, it is nevertheless important to be aware of the concepts which he sought to express. Whether one happens to agree with them or not is entirely another matter. I have therefore explored the theological significance of these buildings and their contents, and I have also supplied a glossary of ecclesiastical terms, many of which were unfamiliar in Pugin's own day - even to churchmen.

I have received much valuable assistance and advice in the course of my research and the preparation of this book, and I would like to record by thanks to all who have helped me. The clergy of the various churches have allowed me free access to the buildings and to archives and other items in their custody: Fr. David Oakley (S. Giles', Cheadle, and S. Wilfrid, Cotton), Fr. Fred Sheldon (S. Mary's, Uttoxeter and S. John's, Alton), Fr. Michael White (Alton Castle), Fr. David Standen (S. Mary's, Brewood); also Fr. Brian Doolan and the Revd. Dr. John Sharp of S. Chad's Cathedral, Birmingham, Dom Laurence O'Keeffe, OSB, (S. Augustine's, Ramsgate). I am grateful to the Squire de Lisle for answering my queries about Pugin and Ambrose Phillipps, and for providing me with a copy of the relevant section of Abbé Vandrival's Journal. Pugin kept up a voluminous correspondence, but he did not, alas, keep very many of the letters he received once they had been acted upon. A good deal has therefore to be deduced from Pugin's own letters held in various collections. Much of what is known about the relationship between Pugin and Lord Shrewsbury is contained in the private Franklin collection, copies of which are in the House of Lords Record Office. I am most grateful to Mr David Franklin for permission to quote extensively from these letters, and to reproduce extracts from them. I thank Mr M.R. Darley and Mr. B. Astbury, Headmaster and Bursar of Stafford Grammar School (Burton Manor) for answering my queries and allowing me free access to Burton Manor and to relevant archive material; also Michael Hadcroft, Librarian at Oscott College. My selection of illustrative material has been helped by Paul Atterbury who has kindly loaned me photographs taken in 1994 for the Pugin Exhibition at the V & A and its associated publications, and also by Mr. R. Lewis of Stafford. The support and encouragement of other Pugin enthusiasts is also greatly appreciated, particularly that of Dr. Margaret Belcher, Dr. Rory O'Donnell, Brian Andrews, John Scott and James Joll. The staff of Counter Print have undertaken the actual production of the book with characteristic efficiency attention to detail, and interest in the subject-matter. My wife, Isobel, has accompanied me on very many site-visits and helped with the selection of illustrative material, and shown remarkable patience during the long periods when I have been completely absorbed, physically and mentally, in "Pugin-Land".

In the preparation of the text I have benefited from the critical eye of Max Roden, who has read and corrected the proofs and suggested amendments where necessary. As a member of S. Chad's, Stafford, he is well-aware of his parish priest's "Gothic Passion", but then we have a splendid Rood and a superb Gothic altarpiece which would make Pugin turn somersaults. Yet both date from the early twentieth century - the reredos by Walter Tapper (1861-1935) and the Rood by Charles Nicholson (1867-1949) - an indication of the powerful influence of Pugin on much later generations of church architects and designers.

Finally I wish to express my sincere gratitude to Lady Wedgwood, that most eminent of all Pugin scholars, for so kindly consenting to write the Foreword to this book, for her valued encouragement of this project as it has taken shape, and for her enthusiastic support of the current programmes of restoration in the buildings at Alton of which Pugin once wrote, "I am nowhere so happy".

Michael Fisher
Easter 2002

1 THE LANDSCAPE

"Cheadle is *Pugin-land'* declared Sir Nikolaus Pevsner by way of introduction to the North Staffordshire market-town dominated by the 200-foot spire of Pugin's S. Giles'[1]. This magnificent church is but one of a cluster of buildings in Cheadle designed by A.W.N. Pugin between 1841 and 1848; there is also the presbytery, the school, and the convent of S. Joseph, but that is not all. "Pugin-land" extends well beyond the confines of Cheadle into the surrounding countryside with its deep wooded valleys and secluded villages. Four miles away is the village of Cotton, where Pugin's church and adjacent College of S. Wilfrid are to be found. A mile or so further along the Farley road, Alton Towers appears on the horizon; that great Gothic mansion to which Pugin made significant alterations and additions throughout most of his working life. On the opposite side of the Churnet valley is the most dramatic of all of Pugin's domestic buildings: Alton Castle perched on the edge of a rocky precipice like some Rhineland *schloss,* and, behind the castle, the church and hospital of S. John which, along with S. Giles', Pugin considered to be the only buildings on which he could look with complete satisfaction. The nearby town of Uttoxeter is the place where Pugin's career as practising architect can be said seriously to have begun with the building of the little church of S. Marie, Balance Street, in 1838; a keynote building which Pugin himself described as the first true revival of its kind in England. Add to this list three or four houses and lodges in and around Alton which Pugin built or enlarged, and we have a total of thirteen buildings, both ecclesiastical and domestic, all situated within a few square miles of north-east Staffordshire, and including those which he himself considered to be his most successful. This is Pugin-Land indeed; and one can think of no other area of comparable size in which the full range of Pugin's work as an architect, designer, and Gothic propagandist can be so readily studied and appreciated. Nor can one think of a more naturally beautiful part of the country as a setting for these fine buildings. This often comes as a surprise to those who are unfamiliar with North Staffordshire, and who imagine the area to be overwhelmingly industrial. Yet it was the dramatic landscape of deep valleys, sandstone cliffs and dense woodlands which attracted the fifteenth earl of Shrewsbury (d.1827) to enlarge Alton Lodge into what soon became the family's principal home. It delighted Pugin too. He firmly believed that buildings should appear to "grow" from the sites in which they were placed, and he did not miss an opportunity to apply this principle to the Romantic environment of the Churnet Valley.

Augustus Welby Northmore Pugin (1812-1852) is best-remembered as the creator of the majestic interiors of the New Palace of Westminster. This commission included carved woodwork, stained glass, tiles, wallcoverings, chairs and benches, light-fittings, inkstands, door-handles and key-plates, in which he revealed his multi-faceted genius as a Gothic designer. Apart from this, he was the architect of over a hundred buildings including cathedrals and other major churches, the author of eight influential books on Gothic architecture and design, Professor of Ecclesiastical Art at Oscott College, the designer of a wide range of ceramics, jewellery, textile fabrics and stained glass, a collector of medieval antiquities, and the co-founder of a Birmingham metalworking firm. In addition, Pugin found time for three marriages and eight children, plus one or two unsuccessful courtships, a voluminous correspondence with friends, clients and patrons, and also to operate a one-man lifeboat service off the coast of Kent. When his doctors told him that he had tried to pack a hundred years into twoscore, it was an understatement, for most of Pugin's major work was carried out between 1836 and 1850.

1. A.W.N. Pugin allegorically presenting Lord Shrewsbury with a copy of his work. Illuminated letter from the dedication page of An Apology for the Revival of Christian Architecture in England, 1843.

Given Pugin's acknowledged status as the leading exponent of the Gothic Revival, and the one whose influence held sway long after his death, it has to be asked why some of the very best of his work is concentrated in a relatively small and remote area of North Staffordshire rather than in some major town or city. The answer lies in the enthusiastic support and financial backing which Pugin received from John Talbot (1791-1852) sixteenth Earl of Shrewsbury, whose principal seat, Alton Towers, lay close to Cheadle. Without Lord Shrewsbury's patronage, many of Pugin's ideas would have remained on paper or would have been considerably reduced, as indeed was the case in other parts of the country where he was not so fortunate. The scale of the building activities which took place on and around the Shrewsbury estates at Alton has been likened to that of King Ludwig II of Bavaria (1864-1886), for all of the thirteen buildings mentioned above were erected within the space of fourteen years (1838-52). There was, in fact, a link between the Talbots and the Bavarian royal family. In 1834 Ludwig I (1825-1848) elevated the earl's elder daughter, Mary, to the rank of Princess; but that was thirty years before the accession of his castle-building grandson[2]. The aims were in any case very different. Whereas Ludwig II built to glorify himself and the Wittelsbach dynasty, Pugin and Lord Shrewsbury sought to restore the former glories of Catholic England in the wake of the 1829 Catholic Emancipation Act.

The impact of these buildings upon the landscape was dramatic enough, and with them came sights and sounds which had not been seen or heard in the area since the sixteenth century: outdoor processions; priests, monks and nuns in full habit, and the sound of the Angelus ringing out across town and countryside from the new towers and bell-cotes, and from the great bell of the Towers chapel itself, morning, noon and evening. Meanwhile the ceaseless activity on and around the various sites, in the quarries and associated workshops, provided work for large numbers of men who might otherwise have been unemployed during the "hungry forties" when industrial unrest and Chartist agitation manifested themselves in North Staffordshire as in other parts of the country.

"Pugin-land" has its outposts, notably S. Mary's church at Brewood on the Staffordshire-Shropshire border, but here too Lord Shrewsbury had an input; and, nearer to Cheadle, the plain little chapel of S. Anne in Stone. Then there are a number of minor works such as Pugin's additions and alterations to the Benedictine convent at Caverswall Castle, to the Cresswell Mission, and to the second church of S. Austin in Stafford. Pugin's rare Anglican commissions are exemplified locally by his restoration of the chancel at Blithfield, and the Masfen memorial window at S. Mary's, Stafford. The restoration of S. Mary's, Stafford, by George Gilbert Scott (1842-44) took place while Pugin was working on S. Giles', Cheadle, and it is the outstanding example of Pugin's early influence upon a key Anglican architect. This influence reached its apogee after Pugin's death with G.F.Bodley's Church of the Holy Angels at Hoar Cross (1876) which ranked second only to S. Giles' in a recent listing of England's thousand best churches[3]. Not only does Staffordshire have the best of Pugin, it has also some of the best work of celebrated architects who were inspired by him. County boundaries may be arbitrary, nor do they circumscribe architectural taste. It is nevertheless true that Staffordshire was the home of several important landed families who were drawn into the Gothic Revival and who were willing to employ the best architects and designers to build churches for them.

Pugin's first recorded visit to Staffordshire took place in the autumn of 1833, when he visited Lichfield as part of an extensive architectural tour of the West Country and the Midlands "in search of the picturesque and beautiful"[4]. His stay in Lichfield was memorable for two reasons. First of all he arrived at his lodgings late at night, and in the dark he crept unwittingly into the wrong bedroom. Aware of the presence of something soft and warm in the bed, he found it to be "the thigh of a female occupant already turned in". There were loud screams and shouts, chambermaids came rushing in with lighted candles, and Pugin had some difficulty in persuading all concerned that it had been a genuine mistake[5]. He was in for another unpleasant surprise when he visited Lichfield cathedral on the following day. He found that the fabric of the building had been mutilated by "the Wretch" James Wyatt, while he described the town itself as "a dull place - without anything remarkable".

By the time of Pugin's next visit to Staffordshire four years later, some significant developments had taken place in his life and work. In 1835 he became a Roman Catholic, and from that moment onwards his whole career was directed towards the advancement of the Catholic cause. In 1836 he published his seminal book, *Contrasts,* which established his reputation and also marked a turning-point in the Gothic Revival. It was Pugin who invested the Gothic Revival with the high moral and theological dimensions that it had previously lacked: Gothic architecture was primarily *Christian* architecture[6]. It was through *Contrasts* that Pugin first encountered Dr. Rock, domestic chaplain to the Earl of Shrewsbury, and it may have been through Dr Rock that Pugin was first introduced to the Earl himself[7].

In August 1837 Pugin made a three-day visit to Staffordshire in the company of Dr. Henry Weedall, the President of Oscott College where Pugin had already begun to make significant alterations and additions. They took in some notable Catholic sites, and no doubt Pugin was introduced at this stage to members of local Catholic families who later gave him commissions. They visited Stafford, where the Jerningham family had begun to rebuild the medieval castle, and they saw the new Catholic church of S. Austin built by the

2.Reliquary of S. Chad; High Altar, S. Chad's cathedral, Birmingham.

Jerninghams between 1818 and 1819[8]. Pugin would no doubt have been told of William Howard, Viscount Stafford, who had suffered martyrdom in 1680[9]. They went on to Caverswall, a seventeenth-century house built into a thirteenth-century castle, and the home of a community of Benedictine nuns who had escaped from Ghent during the French Revolution. Finally, Pugin and Weedall visited Aston Hall, on the outskirts of Stone, where a Catholic Mission had been established. An exciting discovery was made around this time by the Revd. Benjamin Hulme, the chaplain at Aston, namely the relics of S. Chad of Lichfield which had been brought there in the 1790s by a member of the Fitzherbert family and then temporarily forgotten[10]. Pugin designed a splendid reliquary for them **(2)**, and this was enshrined above the High Altar of S. Chad's cathedral in Birmingham at its opening in June 1841.

After going on to Lancashire where he was carrying out work at Scarisbrick Hall, Pugin returned to Staffordshire at the end of August 1837 when he stayed briefly at Wolseley Hall, between Stafford and Rugeley, the home of Sir Charles Wolseley who was also a recent convert to Catholicism. His conversion had been brought about by their mutual friend, Ambrose Phillipps. Pugin also revisited Lichfield where Joseph Potter - a pupil of "the Wretch" Wyatt, and the current architect at Oscott - built the Catholic Church of Holy Cross, to which Pugin added a screen and other furnishings in 1841. Finally, on August 31st, he arrived for the first time at Alton Towers, where he stayed as a guest of Lord Shrewsbury for the next four days.

Pugin's subsequent visits to Alton Towers were frequent, and they sometimes extended over a week or two. This was especially true while the buildings at Cheadle and Alton were in progress, but it was a convenient base from which to visit a growing number of other commissions in the north of England, while being not a great distance away from Birmingham and Oscott. The railway network did not reach Uttoxeter and Alton until 1849, so before then Pugin would have had to travel by road for the fifteen miles or so between Alton and the nearest main-line stations at Stoke and Derby. Quite clearly he loved the area: "I look forward with delight to get into such a haven", he wrote to Lord Shrewsbury, announcing an impending visit in July 1843[11].

Staffordshire was well-endowed with a variety of suitable building-stones which Pugin and other architects were able to use to great advantage, notably the sandstones and gritstones of the Moorlands. To the south-east, near Tutbury, alabaster was being mined only to be crushed to make plaster, until Pugin pioneered the revival of carving in this fine material for altars and statues. A revival of another kind took place in Stoke-on-Trent where the pottery manufacturer Herbert Minton (1793-1858) began to produce encaustic and printed tiles to Pugin's designs, followed by tableware and decorative ceramics also designed by Pugin. This alone would give Staffordshire a prominent place in the history of the Gothic Revival, since these items found their way into churches, public buildings and private homes all over the country, and abroad too. Likewise the products of North Staffordshire's other great industry, textiles, in the shape of the fabulous silk embroideries worked in Leek in the 1880s and 1890s, fulfilled Pugin's earlier aspiration to see another great medieval craft revived in the service of the Church.

The association with Minton was particularly important to Pugin. He believed that, after stained glass, encaustic tiles were amongst the most important forms of decorative art, and there were some significant medieval survivals, for example at Winchester Cathedral and Westminster Abbey. The recovery of this lost art was an important part of the Gothic Revival, and Pugin and Minton were not the only designers and manufacturers who attempted it. Nevertheless, their partnership was the most successful and productive, and this stemmed partly from the personal friendship which developed between them, and also from Minton's own determination to succeed in perfecting the production methods and also extend the range of what was possible using modern methods. Pugin was himself driven by technology, believing that once a design had been worked out in accordance with ancient authorities, there was no reason why the actual production should not be carried out with the aid of machinery.

The process of encaustic tile production involved pouring liquid clay, or "slip" of a contrasting colour into indented patterns on a prepared base tile. Samuel Wright (1783-1849) of Shelton, Stoke-on-Trent, had developed a process in the 1830s and Minton used the process under licence. A recently-discovered letter shows that Pugin was in contact with Minton in the summer of 1840 in connection with the production of tiles for the Convent of Mercy at Handsworth[12]. This pre-dates what is generally believed to have been Minton's first commission for an encaustic pavement, at the Temple Church in London (1841). The floors of the Hospital of S. John at Alton (3) were also early (1841), which makes the removal of the bulk of these tiles in the 1960's all the more regrettable. The Talbot inconography on the surviving ones is identical to that at Handsworth. From 1841 onwards Pugin travelled frequently to Stoke in connection with his work for Lord Shrewsbury, and the Minton Museum holds a large number of watercolour designs - some

3. Early Minton Tiles: S. John's, Alton.

signed by Pugin - for tablewares, door-plates and majolica ware, as well as encaustic tiles. The most important commission of all was for the encaustic pavements of the New Palace of Westminster. A set of full-colour patterns for these, made up from Pugin's original drawings,

4. Croxden Abbey.

survives at the Tunstall factory of H & R Johnson where the production of Minton-Hollins tiles continues.

Pugin was adept at observing and sketching medieval buildings, and details of them, which he could later use as "authorities" when it came to designing his own buildings. Surviving collections of his drawings include very few of Staffordshire, but there was a good deal to attract his interest, and it is known from other sources that he visited medieval sites on and around the Shrewsbury estates. The most obvious of these is Alton Castle, although in the rebuilding of it Pugin and the earl made little attempt to replicate what was known to have been there prior to 1840. Not far away were the ruins of the twelfth-century Cistercian abbey of Croxden **(4)**, founded by one of Lord Shrewsbury's ancestors. Certain features of Croxden - including the south transept and west front - were utilised by Pugin in his design for S. Barnabas' cathedral in Nottingham (1841-44) which was partly financed by Lord Shrewsbury, so Pugin must have made sketches of these. The earl himself greatly influenced the design of S. Barnabas', and said that he envisaged it as a revival of Croxden[13]. In contrast to most of Pugin's other buildings, Nottingham is therefore in the First Pointed or "lancet" style. It is cruciform in plan, has a large retro-choir furnished with three chapels, and as originally built it had an enclosed choir and presbytery; i.e. it is basically monastic in concept.

A few miles east of Alton, and just inside Derbyshire, is the fine medieval church of S. Barlok at Norbury, the ancestral home of the Fitzherbert family who were noted for their adherence to the Catholic Faith, at great personal cost, during the Penal Years[14]. The chancel retains its full complement of medieval glass, which would have delighted Pugin, as would the alabaster monuments to the Fitzherberts. He arranged for a plaster replica of one of these to be made for Alton Towers[15]. Pugin also visited some medieval sites near the Shrewsbury estates on the Staffordshire-Shropshire border, including the church at Albrighton where he noted the alabaster tomb of Sir John Talbot; and he was particularly moved by the ruins of White Ladies Priory[16]. The survival of Catholicism in these areas was remarkable. To see the old hiding-places and secret chapels at Boscobel House and Moseley Hall brings home the totalitarian nature of the governments of the sixteenth and seventeenth centuries, and the fortitude of those who suffered. It also helps to account for the triumphalism and euphoria which accompanied Catholic Emancipation in 1829. The work of Pugin, Lord Shrewsbury and Ambrose Phillipps needs to be viewed against that landscape; buildings of what Newman called the Second Spring of English Catholicism.

Yet the signs of Spring were there before 1829, for example in the Relief Act of 1791, and in the widespread sympathy felt for those who sought refuge in England from anti-Catholic persecution during the French Revolution. Under the 1791 legislation Catholics were allowed to worship openly, and, subject to certain conditions, Catholic chapels could be built. Significantly, perhaps, they had to be called chapels rather than churches, no crosses or other obvious iconography were to be placed on the outsides of such buildings, and worshippers would cling to old habits such as talking euphemistically about going to "Prayers" rather than to "Mass"[17]. Old prejudices died hard too. On a railway journey, Pugin inadvertently upset another passenger by crossing himself while saying private prayers. "You are a Catholic, sir," the lady declared. "Guard, guard, let me out - I must get into another carriage" [18].

In North Staffordshire private chapels in the homes of Catholic nobility and gentry were supplemented by a number of missions following the Toleration Act. Chief among these was the Cresswell Mission which replaced the private chapel at Painsley Hall, the home of the Draycott family and their descendants, the Langdales and Stourtons. The Cresswell Mission became the mother church of the whole of North Staffordshire, and by 1835 eight chapels had been built within its circuit[19]. These included a new chapel - S. Filumena's - at Caverswall (1813), built so that the growing congregation no longer had to use the nuns' chapel at the Castle; and the Lane End chapel on the outskirts of Longton (1819). A small chapel at Cobridge (Stoke-on-Trent) dating from 1781 was considerably enlarged in the 1830s. The enlargement of Alton Lodge into Alton Abbey (later Alton Towers) included the building of a chapel which was from the beginning intended for the local Catholic population as well as for the Shrewsbury family. It was complete by 1819, and the Baptism Register dates from 1820. A chapel was built in Cheadle in the 1820s, and its first resident priest, Fr. James Jeffries, also looked after the mission in Leek to which Lord Shrewsbury contributed £130 and which opened in 1829. A Mission-room was opened at Uttoxeter in 1830.

With the exception of the Towers chapel, all of these buildings were plain structures, and all were later replaced by larger and finer churches of the "Second Spring". Even the

5. *The Cresswell Mission.*

Towers chapel was replaced in 1833 with a building several times bigger than the original one. Only the "mother church", the Cresswell Mission itself, has survived intact, and this is in many ways fortunate. Now known as S. Mary's, and refurnished at different times since it was built in 1816, its basic structure is typical of Catholic chapels generally at the beginning of the nineteenth century. Built of brick, with pointed windows and buttresses, it has neither aisles, nor chancel, nor an east window (**5**),

6. *Cresswell Mission - The Pugin window.*

and at the west end there is a large gallery supported on cast-iron columns. In other words, it is little different structurally from the nonconformist chapels of the period. Pugin added a few refinements, including a stained-glass window depicting the Annunciation (**6**), and possibly the churchyard cross. The window was given in 1841 in memory of the Dowager Lady Stourton.

The significance of Cresswell lies not in its architecture, but in its function as the hub of the North Staffordshire missions. Adjoining the east end of the chapel are the domestic buildings which housed not just the priest, but also a small seminary established in about 1816 by the Revd. Thomas Baddeley who was assisted there from 1819 by William Wareing, later Bishop of Northampton. Among the priests trained at Cresswell were Fr James Jeffries and Fr. Francis Fairfax, the first priests to reside at Cheadle.

A similar story of dogged survival and revival could be told of the district around the Shrewsbury estates on the Staffordshire-Shropshire border, where the Catholic Faith was flourishing in the missions at Longbirch and Black Ladies close to Brewood, and where families such as the Giffards and the Whitgreaves had maintained private chapels and priests. Thus the Staffordshire landscape was well-prepared for the arrival, in 1837, of Pugin, with his high hopes of converting England through Gothic art and architecture, of demonstrating to the nation that, far from being foreign, Catholicism was a part of the English climate, and of proving that, far from being a paradox, to be English *and* Catholic was the most natural thing in the world.

Italian missionary priests nevertheless played their part in the Catholic Revival, and they found their way into Staffordshire. Lord Shrewsbury's friend, Ambrose Phillipps, had brought Fr. Gentili and the Rosminians to work in the rural communities near his Leicestershire home of Grace Dieu, and in 1842 Pugin built a small church and school for them at Shepshed. With Phillipps' encouragement, Fr. Dominic Barberi and the Passionists came to England, and they settled at Aston Hall near Stone. In spite of some initial opposition they achieved remarkable success, so much so that a small school/church was established in Stone in 1843. Again, Pugin was the architect. Dedicated to S. Anne, this simple little church consists of a buttressed nave, and a chancel, built of brick with stone dressings (**7**). There are few refinements apart from the three-light east window, the gable crosses (now missing), the statue of S. Anne over the west door, and some Minton tiles. "Poor Pugin", commented Pevsner, "nearly always what he dreamt to be rich, dignified, elevating, turned out to be mean - for lack of money"[20]; but in this instance Pevsner misjudged. Like the church at Shepshed, S. Anne's was a new mission rather than the aggrandisement of an existing one, and it was built to fulfil an immediate need. Richness was not a consideration. In terms of its structure, however, S. Anne's is no less a "True Principles" church than S. Giles', Cheadle. It has a clearly-defined nave and chancel, there is nothing flimsy about it, and it could not possibly be taken for anything other than a church.

7. S. Anne's Church, Stone.

The premature deaths - both in the autumn of 1852 - of Pugin and Lord Shrewsbury left much unfinished work to be completed by the younger Pugins and by the seventeenth earl. The death of Earl Bertram in 1856 marked the end of the senior, Catholic, line of the Talbot family, with serious consequences for the churches of the Pugin-Shrewsbury partnership. Some noteworthy buildings do, however, date from this later period including the little-known Burton Manor, Stafford, (1854), S. Mary's Abbey at Oulton, near Stone (1854), the new S. Austin's Church, Stafford (1862), and S. Gregory's, Longton, built in 1869 to replace the Lane End chapel[21]. Significantly, the architect of all of these was Edward Welby Pugin (1834-1875).

Among the criticisms levelled at A.W.N. Pugin were that much of his work was left unfinished, that some of his buildings were starved, and that many looked far better on the drawing-board than they did in reality. If this was the case, then it was due to circumstances beyond his control, such as shortage of money on the part of those who commissioned him. Pugin himself confessed that he had spent his life in "thinking of fine things, studying fine things, designing fine things, and realising very poor ones"[22]. He could not say that of his work for Lord Shrewsbury. If Alton Castle was left unfinished, it was only because death intervened; and Cheadle as completed in 1846 far exceeded the expectations of 1841. S. Giles' was, if anything over-done. Pugin's church at Brewood is as much a "True Principles" church as S. Giles', and in terms of seating-capacity it is just as commodious. It has aisles, a properly-furnished chancel, a porch and a spire. Twenty such churches could have been built for the sum that Lord Shrewsbury expended on Cheadle. S. Giles', however, was built for a different purpose. Here Pugin set out to give practical expression to all of his ideas on architecture and ornament as propounded in publications such as *The True Principles, The Present State,* and *The Glossary;* and he drew together the widest possible range of "authorities", both English and continental, that it was possible to do in one place. Everything that he wrote and spoke about - passionately - is here translated into three-dimensional reality. S. Giles' is above all the full expression of the theological basis of what Pugin believed was *Christian* architecture. The same can be said of his buildings in Alton village, embodiments of the social dimensions of Catholicism set out in *Contrasts*. Uttoxeter, Cheadle, Alton, the Towers Chapel - all of these attracted unprecedented attention from English and foreign visitors, and from the Press, even while in the course of construction. They were studied, sketched and imitated by both Catholic and Anglican architects and designers. "It will be a text book for all good people," Lord Shrewsbury said of S. Giles'. "It will surely do good, and improve the taste of young England"[23], and so it did. For this reason alone, North Staffordshire deserves to be known as "Pugin-land".

2 PREST D'ACCOMPLIR
- JOHN TALBOT, SIXTEENTH EARL OF SHREWSBURY

"The redie minde regardeth never toyle,
But still is Prest t'accomplish heartes intent;
Abrode, at home, in every coste or soyle
The dede is done, that inwardly is mente,
Which makes me saye to every virtuous dede
I am still prest t'accomplish whats decrede"[1]

Prest d'accomplir - "ready to accomplish" - is the Talbot family motto which, along with the rampant lion, was repeated time and again in the wallcoverings, cornices, ceilings, windows, metalwork, and other items designed by Pugin for Alton Towers. It also expresses something of that enterprising spirit of earl and architect through whose efforts so much was accomplished on and around the Alton estate between 1837 and 1852. "Prest d'Accomplir" though he may have been, it was Pugin's own battle cry, *En Avant!* which impelled the sixteenth Earl to undertake far more than he sometimes considered desirable or affordable, and not all of it was accomplished without controversy between Pugin and his most illustrious and enthusiastic patron.

Although much has been said and written about Pugin's extraordinary career and achievements, the sixteenth Earl of Shrewsbury **(8)** has remained a shadowy figure. A biography planned shortly after his death never materialised[2], the first edition of the *Dictionary of National Biography* ignored him altogether, and Denis Gwynn's examination of the earl's role in promoting the Catholic cause - *Lord Shrewsbury, Pugin and the Catholic Revival* (1946) - has been out of print for many years.

Where facts are lacking, myths and legends often abound, and not a few have attached themselves to Lord Shrewsbury. On the one hand, the extent of his benefactions was subject to popular exaggeration even in the 1850s, and one of Denis Gwynn's objectives was to set that particular record straight. More recent and local myths of a somewhat sinister kind have included the monstrous suggestion that the earl had built Alton Towers as a residence for his mistress, and

8. *John Talbot (1791-1852) 16th Earl of Shrewsbury: engraving by Joseph Lynch after a painting by Carl Blaas.*

that the building of S. Giles', Cheadle, had been undertaken as a penance. There was, of course, no mistress[3]. The earl inherited the Towers from his uncle when it was to all intents

THE TALBOT EARLS OF SHREWSBURY

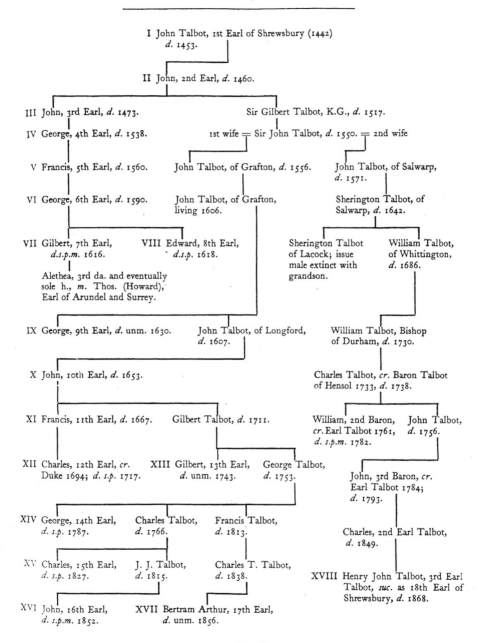

I John Talbot, 1st Earl of Shrewsbury (1442)
d. 1453.

II John, 2nd Earl, *d.* 1460.

III John, 3rd Earl, *d.* 1473.

Sir Gilbert Talbot, K.G., *d.* 1517.

IV George, 4th Earl, *d.* 1538.

1st wife ═ Sir John Talbot, *d.* 1550. ═ 2nd wife

V Francis, 5th Earl, *d.* 1560.

John Talbot, of Grafton, *d.* 1556.

John Talbot, of Salwarp, *d.* 1571.

VI George, 6th Earl, *d.* 1590.

John Talbot, of Grafton, living 1606.

Sherington Talbot, of Salwarp, *d.* 1642.

VII Gilbert, 7th Earl, *d.s.p.m.* 1616.

VIII Edward, 8th Earl, *d.s.p.* 1618.

Sherington Talbot, of Lacock; issue male extinct with grandson.

William Talbot, of Whittington, *d.* 1686.

Alethea, 3rd da. and eventually sole h., *m.* Thos. (Howard), Earl of Arundel and Surrey.

IX George, 9th Earl, *d.* unm. 1630.

John Talbot, of Longford, *d.* 1607.

William Talbot, Bishop of Durham, *d.* 1730.

X John, 10th Earl, *d.* 1653.

Charles Talbot, *cr.* Baron Talbot of Hensol 1733, *d.* 1738.

XI Francis, 11th Earl, *d.* 1667.

Gilbert Talbot, *d.* 1711.

William, 2nd Baron, *cr.* Earl Talbot 1761, *d.s.p.m.* 1782.

John Talbot, *d.* 1756.

XII Charles, 12th Earl, *cr.* Duke 1694; *d.s.p.* 1717.

XIII Gilbert, 13th Earl, *d.* unm. 1743.

George Talbot, *d.* 1753.

John, 3rd Baron, *cr.* Earl Talbot 1784; *d.* 1793.

XIV George, 14th Earl, *d.s.p.* 1787.

Charles Talbot, *d.* 1766.

Francis Talbot, *d.* 1813.

Charles, 2nd Earl Talbot, *d.* 1849.

XV Charles, 15th Earl, *d.s.p.* 1827.

J. J. Talbot, *d.* 1815.

Charles T. Talbot, *d.* 1838.

XVIII Henry John Talbot, 3rd Earl Talbot, *suc.* as 18th Earl of Shrewsbury, *d.* 1868.

XVI John, 16th Earl, *d.s.p.m.* 1852.

XVII Bertram Arthur, 17th Earl, *d.* unm. 1856.

Fig. 2

22

and purposes finished; he practised a near-ascetic lifestyle, and the building of S. Giles' was a part of his widespread promotion of the Catholic cause in which he passionately believed. If there was an unseen hand at work, it was that of A.W.N. Pugin, impelling him to undertake more than he had originally intended. Then there is the legend of the oak-tree in the woods below the Towers, bound with chains lest a falling branch should signal the untimely death of member of the earl's family. The chained oak is there for sure: the sole survivor of a number of "spar-oaks" anciently used as anchor-points in a haulage system for bringing heavy goods up the steep side of the Churnet valley. When its original function was forgotten, folklore supplied a new one to satisfy those for whom natural causes did not adequately explain the early demise of several of the earl's relatives. It is time that the real John Talbot - "The Good Earl" - emerged from the shadows.

John Talbot was born on 18th March 1791, the second son of John Joseph Talbot, younger brother of Charles, fifteenth Earl of Shrewsbury. His mother was Catherine, daughter of Thomas Clifton of Lytham Hall. John Joseph was heir presumptive to the Shrewsbury titles and estates, in the event of the fifteenth earl dying without male issue. The Talbots were indeed notoriously bad at producing male heirs who survived infancy. Not since 1667 had the titles passed directly from father to son. All, however, could trace descent from John, the "Grand Talbot" (d.1453), who had won fame - and his earldom - on the battlefields of the Hundred Years' War **(figs. 2 & 3)**.

The home of this particular branch of the Talbot family was Grafton Manor, on the outskirts of Bromsgrove, Worcestershire, which had been in Talbot hands at least since the early sixteenth century. It had been the home of John Talbot of Grafton (d. 1556), effectively the founder of the second line of the Talbots who succeeded to the Shrewsbury titles and estates on the death without issue of the eighth earl in 1618, remaining in possession until the death of the seventeenth earl in 1856. The early-sixteenth-century manor-house **(9)** was given a new Renaissance-style entrance in 1567, and further additions were made by the architect David Brandon in the 1860s. To the west of the house, and connected to it, is a late-medieval chapel for which Pugin designed a reredos in 1850[4]. The

9. Grafton Manor, Worcestershire.

chapel served as the local Catholic Mission until the opening of S. Peter's, Bromsgrove, in 1863.

At the Reformation the Talbots remained firmly Catholic, and with few exceptions continued so in the first and second lines of succession. Gilbert Talbot, who became the thirteenth earl (1717-1743) on the death of his cousin, was also a Jesuit priest. On account of their religion the Talbots were effectively barred from public life, from the universities, the armed services, and from parliament, until the repeal of most of the Penal Laws in the 1820s. Young John Talbot was therefore educated in various Catholic institutions, and by private tutors. His early life was plagued by misfortune. His mother died when he was only a few weeks old, and in 1797 John Joseph took a second wife, Harriet Ann Bedingfield, who bore him a son, George Henry, and a daughter, Mary. Following this second marriage, John, and his elder brother Charles, seem to have become progressively distanced from their father. First of all they were placed in the care of the Dowager Countess of Shrewsbury, who lived at Lacock Abbey, Wiltshire, and as soon as they were old enough they were sent to the preparatory school attached to the Benedictine College at Vernon Hall, Lancashire. In 1802 Charles died tragically while at the school, and John was removed almost immediately to Stonyhurst. From 1806 to 1810 he was at S. Edmund's College, Ware[5]. During his time at S. Edmund's he displayed his emerging talent as a creative writer by publishing an ode entitled, *A Farewell to the Muses*[6], which was the winning entry in a poetry competition. John excelled at Greek, and he won a medal for rhetoric. In 1810 he was placed under the care of the Revd. Dr. John Kirk (1760-1851) of Lichfield, an author and scholar who was later to have an active role in the founding of Oscott College. Then, to complete his education, he was sent to the Revd. John Chetwode Eustace of Cambridge, whose fame as a classical tourist was established in 1813 with the publication of his two-volume *Tour through Italy*[7].

It was no doubt through Fr. Eustace that John Talbot initially acquired the love of Italy that was to stay with him for the rest of his life. The conditions of the time - the Napoleonic

Wars raging across Europe and the high seas - made it practically impossible for him to undertake the Grand Tour which had once formed an essential part of many a young English gentleman's education. Foreign travel was not, however, totally impossible, and in 1812 John made an extensive tour through Spain, Portugal, and many parts of the Mediterranean coast including North Africa. In Spain he even entered the war-zone itself, and was so sickened by the carnage of the Peninsular War that he determined to return to England as soon as possible. He embarked on a small brig, which, after a stiff engagement, was captured by a Yankee privateer. John Talbot himself took an active part in the fight, was taken prisoner, but was later released minus all his belongings, so he made his way back to England as best he could[8].

On the 27th June 1814 John married nineteen-year-old Maria Theresa (**10**), eldest daughter of William and Anne Talbot of Castle Talbot, County Wexford; a distant relative, and strikingly beautiful. For the next thirty-eight years they were hardly ever apart, and their devotion to each other is movingly expressed in

10. Maria Theresa, Countess of Shrewsbury, (1795-1856): portrait by Julius Hamburger (Ingestre Hall, Staffs).

the simple inscription on Maria's memorial in S. John's church, Alton[9]. They had two daughters: Mary Alethea Beatrix, born in 1815, and Gwendaline Catherine, born two years later. Between the two daughters was born a son, John, who died in 1817 aged only four months. For a time they lived at Hampton-on-the Hill, near Warwick, in a house made available to them by their friend, Lord Dormer; and later at Littleover Hall. They were not at this time particularly wealthy, and from 1821 they spent a good deal of time abroad, mainly in Italy, where the cost of living and of raising children was less than in England. In the 1820s they became absorbed into the social and artistic life of Rome, and this was reflected in the future earl's tastes as a student and collector of fine art. As one might expect, they made friends amongst the Catholic hierarchy, and even became acquainted with Pope Pius VII. In 1824 the painter J.P. Davis (1784-1862) painted a very large canvas showing Pius VII giving a blessing to the kneeling figures of John and Maria Talbot and their two daughters. Shown standing close to the Pope were Cardinal Gonsalvi and the sculptor Canova. The painting was later hung in the dining-room at Alton Towers, and it earned the artist the nickname of "Pope" Davis.

On the 6th April 1827 Charles, fifteenth earl of Shrewsbury, died at his London residence in Stanhope Street, after a long illness. The funeral took place on the 18th April at what was then the Bavarian Embassy Chapel in Warwick Street, "in a style of extraordinary pomp and splendour"[10]. From being plain Mr & Mrs Talbot, John and Maria Theresa now became the Earl and Countess of Shrewsbury in England, and of Wexford and Waterford in Ireland. After the various legacies, annuities and charitable bequests had been settled under the terms of his uncle's will, John received a residual legacy of approximately £400,000 - a fabulous sum in those days - along with all the estates, furniture and other personal property. The Shrewsbury estates were spread over several counties including Derbyshire, Shropshire, Staffordshire, Nottinghamshire and Yorkshire. The principal houses were Heythrop, Oxfordshire, a Baroque palace built c.1706 by Thomas Archer for the twelfth earl; and the Gothic Alton Abbey which had been developed and extended by the fifteenth earl as a summer residence[11].

In 1831 Heythrop was gutted by a disastrous fire which destroyed most of the furniture, paintings and other items accumulated by the family over the previous hundred years or

11. Alton Abbey c.1820: Lithograph by Hopwood after drawing by Thomas Allason

more. Such as survived were taken to Alton Abbey which - now renamed Alton Towers - became the principal Talbot residence **(11)**. Though Earl John may have intended originally to do no more than complete the structural work in the house and gardens which his uncle had left unfinished, he soon embarked upon a building programme of his own to accommodate vast new collections of art, armour and furniture. This included the great galleries on the south side of the house, and a big West Wing extension containing a State Drawing Room, Libraries, and State Bedrooms and Boudoirs for the exclusive use of visiting royalty. In October 1832 the Princess Victoria, then aged thirteen, visited Alton with her mother, the Duchess of Kent, and she recorded her impressions in her diary. The dowager Queen Adelaide stayed at the Towers in August 1840 when a hundred beds were made up for the accommodation of distinguished guests[12]. Three years later Henri, Duke of Bordeaux, the Legitimist Pretender to the French Throne, paid a five-day visit with his entourage[13].

Earl John's education, and his travels on the Continent, had given him a taste for fine art and antiquities, and now that he had considerable resources at his disposal, he was in a position to make extensive additions to the collections which his uncle had started to accumulate at Alton from about 1810 onwards. The most conspicuous of these was the collection of pictures, which by the time of the 1857 sale numbered just over seven hundred. They were hung throughout the house, but the biggest displays were in the linked galleries which formed a part of the grand entrance. The Picture Gallery appears to have been purpose-built to accommodate an entire collection of paintings once belonging to Laetitia Bonaparte - the mother of the deposed Emperor - which the earl had acquired on one of his visits to Rome. It included works by Canaletto, Guercino, Poussin, Titian, Tiepolo, Tintoretto, Velasquez and Van Eyck; and the celebrated *Belisarius,* painted in 1780 by J-L David (1748-1824)[14].

Earl John also commissioned new work from leading painters and sculptors. The focal-point of the Talbot Gallery, added to the gallery range in 1840, was a full-size statue in marble of Raphael done in 1833 by Ceccarini, a pupil of Canova. Pietro Tenerani (1789-1870), the sculptor who also became General Director of the Museums and Galleries of Rome, executed busts of Gwendaline, the earl's younger daughter, and of Henri, Duke of Bordeaux. Among the painters from whom the earl commissioned work was Durantini who copied Domenichino's *Communion of St. Jerome* and Raphael's *The Transfiguration* to hang in the new chapel[15]. The earl seems especially to have admired the work of the Riepenhausen brothers, Franz (1786-1830) and Johann (1788-1860) who lived and worked as members of the German artistic community in Rome. They had close links with the "Nazarene" movement, and were much influenced by Italian art of the late medieval and renaissance period, notably that of Raphael in whom Lord Shrewsbury had a particular interest. Amongst the works which Lord Shrewsbury bought from them was a portrait of S. Elizabeth of Hungary[16] for the Music Room, also pictures of S. Thomas Becket and Archbishop Lawrence O'Toole (of Dublin) for the chapel, and an immense canvas - said to have been the largest ever framed in England[17] - showing an insurrection which took place in Rome after the coronation of the Emperor Frederick Barbarossa (1123-1190). As well as the emperor himself, the picture included King Henry "the Lion" of Saxony, and Pope

Adrian IV. The picture occupied almost the whole of the east wall of the state dining room at Alton. In 1832 Johann Riepenhausen presented the earl with an album of twelve watercolour drawings representing scenes from the life of Raphael[18]. Another member of the German community in Rome was Hauser, whom the earl commissioned to paint the Last Judgement for the chancel-arch of S. Giles' Cheadle.

The Armoury at Alton Towers contained one of the largest private collections of armour in the country[19], while elsewhere in the house were large quantities of fine china and porcelain, including a Dresden chandelier valued in 1851 at a thousand guineas[20], and of course some costly furniture. Far from being hidden away for the enjoyment of a privileged few, the treasures of Alton Towers were seen by many. Not only did the earl allow free access to the park and gardens for people of the locality and further afield; he also opened the galleries and state rooms, and "though hundreds daily wandered through its beautiful saloons, a shilling's worth of loss or damage was never sustained"[21]. Meanwhile, when in residence at Alton, the family lived in the secluded eastern part of the house, in the smaller rooms surviving from the old Alveton Lodge, the original building to occupy the site. When, at the time of the great sale in 1857, these areas were finally open to view, Earl John's bedroom attracted attention and comment not on account of its splendour, but because it was the plainest room in the house, and the simplest in its furniture[22].

The opening of the gardens and the house to the public was perceived as a part of the general philanthropic attitude of Earl John towards the local community. Though he

12. Alton Towers: the tower of the new chapel, 1833.

slipped easily into the role of *grand seigneur*, he was well-aware of his duties and responsibilities. He was generous in his support of schools and hospitals, and was a founder Governor of the Staffordshire Infirmary. When it was suggested that he should build a monastery close to Alton, he chose instead to build the Hospital of S. John in Alton village, along with the school and Guildhall for the local people. He set up a fund for the insurance of cottagers' cows, and on hearing that a Cheadle resident had been attacked and robbed on the road to Ashbourne, he sent him a gift of money[23]. A foreign observer noted that in cases of illness or hardship among the tenantry the earl would freely provide whatever was needed, including medicines and the services of a doctor[24]. In the "hungry forties" when there was much hardship and unemployment, anyone out of work could apply to Lord Shrewsbury's agent and be given a job on road-building or other construction work. During this time, something in the order of sixty-six miles of roads and carriage-drives were laid in and around the Alton estate[25].

The Shrewsburys' family chapel at Alton Abbey had, from its opening in 1820, been attended by Catholics from the villages of Alton and Farley as well as by domestic servants and estate-workers. The earl was particularly devout. It was his custom to rise punctually at six in the morning, spend over an hour in prayer, hear Mass daily in the chapel, and set aside time each day for meditation and spiritual reading[26]. In 1832-33 a large new chapel (12) was built on to the east end of the house. In these pre-Pugin days the earl continued to employ Thomas Fradgley of Uttoxeter, the architect he had inherited from his uncle, and also Joseph Potter of Lichfield whom he commissioned in 1832 to build a substantial church and presbytery at Newport, Shropshire, where there had been a Talbot mission since the seventeenth century. He also subscribed to the church in Leek which opened in 1829 as a offshoot of the Cheadle Mission.

In 1828-9 most of the remaining Penal Laws discriminating against Catholics were repealed. The first to go was the Test Act, which had effectively barred Catholics from public office by requiring office-holders under the Crown to make a declaration against the doctrine of Transubstantiation[27]. Lord Shrewsbury himself published a weighty volume running to 432 pages explaining why Catholics could not conform, under the title of *Reasons for Not Taking the Test,* in the very year that the Act was repealed. Then in 1829 came the Catholic Emancipation Act, which meant, among other things, that Lord Shrewsbury and the other Catholic peers were able to take their seats in the House of Lords and to assume an active role in public affairs. Lord Shrewsbury was admitted to the House on the 13th April 1831. In 1837 he attended the funeral of William IV, not just as the premier earl, but also as hereditary High Steward of Ireland, and he carried the Banner of Ireland in the procession. In politics he confessed that he was by nature a Whig rather than a Tory, because he believed in civil liberties and religious toleration which the Tories had generally opposed; but he acknowledged too that by the early 1840s so many major reforms had been accomplished that the difference between the two parties had become very narrow[28]. He nevertheless opposed the repeal of the protectionist Corn Laws which kept the price of wheat - and hence of bread - artificially high.

Being an earl of Ireland as well as of England, and with an Irish wife, Lord Shrewsbury was deeply involved in Irish affairs. Both the earl and countess were distressed by the tragedy of the Irish famine of the 1840s, and they abhorred the sharp practices of many absentee landlords. Yet the earl was wholly opposed to the movement for the repeal of the 1801 Act of Union spearheaded by Daniel O'Connell, whose election to Westminster had precipitated Catholic Emancipation. He also criticised Irish clergy whose public denunciations of iniquitous landlords allegedly provoked acts of violence and even murder. The Earl's letters on this subject in the *Morning Chronicle,* and his criticism of the Irish bishops for not taking a firmer line with their clergy and not doing enough to relieve the plight of the poor, involved him in a bitter war of words with Dr. McHale, Archbishop of Tuam, and with Frederick Lucas, the somewhat abrasive editor of the Catholic magazine, the *Tablet.* Both Lord Shrewsbury and his friend, Ambrose Phillipps, believed that the continuing presence at Westminster of Irish peers and members of Parliament was vital to the furtherance of the Catholic cause in England; hence their opposition to O'Connell and the repealers, and their dismay at the apparent indifference of the Irish Catholics - preoccupied as they were with economic and political matters - to the conversion of England. The earl's views on the Irish Question in general were expressed in yet another publication, *Hints Towards the Pacification of Ireland* (1844) which ran to a second edition.

In the 1830s family affairs came to the fore. Both of the Shrewsbury daughters had inherited their mother's noted good looks, and, given their cosmopolitan background, it is hardly surprising that they found suitors amongst European royalty and aristocracy. In the summer of 1834 Lady Mary, then aged nineteen, was betrothed to the thirty-three-year-old Prince Frederick of Saxe-Altenburg, a close relative of King Ludwig I of Bavaria. Both Queen Adelaide (herself a German princess) and the Queen of Bavaria were instrumental in arranging the match

13. Oriel window, Doria Apartments, Alton Towers.

which was widely applauded around the courts of Europe. The Emperor of Austria proposed to make Mary a Princess of the Empire, but King Ludwig insisted on raising her to the rank of Princess himself, under the title of Princess Talbot[29]. For reasons which are not clear, the marriage - planned for September 1834 - never took place[30], but Mary retained the title of Princess in her own right, which doubtless enhanced her eligibility.

A second match was eventually found amongst the aristocracy of Italy. On the 6th April 1839 Princess Mary married Filippo Andrea, Prince Doria Pamphili-Landi, a member of a noted Roman and Neapolitan family whose vast residence - the Palazzo Doria Pamphili - was the repository of art-collections on the scale of the Shrewsburys'. Cardinal Guistiani officiated at the marriage, which took place in the chapel of the Shrewburys' own residence in the Via del Corso, and this was followed by a service of thanksgiving in S. Peter's[31]. In the summer of 1839 the newly-weds joined the earl and countess at Alton, where they were greeted enthusiastically by a large crowd of villagers and tenantry on their arrival on the 3rd July. Dancing, entertainment and refreshments were laid on for all comers. The family joined "with the greatest hilarity in tripping the light fantastical toe" during the dancing on the lawns in front of the house, "Such a day of grandeur and festivity has seldom been witnessed in the county of Stafford", concluded one observer[32].

It was the intention of earl and countess that the prince and princess would return to Alton at regular intervals. A suite of rooms - designed by Pugin - was built as an extension to the family apartments at the north east corner of the Towers[33]. Known as the Doria Suite, one of its finest features was an oriel window **(13)**, which gave unrivalled views into the famous gardens. Mary and Filippo did in fact spend a few more summers at Alton - they were there, for example, in 1842, and in 1846 when S. Giles' church, Cheadle was

14. Gwendaline Talbot, Princess Borghese, 1817-1840
(Frontispiece: A. Zeloni, Vie de la Princess Borghese, *1843.*

opened. They had four children, one of whom was born at Alton in August 1846 and was named, appropriately, Gwendaline. Mary died in 1857 and was buried behind the High Altar in the church of Santa Agnese in Rome. The Prince commissioned a fine monument by Tenarani, and was himself buried there in 1876.

The younger daughter of the earl and countess, Gwendaline Catherine **(14)** grew up into a young woman of great beauty, charm and intelligence. She became fluent in French, German, Italian and Spanish, and at least part of her education took place abroad. Her biographer, Zeloni, treats her with such reverence and adulation that one might be forgiven for thinking that he was writing for the *Lives of the Saints*[34]. When only a few days old she displayed a degree of alertness that was noted and remembered by her mother. The child was apparently fascinated by a garland of white flowers which the countess was wearing in her hair, and this may well explain why Gwendaline is shown wearing such a garland in Hauser's painting of the Last Judgement over the chancel-arch of S. Giles', Cheadle. In May 1835 she married Marc Antonio Aldobrandi, Prince of Salmona, who became Prince Borghese on the death of his father in 1839. They had a daughter, Agnes, and three sons. They spent the summer of 1840 at Alton, and attended the grand reception for Queen Adelaide at the Towers in July. Following their return to Rome in the autumn, Gwendaline contracted scarlet fever and died on the 27th October, just a few weeks short of her twenty-third birthday. The three boys also died, within a few weeks of their mother, from rubella.

The princess was given what was tantamount to a state funeral. Rome came to a standstill as the cortège progressed to the church of Santa Maria Maggiore. Pope Gregory XVI, who had a high regard for Gwendaline, and spoke of her death as a public calamity, himself appeared at a window along the route, and blessed the coffin as it passed by. He also ordered the great central doors of the basilica to be opened to admit the cortège - an honour strictly reserved for royalty. After the funeral Mass, the coffin was interred in the magnificent Borghese chapel, within the basilica itself[35].

Lord Shrewsbury - to whom Gwendaline had always been, according to Zeloni, *l'ange du papa* - was devastated with grief, and for a time he seriously considered leaving England altogether to live in Rome so as to be near her burial-place. Indeed, the Shrewsburys were already spending an increasing amount of time abroad. They had given up the London house in Stanhope Street, and when in the capital they took rooms at Mivart's Hotel (later Claridges) in Brook Street. In addition to their residence in Rome, they had the Villa Belmonte in Palermo.

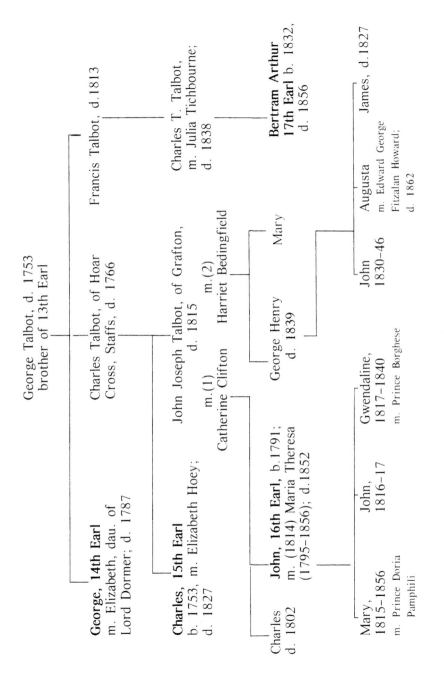

George Talbot, d. 1753
brother of 13th Earl

Francis Talbot, d. 1813

Charles Talbot, of Hoar
Cross, Staffs, d. 1766

Charles T. Talbot,
m. Julia Tichbourne;
d. 1838

George, 14th Earl
m. Elizabeth, dau. of
Lord Dormer; d. 1787

John Joseph Talbot, of Grafton,
d. 1815

m.(1)   m.(2)
Catherine Clifton   Harriet Bedingfield

Charles, 15th Earl
b. 1753, m. Elizabeth Hoey;
d. 1827

George Henry
d. 1839   Mary

Bertram Arthur
17th Earl b. 1832,
d. 1856

Charles
d. 1802

John, 16th Earl, b.1791;
m. (1814) Maria Theresa
(1795–1856); d.1852

John,
1816–17

Gwendaline,
1817–1840

m. Prince Borghese

John
1830–46

Augusta
m. Edward George
Fitzalan Howard;
d. 1862

James, d.1827

Mary,
1815–1856

m. Prince Doria
Pamphili

Fig. 3   THE FAMILY OF JOHN TALBOT, SIXTEENTH EARL OF SHREWSBURY

The death of the Princess Borghese and her sons was not the only set of tragic circumstances seriously to affect the future prospects of the Talbot family. Though the hopes of having a son and heir had all but faded by the 1830s, the earl had a half-brother, George Henry, from his father's second marriage. He died in 1839 leaving a nine-year-old son, John. The earl now looked upon this nephew as his heir and successor, but then John also died - aged only sixteen - in 1846. All hopes for the survival of the second, Catholic, line of the family now lay with thirteen-year-old Bertram Arthur, son of Charles Talbot, cousin to the earl[36]. Bertram was brought under the tutelage of the earl and countess who provided him with rooms at Alton Towers and a private tutor. They also took him on their visits to Italy, which they thought would benefit the boy's delicate health[37]. The French traveller and writer, the Abbé Vandrival, who visited Alton in May 1847, was shown around the Towers by Bertram himself, and he was greatly impressed by the boy's knowledge, his fluency in four languages, and his general demeanour[38]. The earl's half-sister, Mary, was also living at the Towers at this time. "This lady is wonderfully kind and very pious", Vandrival observed; "she has refused several advantageous marriage proposals and prefers to stay as she is".

At the time of his visit to Alton, Vandrival was staying with Ambrose Phillipps de Lisle (1809-1878) **(15)** of Grace Dieu, Leicestershire, a close friend of Lord Shrewsbury. Phillipps had converted to the Catholic Faith - much to the annoyance of his father - in 1825, and he was subsequently responsible for the conversion of a good many others including a near neighbour of Lord Shrewsbury's, Sir Charles Wolseley, and George Spencer, youngest son of Earl Spencer of Althorp[39]. He had some important Staffordshire connections. Henry Ryder, Bishop of Lichfield from 1824 to 1836, was an uncle by marriage, and the bishop himself was a younger son of Lord Harrowby of Sandon Hall. Phillipps was recklessly generous in his promotion of the Catholic cause in the rural communities around Grace Dieu, and he encouraged Lord Shrewsbury to display similar generosity on a grander scale[40]. Several of the earl's publications were written in the form of Letters to Ambrose Phillipps. In reality they are erudite works running, in some cases, to more then three hundred pages, and with copious footnotes. His *Letter Descriptive of the Estatica of Caldaro and the Addolorata of Capriana* (1841) ran to a revised and enlarged second edition. It concerns Lord Shrewsbury's visits to the

My dear dear Shrewsbury
from your most gratefully devoted
Ambrose Lisle Phillipps

15. *Ambrose Phillipps de Lisle, 1809-1879 (frontispiece, E.S. Purcell,* Life and Letters of Ambrose Phillipps de Lisle, *1900, vol 1).*

celebrated holy women of South Tyrol: Maria von Mörl of Caldaro who was a visionary, and Domenica Lazzari of Capriana who had received the *stigmata*[41]. The earl's *Letters On the Present Posture of Affairs* (1841 and 1842) were concerned, amongst other things, with Irish affairs and the disputes with O'Connell. They reveal his quite remarkable historical perspectives and breadth of scholarship, and his intellectual and spiritual relationship with Ambrose Phillipps, who clearly regarded Lord Shrewsbury - eighteen years his senior - as his principal guide and mentor. It was, however, the earl's encounter with A.W.N. Pugin which did more than anything else to change the direction of his life, and the scale of his benefactions. Pugin also found in Ambrose Phillipps a man after his own heart, who shared his enthusiasm for Gothic architecture and the revival of the "English" Catholic Church, and they became lifelong friends[42].

16. Daniel Rock, 1799-1876 (frontispiece, Daniel Rock, The Church of Our Fathers, *1854).*

The precise date and circumstances of Lord Shrewsbury's first acquaintance with the work of A.W.N. Pugin are somewhat uncertain. Pugin's biographer, Benjamin Ferrey, gives the date as 1832 and the location as Edward Hull's furniture shop in Wardour Street, London[43], where the earl saw some of Pugin's drawings and asked for an introduction. Lord Shrewsbury was indeed furnishing the new West Wing at Alton Towers at this very time, and it is known that Pugin designed some Gothic furniture for it[44], but Hull did not set up in Wardour Street until 1834. A similar story was told by Sir Thomas Wyse, M.P., (1791-1862) who had been a friend of Lord Shrewsbury's since their schooldays at Stonyhurst[45]. Pugin's diary, however, makes no mention of Lord Shrewsbury until 3rd October 1836, when he replied to some earlier communication from the earl.

By the summer of 1836 Dr Daniel Rock (1799-1876) **(16)**, domestic chaplain to Lord Shrewsbury from 1827 to 1840, had read some of Pugin's works. He wrote to congratulate him specifically on his designs for church silverwork, and offered to show him a medieval chalice and a processional cross in his possession[46]. It is therefore quite possible that it was Dr Rock who effected Pugin's introduction to the earl. Rock was himself keen to revive the English Liturgy and the ornaments and vestments which went with it. In 1833 he had published *Hierurgia,* a detailed study of the Mass written mainly for the benefit of Protestants **(17)**. It carries a dedication to Lord Shrewsbury dated 18th March - the earl's birthday. Rock's zeal for the Gothic Revival, and for the Sarum Rite which had prevailed in England prior to 1549, were later expressed in his three-volume work, *The Church of Our*

17. Illustration from Daniel Rock's Hierurgia *(1833) showing a priest at what is recognisably the altar of Alton Towers Chapel as it was before Pugin's alterations.*

Fathers (1849-54)[47]. To have found such a man already installed as chaplain at Alton must have been a source of great delight to Pugin, and there is no doubt that they furthered each other's scholarship and research. Their correspondence about ornaments and vestments continued long after Dr. Rock had left Alton to become chaplain to Sir Robert Throckmorton at Buckland, Berkshire. His departure from Alton came about as the result of disagreements with Lord Shrewsbury who concluded that, whatever his abilities as a scholar, Rock was not the effective missionary needed to further the Catholic cause in the neighbouring villages, which had now become a priority. "He has some good qualities, but a very weak mind which study and seclusion seem to have altogether overpowered..... I can assure you it will be a great relief to us all to be quit of him, for he has long made himself very disagreeable"[48]. Like Pugin, however, the earl continued to correspond with Dr. Rock, who was invited back to Alton as a guest from time to time, and shortly before his death the earl invited him to stay at the Villa Belmonte in Palermo[49]. Rock's successor at Alton was Dr. Henry Winter, who stayed until 1866. He took up residence in the new buildings at S. John's, Alton, for Lord Shrewsbury had declared that after his experiences with Dr. Rock he would have no more chaplains in residence at the Towers; "they are almost sure to be spoilt"[50].

Meanwhile, following his first visits to Alton in the autumn of 1837, Pugin had begun to work for Lord Shrewsbury as architect at the Towers, and as the designer of the many churches which - encouraged by Ambrose Phillipps - the earl financed wholly or in part. Though the extent of Lord Shrewsbury's benefactions has sometimes been exaggerated[51], his financial support for the Catholic Revival was considerably greater than that of any other individual. The three buildings - or groups of buildings - which he financed entirely were S. John's Hospital, Alton, and Alton Castle (1840-51), and S. Giles' Church, Cheadle, and its associated school, convent and presbytery (1841-46). Elsewhere in Staffordshire he made very substantial contributions to S. Mary's, Uttoxeter (1838-9), and S. Wilfrid's, Cotton (1846-8); and a much more modest one to S, Mary's, Brewood (1844). Outside the county he was the principal benefactor of Mount Saint Bernard Abbey (1840-44), and S. Barnabas', Nottingham (1841-44), and he made large donations to S. Mary's, Derby (1837-9), S. Alban's, Macclesfield (1839-41), S. George's, Southwark (1838-48), and the Convent of Mercy, Handsworth (1840-41). Lord Shrewsbury's benefactions were made conditional upon the appointment of Pugin as architect. In September 1839 he wrote to Bishop Briggs that "in consequence of the lamentable failure of most of our modern chapels, I have come to the resolution to subscribe to no buildings which are not erected under the designs and superintendence of Mr. Pugin"[52]. Two years earlier he had written to Ambrose Phillipps, "I look upon Pugin as the greatest acquisition for our body (i.e. the Catholic Church) for an immense time past..... He is the man to encourage"[53].

In addition to his financial contributions, Lord Shrewsbury made gifts of vestments, statues, furnishings, metalwork and stained glass to the churches which Pugin designed. Some of these were specially commissioned, but others were medieval antiquities which formed part of the eart's collections or which Pugin encouraged him to buy. He gave a magnificent fifteenth-century brass eagle-lectern to S. Chad's cathedral[54], and a parcel-gilt altar-cross of similar date to S. John's, Alton[55]. His private collections included items formerly belonging to the Bridgettine convent of Syon, near Brentford. Among them was the Syon Cope **(colour plate 1)**, a rare and beautiful example of English medieval needlework which had survived the final dissolution of the convent in 1558 and had been taken by the nuns to continental Europe[56]. Other medieval vestments in his possession were given to Oscott, including a fifteenth-century set from Wexford Cathedral. He also had rare copies of the Sarum Missal and Antiphonal of fifteenth- and sixteenth-century dates[57], and a number of altarpieces.

For his part, Pugin freely acknowledged his indebtedness to Lord Shrewsbury, not only for the patronage which came directly from him, but also for the introductions which he was able to arrange - often at gatherings at Alton Towers to other potential clients and to leading churchmen. When, in 1843, Pugin published his *Apology for the Revival of Christian Architecture in England,* he prefaced it with a dedication to Lord Shrewsbury, paying tribute to the earl's encouragement of the Revival, and praying that he might "continue to increase the spiritual welfare of these realms by reviving the ancient glories of the English Church". Nor were these activities confined to England. Among the people whom Pugin met at Alton Towers was John Hyacinth Talbot (1794-1868), an uncle of the countess and an Irish M.P. and landowner. It was largely through him that Pugin secured a number of important Irish contracts, including S. Peter's College, Wexford, to which Lord Shrewsbury also contributed[58].

The extensive correspondence that passed between Pugin and Lord Shrewsbury reveals a relationship that ran much deeper than the purely professional one of architect and patron. Their letters ranged over many subjects, such as the Irish Question, Chartism, the restoration of the Catholic hierarchy, foreign travel, and family matters too. They consoled each other in bereavement, as for example when the Princess Borghese and her children died in 1840, and when Pugin's second wife, Louisa. died in 1844. When Pugin plunged himself into a fit of black despair following the frustration of his plan to marry Mary Amherst as his third wife, it was to Lord Shrewsbury that he poured out his grief: "I cannot eat, I cannot work .... I propose quitting England and giving up my profession .... I am ruined in mind and body, broken down and destroyed"[59]. Earl and architect were as different in temperament as they were in background and upbringing: the gentle, eirenic and self-effacing Lord Shrewsbury, and the ebullient, passionate Pugin. There were many disagreements - for example over the design of the new dining room at Alton Towers, and

18. Thomas Walsh (1776-1849) Vicar Apostolic, wearing Gothic chausuble and mitre designed by Pugin: from a painting by J.R. Herbert at Oscott (Ward, Sequel to Catholic Emancipation, *Vol II).*

the plan and furnishing of S. Giles', Cheadle - and Pugin pushed his ideas to the limit with an alarming degree of forthrightness and candour. Yet through all of Pugin's bluff and bluster, the relationship held firm, and the factor which outweighed all others in the earl's estimation of him was that, uniquely, Pugin viewed his whole career as an architect and designer as subservient to the Catholic cause.

Lord Shrewsbury's broad knowledge of art and sculpture, and his renown as a collector, were no doubt significant factors in his appointment in December 1841 to the Royal Fine Arts Commission set up under the presidency of Prince Albert to superintend the decoration of the New Palace of Westminster. It seems that he may not have taken up this appointment[60], but nevertheless, Pugin later expected him to take action over "the monstrous selection of statues for the Palace... there are the names of Wicliff, John Knox, Bunyan, and John Westley *(sic)* !!"[61]. The earl's tastes in matters of art and architecture were much broader than Pugin's, and on account of his education and subsequent career, he had a deep love of Italy and of all things Italian. How then he coped with some of Pugin's violent condemnations of "pagan" Rome - "the Vatican is a hideous mass, and St. Peter's is the greatest failure of all"[62] - is something of a puzzle. The Warwick Street Chapel, where the Talbots worshipped when in London, was, in Pugin's eyes, the epitomy of everything that was bad in current Catholic architecture, decoration and worship. The new chapel at Alton Towers - though vaguely Gothic in form - was little better internally when Pugin arrived in 1837, and as part of his attempts to improve things he set about removing and disposing of pictures and cast-iron statues which he considered inappropriate[63].

Many of Lord Shrewsbury's gifts and benefactions in the Midlands were in support of projects initiated by Bishop Thomas Walsh (1776-1849), Vicar Apostolic of the Midlands District from 1826 to 1840, and then of the new Central District from 1840 to 1847 **(18)**. In Pugin's view, Walsh was the only bishop in England to have advanced the dignity of the Catholic Faith through his encouragement of the revival of "true" art and architecture. "Dr. Walsh found the churches in his district worse than barns; he will leave them sumptuous..... The greater part of the vestments were filthy rags, and he has replaced them with silk and gold"[64]. A project dear to the heart of Walsh, Pugin and Lord Shrewsbury was the establishment of the new College of S. Mary at Oscott for the training of a new breed of English missionary priests, distinct from the homespun variety trained in small establishments such as the Cresswell Mission, and from the Italian Passionists favoured by Ambrose Phillipps. Much as he himself loved Italy, the earl knew that importing Italian priests who had little knowledge of English might only serve to reinforce the prejudices of those who were wont to refer to the Catholic Church as "the Italian mission". "We must", he wrote to Phillipps, "have a new race of zealous English missionaries such as are now bringing up at Oscott, under the good Bishop and Pugin"[65]. Pugin was appointed Professor of Ecclesiastical Antiquities at Oscott, where he established a Museum for the instruction of ordinands in the refinements of the English Catholic Liturgy.

It was Walsh who undertook the building of S. Chad's Cathedral, Birmingham (1839-41), designed by Pugin with a full complement of appropriate furnishings including a controversial rood-screen. Pugin viewed Walsh almost as a reincarnation of the great fourteenth-century church-building bishop, William Wykeham, with Lord Shrewsbury as the bountiful *grand seigneur* - a quasi-medieval vision which he vastly preferred to the squabbling congregational church-building committees which generally held sway at this time.

Not all shared Pugin's Gothic passion as readily as Walsh and Lord Shrewsbury, and some were positively hostile to it. When, therefore, Pugin found that his ideas were being welcomed warmly by some influential Anglicans, he further alienated many of his own Church by expressing sympathy with "the Oxford men", and applauding their achievements. Ambrose Phillipps went even further and dreamed of a re-union of the two Churches. Bishop Wiseman (President of Oscott from 1840 to 1847) was also for a time sympathetic, but Lord Shrewsbury was much more cautious. Though knowledgeable of Anglican history and of the Catholic Revival in the Church of England[66], he doubted the sincerity of some of the "Oxford men"; and while he too hoped for reconciliation, he concluded that "there is but one ground upon which we can meet - the authority of the Church, the doctrines of primitive antiquity, as defined by (the Council of) Trent, and promulgated and received as such"[67].

Lord Shrewsbury's confidence even in clergymen of other churches who did submit to Rome must have been severely shaken by the scandalous conduct of one in whom he took a particular interest, and to whom he showed exceptional kindness - the Revd. Pierce Connelly. A minister of the American Episcopal Church, and of Irish ancestry, Connelly resigned his parish in Natchez, Mississippi, and along with his wife, Cornelia, travelled to Rome in the winter of 1835-6 with the intention of being received into the Catholic Church[68]. Among those whom they met soon after their arrival in Rome were Lord and Lady Shrewsbury who were wintering there, and the earl stood sponsor for Mr & Mrs Connelly when they were eventually received in Holy Week. Later in the year, Pierce visited England at Lord Shrewsbury's invitation, and stayed at Alton Towers as a house-guest while the family were in residence during the summer. By 1841 Pierce had become convinced that he had a vocation to the priesthood. Cornelia concurred with the view, even though she knew this would involve separation from herself and the children, and that she herself would have to enter a Religious Order. Pierce took their eldest son, Mercer, to England, where he was sent to Stonyhurst at Lord Shrewsbury's expense. The earl also found

Pierce an appointment - pending a final decision from Rome about possible ordination - as travelling companion to a young Catholic gentleman, Robert Berkeley[69]. Both Pierce and Cornelia were together at Alton in the summer of 1843, before setting off to Rome to lay their petition for separation before the authorities.

One of the most remarkable facets of this bizarre story is the ease with which the Connellys were rapidly absorbed into the society of the rich and famous, both in England and in Europe. Lord Shrewsbury had formed a high opinion of Connelly's character and talents, and that undoubtedly carried weight. While at Alton, Pierce and Cornelia were introduced to George Spencer, Ambrose Phillipps, Pugin, and Bishop Walsh. En route for the Vatican in the autumn of 1843 they attended half a dozen aristocratic dinner-parties in Paris, and on arrival at Rome they were welcomed by Lord Shrewsbury's son-in-law, the Prince Borghese, who undertook to provide for the education of the Connelly's youngest son, Frank. They had at least two audiences with Pope Gregory XVI who appeared to take a personal interest in them.

In April 1844 the Holy See issued a deed of separation. Cornelia became a postulant at the convent of Trinità Dei Monti, and just over a year later Pierce was ordained priest in the chapel of the Trinità, where he also said his first Mass while Cornelia sang in the choir. In spite of his earlier avowal never to have another chaplain living in the house, Lord Shrewsbury installed Fr. Connelly as chaplain at Alton Towers in May 1846, and gave him special responsibility for the education of his cousin and heir, Bertram. It was Connelly who welcomed the Abbé Vandrival to the Towers in May 1847 and introduced him to young Bertram. Having heard Connelly's own account of his conversion, Vandrival concluded that here was "a great soul, strong and profoundly devout", and an admirable example of those "who pass each day from Anglicanism to Catholicism"[70].

Meanwhile, with the encouragement of the Pope and Bishop Wiseman, Cornelia too had come to England as foundress of the Society of the Holy Child Jesus, established first in Derby and then at St. Leonard's-on-Sea. Pierce intervened, first to try to establish some control over the Society and its Constitutions, and hence over his former wife. When this failed, he instituted proceedings in the (Anglican) Court of Arches to reclaim Cornelia and have conjugal rights restored; Cornelia, of course, contesting this. In May 1849 the Court of Arches ruled against him, likewise the Judicial Committee of the Privy Council to which Pierce appealed in 1851. His fury at this outcome knew no bounds. He renounced his priestly Orders and the Catholic Faith, and published a series of scurrilous pamphlets on the "detestable enormities" of Rome. These culminated in an open letter addressed to Lord Shrewsbury under the title, *Reasons for Abjuring Allegiance to the See of Rome* (1852). In the same year he made a final appeal to the House of Commons in terms so slanderous that a debate was held as to whether or not it ought to be printed. Nothing came of it, and Connelly eventually went to Italy where he acted as Rector of the American Episcopal Church in Florence until his death in 1883.

Possibly because of the exalted circles in which he had moved, in Rome, Paris, at Alton Towers and elsewhere, and because of his spectacular rise in the estimation of Lord Shrewsbury and some of the cardinals, including Fransoni, the Prefect of Propaganda,

Pierce Connelly seems to have entertained false hopes of rapid preferment in the Church. The disappointment of these hopes, and the failure of his subsequent attempts to regain influence over Cornelia, exposed a sinister side to his character. Wiseman - who had been on the receiving end of some vitriolic letters from Connelly - believed that he was now revealing himself in his true colours, and he wrote anxiously to Lord Shrewsbury:

> "....But, my dear Lord, I do feel myself called to say that if on action, or otherwise, Mr Connelly's letters are published, he will appear to Your Lordship and to others in a very different light from what he has been till now. His shallowness, vanity, wild fanaticism...... his presumption, and his ingratitude to the noble house that has given him its confidence, will I think make Your Lordship not regret that Providence has removed a *baleful* influence from the heir of your line..."[71]

Quite apart from the anguish and embarrassment caused personally to Lord Shrewsbury by the actions of one in whom he had placed such great trust, the Connelly affair came at a most inopportune moment for the Catholic cause in general. Plans were afoot to end the missionary status of the English Catholic Church and to replace it with a regular hierarchy of bishops with English territorial titles, and with an Archbishop of Westminster at its head. Wiseman was in Rome to conduct the negotiations, and at Michaelmas 1850 Pope Pius IX issued a brief establishing thirteen dioceses. Monsignor George Talbot, a relative of Lord Shrewsbury's who had the ear of Pius IX, claimed to have influenced the pope to send Wiseman back to England as cardinal and first Archbishop of Westminster[72]. Prior to his return to England, Wiseman issued a pastoral letter, *From out of the Flaminian Gate,* announcing the hierarchy and his own appointment. It provoked allegations of "Papal Aggression", and the last serious outbreak of "no popery" violence to be seen in England. The Pierce Connelly affair served only to reinforce the prejudices of those who wished to beat the anti-Catholic - and anti-Tractarian - drum[73].

Lord Shrewsbury was in Rome when the storm broke, and he was horrified by what he heard of the disturbances, "All Europe is astounded at the folly and tragedy of England", he wrote to Pugin, "and no-one can comprehend how to reconcile such absurdity with the wisdom of so great a nation"[74]. Though he supported the restoration of the hierarchy, he strongly disapproved of the insensitive way in which it had been introduced by Wiseman without any reference to the leading Catholic laity of England. He would also have liked to have seen the restoration of the Convocations, and a regular system of Catholic parishes, as a way of safeguarding the interests of the lower clergy. The earl also objected to the clumsy way in which the Prime Minister, Lord John Russell, reacted to Wiseman's pastoral letter by introducing the Ecclesiastical Titles Bill of 1851. The Bill sought to make all territorial titles illegal for Catholic bishops. He voiced his opposition to it through an open letter addressed to the Prime Minister[75], and in a portrait painted at this time (**8**), the earl is shown holding this letter in his right hand. Though the Bill became law, it was never enforced, and it was repealed twenty years later.

Pugin played his own part in the *furore* of 1851. First he published *An Earnest Address on the Establishment of the English Catholic Hierarchy* in which he set out the contentious thesis that in the sixteenth century the English Catholic Church had been betrayed by bishops who had concurred with the policies of Henry VIII rather than lose their wealth and influence. At the time of his death he was working on *An Apology for the Separated Church of England* in which he carried his earlier argument further to the extent that it came to be believed that Pugin - disappointed by the hostility of many of the hierarchy to his views on church architecture, and alarmed by the growth of Ultramontanism - may even have considered becoming an Anglican.

Following the death of the Princess Borghese in 1840, Lord and Lady Shrewsbury had been spending an increasing amount of time in Italy. The earl had come to the conclusion that the most practical and lasting way in which he could further the Catholic cause was by putting money into church-building, and he calculated that by staying away from Alton during the summer months he could save at least £2,000 per year which was enough for half a small church or a whole monastery; "and a church, or chapel, or monastery will endure (it is to be hoped) for many a long day, and be <u>infinitely</u> more instrumental in the conversion of the people than any personal exertions we can make at home. Of course we must come sometimes, but I hope not often"[76]. Though the Shrewsbury estates were vast, they were strictly entailed, and there were definite limits to the resources which the earl could allocate to church-building; and he was conscious more than anyone else of the contrast between the enormous private expenditures that were required to fulfil his social obligations at Alton Towers, and the relatively small sums of money which he was able to give to the Church[77]. The virtual closure of Alton Towers as a residence for long periods was a sacrifice he was pleased to make; the Census Returns for 1851 reveal that the number of domestic staff had been pared to a minimum, and the earl also sold off all but a very few of his fine horses and closed down the stud farm for which Alton had once been famous[78]. He dressed simply, ate frugally, abstained almost totally from alcohol, and accounted very strictly for every penny of expenditure, This latter point is made very clear in his correspondence with Pugin. He considered postal envelopes to be a complete waste of money, and continued instead simply to fold his letters and seal them with wax in the old-fashioned way. "You should write on a <u>single</u> sheet", he told Pugin, "and not put it into an envelope - if it weighs ever so little it pays <u>double</u> and that is a heavy charge in these sad times"[79]. Such economies were not born of miserliness, but of the earl's overwhelming desire to divert as much of his disposable income as possible into the furtherance of the Catholic cause. In addition to donations and gifts of furnishings and vestments to individual churches, he was able to make regular contributions to Bishop Walsh's general fund for the support of the Catholic missions. Lord Shrewsbury was the first President of the Catholic Institute established in 1838 to circulate Catholic tracts, organise lectures, and support schools; and also lay President of the *Oeuvre* set up in the following year to organise nation-wide collections in aid of the propagation of the Faith[80]. In 1846 he was honoured by the Pope, who appointed him Knight Grand Cross of the Order of S. Gregory, an award which he doubtless valued more than all his territorial lordships.

Among those who were in regular contact with the earl and countess during their absences in Italy were Pugin and Ambrose Phillipps. Pugin kept them informed of the continuing work at Alton Towers, S. John's Hospital and the Castle, and in 1851 Lord

Shrewsbury asked him to send sketches of the north and south fronts of the Towers to show how the great dining hall and other new rooms were progressing[81]. When Pugin became seriously ill at the beginning of 1852, the earl wrote twice offering to accommodate him at the Villa Belmonte in Palermo, and sending details of trains and steamers. "I know of no place where he could pass the Spring and summer with such advantage", he wrote to Jane Pugin. "If he would make up his mind to remain a whole twelve month with us, so much the better"[82]. Pugin had never been convinced that Sicily was a healthy place in which to live, and wondered how Lord Shrewsbury could stand the summer heat in Palermo. In spite of his temporary recovery in March 1852 - news of which clearly delighted the earl and countess - it was too late, and earl and architect never met again. Pugin soon relapsed into serious illness, and died on 14th September 1852. Lord Shrewsbury's reaction to the news is contained in a letter to Dr Rock, sent from Geneva on 25th September:

> "...Poor Pugin's very sudden departure really makes me sad; tho' I fancy we shall miss him more on our return than now. It is most fortunate, however, that he lived long enough to found and leave a complete school behind him in every branch of his art, his son will prove the most effective as well as the brightest ornament"[83]

19. Funeral of the sixteenth Earl of Shrewsbury, 14th December 1852 (Illustrated London News, 25th December 1852).

The fears which Pugin had earlier expressed for Lord Shrewsbury's health were not unjustified. In October 1852 the earl and countess left Rome for the Villa Belmonte, but the heat in Palermo was too excessive for Lady Shrewsbury, and they decided to return to Rome. Before they could start back the earl fell ill with malaria. His local physician advised that he be taken to Naples, where he was attended by Mr Roskelly, the surgeon to the British Embassy, but he died on November 9th, aged sixty-one. The grief-stricken countess was herself taken ill with malaria, but recovered; meanwhile the Prince and Princess Doria made the preliminary arrangements for the funeral.

The earl's body was placed in a copper coffin which was then filled with spirits of wine, and sealed, before being brought back to England where it first lay in state in S. George's Cathedral in Southwark, the last of Pugin's great churches to have been opened, and where a magnificent east window and other gifts testified to Lord Shrewsbury's generosity. An outer coffin of Spanish mahogany with elaborate metal fittings was made by Hardmans, while Edward Pugin superintended the funeral arrangements at Alton. The funeral itself took place on the 14th December in the Towers Chapel which had been redecorated and draped in black for the occasion **(19)**. Bishop Ullathorne presided, assisted by the Bishops of Shrewsbury and Clifton; and 150 secular priests were present, along with representatives of the various religious Orders[84]. The eulogy was given by Dr Henry Weedall, who had been President of Oscott in the 1830s, and who paid tribute to the earl's role as benefactor and as the recognised leader of the Catholic laity. He also quoted from a tribute written by Ambrose Phillipps testifying to the simplicity and gentleness of the earl's character:

> "...God had placed him amongst the princes of his people, but he walked through the gorgeous Halls of his glorious Palace as few poor men would pace the lowliest cabin. No one ever saw a haughty look or a disdainful smile on his placid face. No one ever heard a discourteous word from his lips".

Weedall's eulogy was subsequently printed as a pamphlet[85], and other tributes followed. Wiseman praised the earl's social work as much as his generosity to the Church[86], while the *Catholic Directory* for 1854 carried a twenty-page Memoir written by the Revd. Edward Price. This was quite exceptional, and not only on account of its length, for, as it was pointed out, it was the policy of the *Directory* to print tributes only to clergy of the highest rank. The most telling testimonial of all, however, was the silent one paid by the ordinary people of Alton and Farley on the day of the funeral itself. After the Requiem in the Towers Chapel the coffin was taken for burial on the Gospel side of the altar in S. John's church, Alton. Crowds of people joined in the funeral procession, and it was remembered that when the head of the procession reached the doors of the church, the coffin could be seen just emerging from the gates of Station Lodge nearly a mile away in the valley below[87]. Whatever else Lord Shrewsbury may have been - England's premier earl, the leading Catholic layman of his day, the wealthy patron of Pugin, and the father-in-law of princes - to the people of the locality he was known by that grandly simple title "the Good Earl". The "gorgeous Halls of his glorious Palace" were stripped of their fabulous treasures within a few years of his death, but on the opposite side of the valley the cluster of buildings in Alton village, along with the churches at Cheadle, Cotton and Uttoxeter, continue to serve the purposes for which they conceived and built, and these are his enduring memorial.

3 S. MARY'S, UTTOXETER

"It was a lovely sight to gaze around
That Gothic fane while gazing there to feel
That he whose genius framed the sacred pile
Is one whose noble aim it is to raise
God's fallen altars thro' the land - to blend
The holy and the beautiful once more!"
- BRITANNICUS, *Orthodox Journal. 1839*

The Catholic church of S. Mary, Uttoxeter, is hidden away in a side street - Balance Street - a few hundred yards distant from the medieval tower and spire of the Anglican S. Mary's, which had its nave rebuilt in 1828 in the Georgian Gothic style. Pugin's church has also been considerably altered since its opening **(20)**, while its location and the original smallness of the building belie its profound significance in the history of the Gothic Revival, and in Pugin's own career as an ecclesiastical architect and designer. It was the first church of the Shrewsbury-Pugin partnership to be completed, and, in Pugin's own words, it "may truly be described as the first Catholic structure erected in this country in strict accordance with the rules of ancient ecclesiastical architecture since the days of the pretended Reformation"[1]. Though situated in a town, S. Mary's was the prototype of Pugin's basic parish church, consisting of a simple nave and chancel without aisles or a tower, which could be built inexpensively to serve the needs of a small congregation. It was widely imitated by other architects, and in other countries. Though simple in design,

20. S. Mary's, Uttoxeter, 2001

S. Mary's did not lack any of the features regarded by Pugin as essential for the proper celebration of the English Catholic Rite. S. Mary's thus represented a revival of liturgical furnishings and practices not seen or used since the sixteenth century, and they plunged Pugin straight away into conflict with members of the Catholic hierarchy who viewed such revivals as archaic and irrelevant. Even before it was finished, this church received much publicity, while its opening in August 1839 was hailed in prose and in verse. Of all of Pugin's Staffordshire buildings, it is the one for which the most complete set of detailed plans and drawings has survived. For all of these reasons, S. Mary's is a key building, and of more than local significance.

The Uttoxeter Mission was established in about 1832 at the instigation of the Revd. J. Dunne of the Cresswell Mission who held weekly services and lectures, first in an outbuilding in the yard of the "Old Star" in Queen Street, and then in a building at the back of the Blue Bell Inn in High Street. In 1835 the Revd. George Morgan joined the Cresswell Mission. He was given responsibility for Uttoxeter, and it was he who initiated the scheme to build a proper chapel. Described as "a man of action who met difficulties merely as something to be overcome", Morgan - who came from an old Catholic yeoman family in Monmouthshire – is said to have sold his paternal estate to help build the chapel, and he also set about raising subscriptions from other sources[2]. His greatest opportunity came about in December 1836 when he temporarily took charge of Alton while Dr. Daniel Rock, chaplain to the Earl of Shrewsbury, went to Rome, partly for the benefit of his health. This brought Fr. Morgan into direct contact with Lord Shrewsbury, who became the principal benefactor. By this time the Earl was already in contact with Pugin, who began to work for him in the following year. Thus it was that Uttoxeter came to be the location of the first of Pugin's "True Principles" churches.

"A bicycle shed is a building; Lincoln Cathedral is a piece of architecture" - so Pevsner introduces his classic work, *An Outline of European Architecture* (1960), by drawing a distinction between structures which are purely utilitarian - such as a bicycle shed - and ones which are expressive, such as a cathedral, or indeed, S. Mary's, Uttoxeter. The church buildings of the first Christian centuries were of course largely utilitarian; practical buildings where the faithful could assemble under cover and set up an altar; and their architectural style was essentially no different from that of the secular buildings of the period. But then - and this is one of the major arguments of A.W.N. Pugin - the Christian era produced its own distinctive architecture and art; that which later came to be called Gothic. The pointed style, to use one of Pugin's preferred terms for it, is inseparable from the Christian Faith; hence the title of one of his most influential books, *The True Principles of Pointed or Christian Architecture (1841)*.

Pugin believed that Christian architecture had reached its high point in the fourteenth century with the phase of Gothic which is sometimes referred to as "Decorated". Thereafter it fell into decline, first with the so-called "Perpendicular" style (though, to his subsequent regret, Pugin himself used "perpendicular" for some of his earlier buildings); then came the Renaissance with its reversion to the Classical styles of ancient Greece and Rome which Pugin regarded as thoroughly pagan and therefore totally unsuitable for places of Christian worship. Finally there was the Reformation which led to the wholesale destruction of church interiors and a thousand years' worth of accumulated Christian art: stained glass windows, statuary, metalwork, wood-carving, and embroidery. Yet here and there, in the ancient churches and cathedrals of England, there were vestiges of what once had been: a rood screen here, a complete stained-glass window there; a hammer-beam roof, a painted panel, a fourteenth-century vestment or a late-medieval chalice which had somehow escaped the holocausts of the sixteenth and seventeenth centuries. What had once been, Pugin believed, could be again. Let the newly-liberated Catholic Church in England abandon the pagan art and architecture of Italy and adopt the styles of the High Middle Ages, and Catholicism would cease to be seen as something alien or foreign to England, and would be viewed instead as being as much a part of the English landscape as the ancient towers and spires under whose shadow the Catholic rites had once been performed until the advent of "that sacrilegious tyrant Henry VIII and his successors in church plunder"[3]. The re-marriage of the Catholic Faith with the architectural and artistic styles which were fundamentally expressive of it would contribute more than anything else, so Pugin believed, to the advancement of the Catholic cause. And it would be achieved supremely in and through that fundamental building, the parish church, set at the heart of the community, properly equipped with the right furnishings and fittings, and served by clergy who knew how to use them correctly:

> "It is, in fact, by parish churches, that the faith of a nation is to be sustained and nourished; in them souls are engrafted to the Church by the waters of baptism; they are the tribunals of penance, and the seats of mercy and forgiveness. In them the holy Eucharistic sacrifice is continually offered up, and the sacred body of our Lord received by the faithful. There the holy books are read, and the people instructed; they become the seat and centre of every pious thought and deed,"[4].

It seemed extraordinary to Pugin that while mistakenly viewing Catholicism as "foreign", so many English people clung stubbornly to the name of "protestant"; a term which had originated in Lutheran Germany and Calvinist Switzerland. The revival of Christian (i.e. Gothic) art and architecture might help to change their minds, but it was not just a question of doing battle with Protestants, for within the Catholic Church there were many who had no wish to abandon current Italian and French fashions of architecture and liturgy in order to return to the Middle Ages. They were an obstacle too, for their tastes and practices would tend to reinforce the popular myth that Catholicism was somehow alien to Britain:

> "We have a detestable crew to deal with", Pugin wrote in 1839, "ignorance, prejudice, timidity, tepidity. All combined - My dear friend, we have a sorry soil to plant in, and that not from protestantism; actually protestants in many cases are far better inclined to Catholicism than half the soi-disant Catholics of our days. Every attempt to restore religion to its antient dignity and glory is met with sneers, insult, and opposition from those who ought to be foremost in aiding the great work"[5]

As a recent convert to Catholicism - Pugin was received into the Church in 1835, only a year before he published his most famous book, *Contrasts* - he had as yet no influential friends to advance his cause in Catholic circles. *Contrasts* was subtitled, *The Noble Edifices of The Fourteenth And Fifteenth Centuries, And Similar Buildings of the Present Day; Shewing the Present Decay Of Taste,* which gives a fair gist of what the book was all about. Brilliantly illustrated, the accompanying text was in places so scathing that no publisher would accept it, and so Pugin had it printed at his own expense. In 1841 it ran to a second, expanded, edition.

At Uttoxeter Pugin had, in 1838, an early opportunity to move beyond satire and polemic, and to demonstrate what he meant by "the real thing". The buildings were to consist of a small aisleless church with a presbytery attached, of brick with stone trim, and

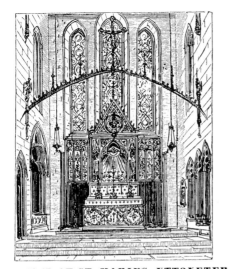

CHANCEL OF ST. MARIES, UTTOXETER.

21. Pugin's original design for Uttoxeter,
Orthodox Journal, *1839*

in the "lancet" style. Pugin was anxious to counter the allegation that Gothic churches were necessarily more expensive to build than the more "normal" type of Catholic chapel of this period, and to evolve at Uttoxeter a type which could be replicated elsewhere. "I am willing to prove, beyond all power of contradiction," he wrote in 1839, "that *more effect can be produced, and greater space gained,* for a given sum, in pointed architecture than in any other style whatsoever... " [6]

This was the first building in which John Bunn Denny (c.1810-1892) was involved as clerk of works, a post which he held, in respect of the Pugin-Shrewsbury buildings in this area until 1856. He later emigrated to Australia where he became a builder-architect in his own right[7]. Working under Denny were stonemasons and builders Peter and John Bailey of Alton, who were likewise involved at Alton Towers and other buildings in the area. Great care was taken over the preparation of detailed working drawings for both the church and the presbytery, and these remained in the possession of the Bailey family until 1987[8].

The foundation stone of S. Marie's[9], Uttoxeter, was laid by Fr. Morgan on 4th October 1 838. As the work progressed, Pugin took up his pen again, and on the 20th July 1839 a view of the proposed interior of the church appeared on the front page of the *Orthodox Journal,* with a three-page descriptive article inside **(21)**. Both the picture and the description made it abundantly clear that this was no ordinary church, but a revival, in every respect, of the ancient ecclesiastical architecture of England which "is so associated with every recollection that should bind the Catholic of this day with the faith of his fathers, and animate him to exertion, that to oppose its restoration is madness indeed"[10.]

Though externally quite plain, and without any structural division between nave and chancel, S. Mary's had all the essential features which made it clearly recognisable as a church, and a "true principles" church at that. Set on the western gable was a double bell-cote, below which was the only major embellishment: a circular window divided into twelve sections,. and filled with stained glass **(22)**. The main entrance was originally under this window, and over the west door on the inside was set the only significant piece of stone-carving: the

22. West window, Uttoxeter.

lion's head from the Shrewsbury coat-of-arms. Pugin took pains to pay early tribute to the earl, "whose pious and zealous exertions are effecting wonders in the restoration of Catholic architecture in this country"[11].

It was inside the building that Pugin proposed his most daring excursions into neomedievalism, all of which were described in advance in the *Orthodox Journal.* He drew attention to the provision of holy-water stoups just inside the entrance, and of a stone font with a locking cover. He hoped that the latter would signal a general restoration of fonts: "Old bottles and jugs are but sorry substitutes for fonts..... It is a most humiliating and shameful consideration, that, in this country modern Catholic chapels and dissenting meeting-houses can alone be pointed at as wanting this most essential object of church furniture".

23. Dove-shaped hanging pyx as shown by Pugin in the Glossary *(1844).*

As might be expected, it was in the chancel that Pugin proposed to introduce his most striking innovations. Over the entrance to the chancel there would be an arched rood-beam with a large crucifix and six tapers. The stone altar would have a carved front panel, painted and gilt, and would be equipped with a triptych reredos, with folding side-panels which could be closed during the penitential season of Lent. Three gilt lamps would hang in front of the altar, while on the altar itself there would be two large candlesticks - as was the universal custom in pre-Reformation England - as opposed to the now more customary "big six". The most unusual feature of all was the hanging pyx for the reservation of the Blessed Sacrament. The usual arrangement was to have a Tabernacle for this purpose fixed centrally on the altar or on the retable behind it. Instead, Pugin proposed a pyx in the form of a silver dove (**23**), which would be suspended over the altar, and the central panel of the reredos would be decorated accordingly with rays of glory to surround the pyx, and adoring angels on either side. Pugin was careful to cite his "authorities" for this, stressing that, far from being an innovation, it marked the revival of "an ancient and formerly general practice". Other revivals included the provision of stone seats, or sedilia, on the south side of the chancel for the priest, deacon and sub-deacon at High Mass, along with a sacrarium for the washing of the sacred vessels and to accommodate the wine and water cruets. In the north wall there was to be an Easter Sepulchre for use during the Holy Week ceremonies which Pugin sought to revive, and which he described in some detail[12].

Some of these features were bound to excite controversy and opposition. The hanging pyx was eventually abandoned in favour of a fixed Tabernacle in the form of a battlemented tower, and for this too Pugin was able to cite medieval precedent[13]. The central panel of the reredos was redesigned to depict the Madonna and Child, but otherwise the furnishings of the chancel were carried out exactly as Pugin had described them, and they were thus illustrated (**24**) in the first of Pugin's *Dublin Review* articles in 1841[14]. A quantity of metalwork, all to Pugin's design, was ordered from Hardman's[15]. Lord Shrewsbury made a special gift of the stained glass for the lancets of the east window, possibly by Thomas

ST. MARY'S, UTTOXETER.

24. Revised scheme for Uttoxeter as published in Dublin Review, *1841*

Willement (1786-1871), who was still working for the earl at Alton Towers in 1839. The glass, which consisted of geometrical patterns, was replaced in 1887. Though by no means as rich as the interiors of some of his later churches, the combined effect of all of these furnishings was quite striking as the contemporary illustrations show. Pugin saw to it that S Mary's lacked nothing that he considered necessary for the correct celebration of the Sarum Rite, and he cited it as an instance that "a Catholic church, complete in every respect, may be erected for a very moderate sum"[16].

The revival of the English Catholic Liturgy advocated by Pugin and Dr. Rock extended to matters of music - they wished to see the almost exclusive use of Gregorian Chant[17] - and to the style of vestments. Regarding the latter, Pugin wanted to revive the very full medieval shape of the surplice, the white robe worn by clerics in choir and by acolytes; and the chasuble, the principal vestment worn by the priest at Mass. Both of these had undergone a process of attenuation in continental Europe over the centuries. The surplice (25) had become much shorter, barely reaching the knees and forearms, and was generally called a cotta. The chasuble was originally a very full vestment, almost circular in shape with a central aperture for putting on over the head (26). This had likewise been cut down, particularly at the sides, to assist the priest's freedom of movement, and was generally shorter. The most extreme examples were the type known, from their shape, as "fiddle-backs". Even surviving medieval chasubles were mutilated to convert them to modern shape, and the left-over remnants used to make smaller items such as stoles[18]. Consequently the original form of these vestments had long been forgotten, so that Pugin's attempted revival of them seemed like innovation, and it was strongly opposed in some quarters.

Pugin saw the opening of S. Mary's, Uttoxeter, as a prime opportunity to introduce the "new" chasubles and surplices into a parish church. Dr Rock had already had an ample Gothic chasuble

25. Priest wearing the full medieval-style surplice (John Purchas, Directorium Anglicanum, *1858).*

made out of purple material in readiness for use in the Towers Chapel at Advent, and in May 1839 Pugin asked to borrow it. "I am fully determined to carry out Uttoxeter," he wrote. "I want all the plain chasubles made like your purple one so pray send it to me." [19] The use of these vestments at the opening of S. Mary's in August brought about an immediate protest from Bishop Baines, the Vicar Apostolic of the Western District, who refused to take part in the ceremonies rather than wear one. He was not alone in his view, and before the end of the year representations had been made to the Propaganda Fidei in Rome which resulted in a reprimand for both Pugin and Bishop Walsh for what were regarded as unauthorised innovations. Pugin pointed out the absurdity of it in a letter to Dr Rock: "..At Uttoxeter Mr Morgan had but one wretched vestment of *no colour* for all days, he procured a *compleat set* & they are prohibited as *not canonical*. What a farce"[20].

26. *Daniel Rock's illustration of a priest wearing alb, stole, and the ancient form of the chasuble* (Hierurgia, *1833, vol.2).*

To the modern mind these disputes over clerical vesture may seem purely academic, but to men like Pugin, Ambrose Phillipps and Bishop Walsh the vestments were significant ingredients in a general confection that would set before the eyes of Englishmen the Church of their forefathers in all its splendour; the Latin Mass - of course - but in a form and setting that was unmistakably English. Pugin and Phillipps urged Lord Shrewsbury to make representations to Rome, and his influence may have helped to prevent any formal censure being promulgated, but this was by no means the end of the matter. The underlying issue was one of authority. Bishop Baines regarded the Pugin chasuble as an innovation which needed the sanction of Rome before he could use it. Pugin, Phillipps and Rock believed that it was the post-medieval deviations which lacked proper authority, and that in any event the sanction of the Vicar Apostolic (in this case Bishop Walsh) was sufficient for the reintroduction of a style which had once been universally approved[21]. S, Mary's, Uttoxeter, was opened on 22nd August 1839. Dr Walsh presided, wearing the cloth-of-gold vestments designed by Pugin. Observers noted the censer, processional cross and acolytes' candlesticks, all of silver, that were carried at the head of the procession; the fourteen priests clad in voluminous surplices of the Old English type, and others arrayed in rich copes[22]. Dr Rock sang the Mass, and the address was given by the Revd. George Spencer. Lord and Lady Shrewsbury were present, along with their son-in-law and daughter, the Prince and Princess Doria Pamphili; and, of course, Pugin. The choir of Alton Towers Chapel sang, and their repertoire included items by Mozart and Haydn - a small concession to "modernism". Later in the year a lengthy poem appeared in the *Orthodox Journal*. Written under the pseudonym "Britannicus" by someone who had actually attended the opening service, the poem described the ceremonies and - without actually naming them - paid eloquent tribute to bishop, preacher and architect[23].

27. *The nave and chancel at Uttoxeter following the alterations of 1879 and 1913* (The Lewis Family Collection).

While extolling the many virtues of Uttoxeter, Pugin could not restrain himself from damning, in the same *Orthodox Journal* article, those who continued to build Catholic churches in the Italian and "meeting-house" styles. The new church of S. Francis Xavier, Hereford, was dismissed as a "hideous mass of semi-Italian building under the very walls of the venerable pile of Hereford cathedral"[24]. A correspondent to the *Orthodox Journal* who, under the pseudonym "Catholicus", attempted to defend the meeting-house style as a cheap way of providing new churches, was told by Pugin that "Methodisticus" would be a more appropriate name for one who dared hold up "that spawn of the original Protestant faction the Methodist body" as an example for imitation[25]. Such intemperate outbursts brought sharp responses even from those who admired Pugin's work; for example:

> "I do think Mr Pugin is getting out of his place, and assuming that dictatorial authority that does not belong to him, and using those abusive epithets that ill accord with the gentleman and the Christian...... We are almost led involuntarily to ask for the Bull appointing him superior of all the Catholics in England...... Mr Pugin is a diamond, and, we thought, a polished one; but he shows that he is not polished on all sides. He is so fond of antiquity that he cannot avoid mixing the rudeness of a Hector with the valour of a Christian knight"[26].

Those in the Catholic hierarchy treated with varying degrees of good humour and indignation the audacity of a convert of only a few years' standing who dressed like a Bohemian yet dared to lecture them on what they should wear at Mass, and who pushed them around the sanctuary at Oscott like pieces on a chess-board. The friendly Bishop Walsh nicknamed him "Archbishop Pugens", probably because of his habit of prefacing his signature with a cross, as the bishops did; while the antagonistic Dr. Bowden of Sedgley Park, irritated by Pugin's influence over Walsh, emphatically declared, "If Archbishop Pugens comes here I shall not do anything he advises"[27]. Pugin did not win all his battles, but it is of significance that from 1839 few churches were built in styles other than Puginesque Gothic. The support of Walsh was crucial in effecting the transition from "chapel" to "church" architecture, and Pugin said of him that no English bishop since the days of William Wykeham[28] had "done so much for the revival of the Glory of the house of God"[29].

28. S. Mary's, Uttoxeter: Angel-corbel from the former rood-beam.

Uttoxeter had an important part in effecting the transition, and it was this church that Pugin was thinking of when he later wrote, "I rebuilt the first sedilia, I set up the first Sacrarium, I erected the first Rood & Rood loft. I restored the 2 candlesticks on the altar & the curtains on each side...."[30]. It was also in some ways a victim of its own success. By the late 1870s the congregation had outgrown the building, and many had to stand out in the street for Sunday Mass. In 1879 a new chancel was added to the design of Pugin's youngest son, Peter Paul (1851-1904), who also provided a new reredos (27). The central panel of his father's triptych was taken to a new Catholic chapel at Draycott-in-the-Clay, about five miles distant, where it remained until the closure of that chapel in 1973. S. Mary's was enlarged again in 1913 by Henry Sandy of Stafford, who added the aisles, narthex, Lady Chapel and sacristies[31]. Pugin's Easter Sepulchre was moved to form the altar and reredos for the Lady Chapel, where the last vestiges of his Rood-beam were also relocated: the moulded corbels with figures of angels (28). For some inexplicable reason the double bell-cote over the western gable was replaced with a single one. If Pugin had not written a description of S. Mary's, and illustrated it, his intentions would now be difficult to understand[32], but in 1839 he was making a bold statement about the service of art to religion, as he had expounded it to the students of Oscott only a few months previously:

> "The Mass, whether offered up in a garret, or a cathedral, is essentially the same sacrifice; yet, who will not allow that, when surrounded by all the holy splendour of Catholic worship, these august mysteries appear ten times more overpowering and majestic?"[33]

4 ALTON CASTLE, AND THE HOSPITAL OF S. JOHN

"It will be the most perfect thing in England"- *A.W.N. Pugin*

When the second edition of *Contrasts* was published in 1841 it contained two additional sets of illustrations which reveal Pugin's thoughts on what he perceived to have been the social consequences of the English Reformation. The first set contrasts a view of a Catholic town in 1440, bristling with Gothic towers and spires, with a view of the same town in 1840, by which time the forces of materialism and secularisation have swept away most of what was overtly Christian, and ugliness reigns. The second pair of illustrations takes up the theme - topical in the 1840s - of the treatment of paupers under the 1834 Poor Law Amendment Act. "Contrasted Residences for the Poor" **(29)** shows a spartan utilitarian structure almost identical to the prison building in the 1840 townscape. Set against this is "The Ancient Poor House": a splendid range of Gothic buildings which are Pugin's idealised view of the medieval almshouse. Vignettes in the border of each illustration carry the contrast further. The medieval poor are well-dressed and amply fed, and after death they receive a dignified burial with full Catholic rites. On the other hand the modern pauper is threatened with a whip and fetters, is fed on gruel, and when he dies his body is sold for dissection. It is a caricature no doubt, but no more so than Dickens' verbal portrayal of Poor Law institutions in *Oliver Twist,* and unlike the novels of Dickens, Pugin's writings suggested antidotes to the ills he saw around him.

Both sets of etchings made a similar point. In the God-centred Middle Ages, so Pugin believed, there had been social cohesion, and true fellowship. Modern man was by contrast materialistic and unspiritual, and society was deeply divided. *Contrasts* was therefore not merely a book about aesthetics: architecture and art were but the means of reviving the spiritual and social values of the Catholic past. Alton was the place where the vision was to be translated into reality once more, and where Pugin sought to demonstrate how Catholic art and Catholic charity could transform a village into something like the ideal community implied in his view of the medieval town of the mid-1400s. As the new edition of *Contrasts* rolled off the press the buildings were already taking shape: the Hospital of S. John the Baptist, built entirely at the expense of John Talbot, sixteenth Earl of Shrewsbury.

"Hospital" in the medieval sense of the word did not signify a medical institution for the treatment of the sick, but what nowadays might be called sheltered accommodation for the poor and the elderly, i.e. almshouses with some communal facilities such as a chapel, a hall, and perhaps a library, and a resident warden. Medieval examples included St. Cross Hospital in Winchester and Browne's Hospital at Stamford, Lincolnshire. Pugin's diary for

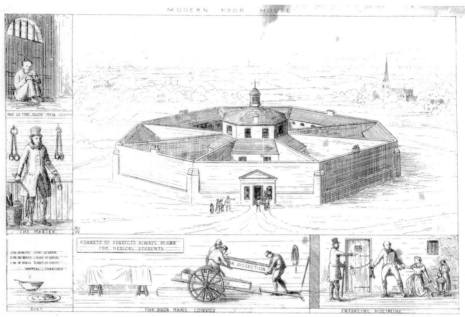

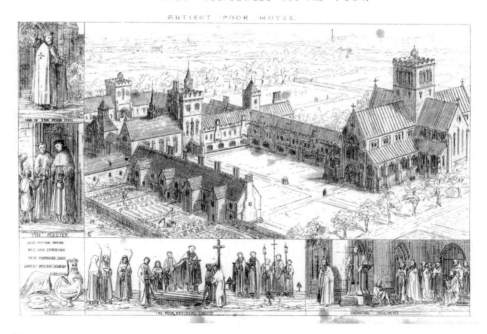

29. A.W.N. Pugin, "Contrasted Residences for the Poor" (Contrasts, 1841).

1840 records a visit to Stamford at the beginning of March, at the start of a tour of East Anglian churches, and he was there again in August 1848. Browne's Hospital, founded in 1475, contains many remarkable survivals including fine woodwork and glass, which Pugin undoubtedly saw and noted.

The notion of establishing such an institution at Alton may have been as much Lord Shrewsbury's as Pugin's. After making a grant of land for the founding of a Cistercian monastery in Charnwood Forest (Mount Saint Bernard), Ambrose Phillipps encouraged Lord Shrewsbury to do something similar at Alton. There were medieval antecedents in either case. The Leicestershire seat of the Phillipps family - Garendon Hall - occupied the site of a former Cistercian monastery, while in a valley close to Alton lay the ruins of Croxden Abbey, also Cistercian, founded and endowed in the twelfth century by Lord Shrewsbury's ancestors, the de Verduns of Alton Castle. Initially the earl promised to follow Phillipps' example, and he went some way towards acquiring a site; but in September 1836 he had a change of heart, and wrote to Phillipps from Alton Towers:

> "….I am apt to think that a society of brothers of Christian Instruction, with almshouses for the poor old people, would be more *useful* than a regular monkery. What think you? I begin to repent of my promise, not that I do not wish, nay ardently desire, to see a *religious* establishment on the premises; but I fancy we might have a much more useful one than a Trappist monastery. The new system of Poor laws makes it once more highly desirable to have almshouses where the poor old forlorn wretches may find a comfortable asylum with the benefits of religion, instead of those horrid haunts the common workhouses"[1]

Whether or not Lord Shrewsbury had by this time already met Pugin and been influenced by him is a matter for some conjecture. They were most certainly in touch with each other by the end of September 1836[2]. In 1839 Lord Shrewsbury contributed £2,000 towards the building of Mount Saint Bernard, and Pugin was appointed as architect; but as far as his own estates were concerned there was to be no monastery. Instead the Hospital of S. John the Baptist - Lord Shrewsbury's patron saint - was planned as a multi-functional complex of buildings. Pugin began work on the drawings at the beginning of September 1839, completing them on December 4th. His diaries record much travelling about during these weeks, and attention given to various other schemes, but the fact that Pugin was working on the hospital plans over a period of several weeks may also be taken as evidence of the great care which he took over a project he ardently believed in. "When completed it will present, both in its exterior and internal arrangements, a perfect revival of a Catholic hospital of the old time, of which so many were seized, demolished, and perverted by the sacrilegious tyrant Henry and his successors in church plunder; and in lieu of these most Christian and pious foundations for our poorer brethren, prisons are now substituted for those convicted of poverty"[3]. Here is the man of *Contrasts* rising to the occasion: a "Gothic passion" indeed!

The site chosen for the hospital was the area of the castle (**fig. 4**), to the south-east of S. Peter's parish church in Alton village; a picturesque location high up on the south side of the Churnet valley, with a sheer drop to the river below. The topography appealed to

Pugin, and there is no doubt that the visual impact of a range of buildings in a location such as this influenced their design and deployment: "The site that has been selected for this hospital", he wrote, "is one of the most beautiful and suitable for such an edifice that can well be imagined....... When viewed from the opposite hills, its turrets and crosses seem to form but one group with the venerable tower of the parochial church and the varied outline of the castle buildings,"[4].

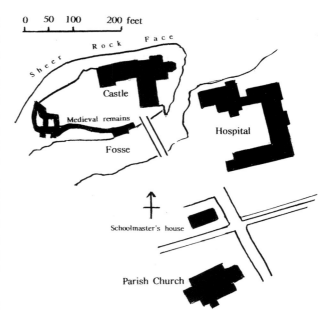

Fig. 4 – ALTON CASTLE and S. JOHN'S HOSPITAL

It is believed that the medieval castle was built by Bertram de Verdun - the founder of Croxden Abbey - in the mid-eleventh century. The Verduns retained possession of Alton until the male line died out in 1316; thereafter it passed by marriage into the hands of the Furnivals. In 1406 John Talbot - later first Earl of Shrewsbury - married Maud Neville, the heiress of the Furnival (and Verdun) properties. Thus the Alton estate, including the castle, came into the hands of the Talbots, though none of the family seems to have used it as a residence. During the Civil War the castle was garrisoned for Parliament, and thereafter it fell into decay. An engraving done by S & N Buck in 1731 shows that considerable portions of the castle were still standing at this time, but it was an easy quarry for building-stone and rubble for road-mending. Plundering of the site continued until the fifteenth Earl put a stop to it[5], and he took steps to stabilise and preserve what remained[6]. He was after all an antiquarian with a deep interest in his family's Staffordshire roots.

It is difficult to know for certain whether the rebuilding of the castle formed part of the original scheme or whether it was an after-thought. Pugin's description of work which in 1842 was either in progress or planned mentions only the chapel and hospital; yet in a footnote he writes that rubbish had been cleared away from the castle site in 1840, that the location of the castle chapel was known, and that a twelfth-century thurible had been found buried in the moat[7]. There was a local precedent for castle-building on old foundations. In September 1837 Pugin had visited Stafford Castle, another victim of the Civil War, which had already been partially rebuilt on its medieval foundations by the Catholic Jerningham family who, like the Talbots, were re-visiting their Staffordshire roots; but there was more to the rebuilding of Alton Castle than mere antiquarianism.

A deep fosse separates Alton castle from the hospital buildings (30), but they are linked by a bridge, and when viewed either from a distance or from the immediate approach from the village they form a coherent group as Pugin intended they should. Though Lord Shrewsbury resided at the Towers, out of sight on the other side of the valley, the restoration of the castle had a symbolic value. Castle and almshouse stand together; the architecture is the same noble Gothic; there is no "contrast" in style, materials, ornament or decoration between mansion and poor-house. In Pugin's vision of England, prince and pauper live cheek-by-jowl in proper dignity and united by a common faith. The church contains no "squire's pew", and when the time came, the premier Earl of England would be laid to rest, not in a grand mausoleum or a lordly family vault, but in a simple grave surrounded by those of his tenantry and bedesmen. Here again is a practical outworking of the social ideal portrayed in the 1841 edition of *Contrasts*.

30. Alton Castle: the fosse, the medieval remains, and Pugin's new buildings (1995).

Medieval Catholic England was, according to Pugin, "merry England, at least for the humbler classes; and the architecture was in keeping with the faith and the manners of the times, - at once strong and hospitable"[8].

Pugin's detailed drawings for the Hospital and the Castle do not appear to have survived. What does exist however, is a bird's-eye view of the hospital scheme which was used in February 1842 to illustrate an article in the *Dublin Review* (31). This was published 1843 as a separate volume under the title of *The Present State of Ecclesiastical Architecture in England*. The view shows the buildings arranged around three sides of a quadrangle; the chapel on the north side, the guildhall buildings on the south, with a residential block connecting them. The northern range had been finished by this time and so the chapel and warden's lodging are shown exactly as built. The remainder of the buildings underwent a degree of modification as the scheme developed, and were the subject of some disagreement between earl and architect. One has to remember too that both Pugin and Lord Shrewsbury died before the buildings were entirely finished; and that although some work continued thereafter, it came to an abrupt end with the death of the seventeenth earl in 1856.

Work began in 1840 on the northern range which comprised the chapel, school, and warden's lodging. The chapel would also serve as the parish church for the Catholic residents of Alton and Farley who at this time attended Mass at the Towers Chapel. The earl's newly-appointed chaplain, Dr. Henry Winter, would take up residence in the warden's

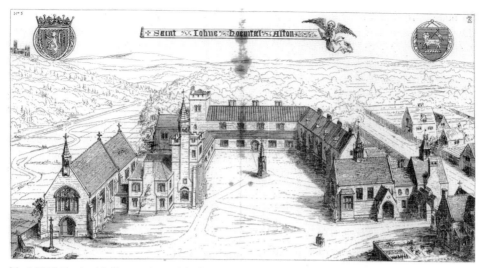

*31. A.W.N. Pugin, bird's-eye view of the hospital buildings (*Present State, *1843)*

lodging, and the school would provide suitable education for local Catholic children. From the very outset the Hospital was seen as much more than a secluded almshouse for the elderly. It was to be rooted in the whole community and to have a role in shaping its future. The school was particularly important. Apart from a small "free school" set up in 1682 for the education of twelve children, there was no provision for the education of the poor in Alton, where the population had increased by 46% between 1801 (1,633) and 1831 (2,391). The (Anglican) National Society did not establish a school there until 1845, partly in response to what the Catholic Church was doing.

32. S. John's, Alton, 2001.

Outwardly the chapel of S. John is typical of Pugin's small churches, similar to those at Uttoxeter and Warwick Bridge (Carlisle), i.e. a basic nave, chancel, and a simple bellcote on the gable (**32**). Subsequent changes in the way in which the building has been used have, however, obscured the fact that as originally built the nave was designed to function as a schoolroom, while the chapel proper lay east of the chancel arch; but clues are still there. In the first place the statue over the west door is not, as might be expected, that of the church's patron, S. John the Baptist, but of S. Nicholas, patron saint of children, and at his feet are three small boys in a tub - an allusion to the saint's miraculous restoration to life of three boys who had been murdered in a brine-vat. Secondly, the chancel-arch is set with large iron hinge-pins from which were originally hung the doors which could be closed when the nave was being used by the school, and opened when needed to provide additional space for worship. For the schoolroom Pugin designed rows of elm benches with hinged flaps which could be raised to form desks, and lowered to turn them into church-seats[9]. Concerned for the comfort of the children, Pugin decided that the seating area should be floored in timber rather than with quarry-tiles which he thought would be too cold for them in winter. Most, if not all of them, would have walked barefoot. The walls were also given a dado of elm "to prevent the plaster being broken"[10]. A house for the schoolmaster was ready by the winter of 1841[11]: one of a pair of cottages facing the north side of S. Peter's churchyard which Pugin adapted and extended for the purpose.

The materials used for the hospital buildings were local ones, principally "Hollington" sandstone which takes its name from a village three miles from Alton, and of which there is a great abundance all over the area, in a variety of colours ranging from deep red to buff. In 1841 Pugin opened a new quarry at Counslow, on a ridge between Cheadle and Alton, and this became the principal source of ready-worked sandstone for S. Giles', Cheadle, and for the continuing work in Alton village and at the Towers[12]. For the altars and for fine carving, Pugin was encouraged by Lord Shrewsbury to revive the use of alabaster which in medieval times had been used extensively for statues, reredoses and monuments[13]. There were alabaster quarries at Fauld, near Tutbury, which Shrewsbury suggested Pugin might use. At this time, however, the material was being mined only for making gypsum for plaster, and Pugin had to send his own quarrymen:

33. S. John's, Alton: west window with statue of S. Nicholas.

> "I have had a deal of trouble to get it for the people the quarry belongs to are so stupid; they blast it & it all flies into small pieces. We were obliged to send off 2 of our men to quarry the blocks at last, but it is well worth the trouble, it looks exactly like the old thing & when some of the mouldings are gilt it will be rich indeed"[14].

To ensure the success of this revival of a lost art, Pugin needed a skilled sculptor who could learn to use alabaster competently, and he found one in Thomas Roddis of the Sutton Coldfield firm of stonemasons who built Oscott College. He had been trained as a sculptor by Francis Chantrey; Pugin had already used him to carve fittings for S.

Augustine's church, Solihull (1838), and he moved to Cheadle in 1842. It is known that Pugin provided examples of genuine medieval sculpture for his craftsmen to work from, and there was a collection at Oscott. Fine examples lay close at hand too, for in the church at Norbury, between Alton and Ashbourne, were the alabaster tombs of the Fitzherbert family dating from the fifteenth century. Early in 1841 Pugin sent a plasterer to make casts of one of these to install in the Octagon at Alton Towers[15]. Around the sides of the tomb-chest are figures in rich canopied niches. The reredos which Roddis carved for S. John's is so remarkably similar in style that these casts may well have served as models before being assembled at the Towers, figures of saints being substituted for the secular figures portrayed on the sarcophagus **(Col. plates 2&3)**. The saints were, in fact, supplied by Pugin ready-made, and they could be of some antiquity[16]. The altar has figures of angels and saints under Gothic arches, all richly coloured and gilt. Pugin was delighted with the result and in February 1842 he wrote from the Towers to Lord Shrewsbury who was spending the winter in Rome:

> "... Roddis has produced a glorious altar in the alabaster. It is an exquisite material. I should never have revived it without your Lordship had urged it, and now I am quite delighted with the effort. It has a very rich appearance and the mouldings show through perfectly. Roddis now works in the most exquisite manner"[17]

Other craftsmen were more local, for example Peter and John Bailey of Alton, stonemasons who had already worked on the buildings at the Towers, Thomas Kearns, Lord Shrewsbury's painter and glazier who carried out the internal decorations at S. John's and in other churches of the Pugin-Shrewsbury partnership, and carpenter Thomas Harris. Superintending the entire operation as clerk-of-works was John Denny who had supervised the church at Uttoxeter, and was in charge of the continuing work at Alton Towers. Though Pugin had many other projects in hand, his diaries for 1840-42 record almost monthly visits to Alton, and some of these were spread over a week or more. This, as well as the regular correspondence which he maintained with the Earl and with Denny as the work progressed, reflect Pugin's enthusiasm for the hospital project, and his determination that everything should be exactly right. Here at any rate his efforts would not be curtailed by lack of funds, and this being the case, he knew that it could make or break his reputation as a working architect. "I am taking the greatest pains with every detail," he wrote to the earl in the autumn

34. Interior of S. John's as illustrated by Pugin in Dublin Review *(1841) and* Present State *(1842).*

of 1841........ Already crowds of people come to see the hospital"[18]

Crowds more would come in the next few months, following the publication of Pugin's enthusiastic description of the work in the *Dublin Review* in February, and the consecration of the altar by Bishop Walsh on July 13[th19]. In addition to the bird's-eye view of the hospital buildings, Pugin included a woodcut of the interior of the chapel **(34)**. In the foreground is the finely-carved rood-screen which stood, not under the chancel arch, but to the east of it close to the sacristy door. This was removed in the 1960s to the Birmingham Museum, but the crucifix from it presently hangs from the roof. The open timber roof is supported on corbels in the form of angels. Other fine woodwork included the poppy-head benches which were made for the chapel itself, although some of these have now been relocated in the "nave". "These are precisely similar to those remaining in some ancient parish churches in Norfolk, with low backs filled with perforated tracery of various patterns; the poppy-heads are all carved representing oak and vine leaves, lilies, roses, lions, angels, and other emblems"[20]. There are similar ones at Browne's Hospital too. It goes almost without saying that the gallery at the west end is not part of Pugin's original scheme.

With the exception of the west window, which is by Paul Woodroffe (1875-1954), all the glass for the windows was made by Thomas Willement (1786-1871) who had provided glass and other decorations for Alton Towers. The seven windows in the nave have armorial devices of the Verdun, Neville and Furnival families, diagonal bands with the Shrewsbury motto *Prest d'accomplir,* emblems of saints, and the inscription, "Of your charity pray for the good estate of John the sixteenth Earl of Shrewsbury, who founded this hospital in honour of S. John the Baptist, Anno Domini 1840. St. John pray for us. Amen". The east window has figures of the Virgin and Child, S. John the Baptist and S. Nicholas **(35)**. All of this glass is listed in Willement's ledger, along with the side-windows and the glass in the cloister and Blessed Sacrament Chapel. Drawings by Pugin of details of the east window are also preserved in the Willement collection[21]. Pugin thought he had been overcharged and vowed never to use Willement again[22], but the quality of the work was never in doubt: "I feel assured when your Lordship sees the glorious effect of the glass in the schoolroom you will not blame me. It is not for the urchins but the elite who will flock to see the building which should be in all respects a perfect specimen of the style"[23]. Pugin was not here slighting the poor children - such a thing was not in his nature. He was rather indicating the propaganda

35. East window, S. John's, Alton.

value of the hospital which would be of absolutely no concern to the pupils but which he hoped would register with visiting members of the Oxford and Cambridge architectural societies; and after all, where else in England were pauper children taught in such a splendid setting?

As at Uttoxeter the arrangements for the Reservation of the Blessed Sacrament were a departure from current practice. No provision was made at the high altar. Instead Pugin added a small chapel on the north side of the sanctuary. Here an alabaster altar carved by Roddis with figures of angels adoring the Blessed Sacrament (36) was furnished with a tabernacle in the form of a gilt tower surmounted by a cross. This

36. S. John's, Alton: alabaster side-altar carved by Thomas Roddis, and tiles by Herbert Minton.

tower is no longer extant, and a tabernacle was later placed at the main altar. Another innovation was the Easter Sepulchre under the arch separating the side-chapel from the main sanctuary[24]. The Minton tiles which once paved the whole area east of the chancel arch survive only in the side chapel. The stencilled patterns which Thomas Kearns applied to the walls, though not as intense as those at Cheadle, were nevertheless quite rich. "A building is nothing without diapering and colour", Pugin wrote to the earl.[25] The painting was, sadly, obliterated in the 1960s, and the hanging *coronae* by Hardman have likewise been removed, but old postcard views (37 & 38) show what S. John's was like when everything was still intact, and the furnishings in their proper place.

The sacristy, on the south side of the chapel, was fitted out with purpose-built almeries and presses for the vestments and vessels which were provided for the proper performance of the liturgy. Among these items was a medieval altar-cross in silver-gilt which Lord Shrewsbury bought from

37. Postcard view of interior of S. John's, c.1910 (The Lewis Family Collection).

*38. S. John's, Alton: postcard view of screen and chancel, c.1910 (*The Lewis Family Collection*).*

Samuel Pratt, a London antique dealer. It was of fifteenth-century date, and an inscription on the base records that it was made by a silversmith named Peter for a German bishop[26]. Pugin promised to design a pair of candlesticks **(39)** to complement it. An annotated drawing for these still exists[27]. The candlesticks have Talbot lions in enamelled shields, and the inscription, taken from S. Matthew, chapter 11: *Praecursor Domini venit de quo ipse testatur nullus major inter natos mulierum Joanne Baptista* (The fore-runner of the Lord comes, of whom the Lord himself bears witness, Among those born of women there is none greater than John the Baptist). The care lavished on these illustrates Pugin's determination: "Everything at the hospital must be perfect". It also illustrates what was quite a common practice of his, namely to put a genuine medieval artefact side-by-side with one of his own designing, as if to show the continuity.

Pugin was concerned that the sacristy and its contents should be properly looked after by someone who was in sympathy with his principles. He complained often enough about his churches being ruined because the clergy did not know how to use them properly. S. Mary's, Derby, was a case in point. Though he had equipped the sacristy with everything, only two years after the opening of the church Pugin found it to be untidy and filthy, and the costly vestments given by Lord Shrewsbury were thrust into a corner instead of being kept in the specially-made almeries. Such a thing could not be allowed to happen at Alton:

> "... What a glorious place the hospital at Alton will be with its Warden, confraternity, brethren, children of the school etc. Why, it could be a little paradise. There is not one

39. S. John's, Alton: medieval cross, and the candlesticks designed by Pugin to complement it.

Catholic hospital existing at the present time in England. What a revival. But I am certain from the very moment the chapel is completed a person must be appointed to fulfil the regular duties of a sacristan or all will be spoilt and he must be a very responsible person for all in his charge..."[28]

To the south of the church is the Warden's lodging with its three-storey tower and with a direct link to the chapel and sacristy **(40)**. This was also complete by February 1842. Over the entrance is a statue of S. John the Baptist, while the label-stops are carved with likenesses of the Earl and Countess of Shrewsbury **(41)**. The north side of the cloister was also completed at this time. In it were placed a memorial brass by Hardman commemorating the 15th Earl (d. 1827) who was buried at Heythrop. Correspondence between Pugin and Lord Shrewsbury about this memorial survives[29]. A brass to the countess's parents, Jane Talbot (d. 1843) and William Talbot (d. 1849) is also located in the cloister. Both of them died at Alton and were buried in the cloister. The other family memorials are of course those of the founder and his widow who were eventually buried (1852 and 1856 respectively) on the north side of the sanctuary, and that of the seventeenth earl (d, 1856) on the south side.

40. *S. John's, Alton: the Warden's lodging.*

Everyone, according to Pugin, should be given a decent burial in consecrated ground with full Catholic rites and a proper memorial. The point was made in the almshouse drawing in *Contrasts,* and reinforced in the *Dublin Review* article. After he settled at Ramsgate Pugin provided graves at S. Augustine's for the bodies of sailors washed ashore after shipwreck, and designed memorials for them. Such memorials had an important instructional value:

> "... nothing can be more calculated to awaken the solemn and devout feelings, than passing through this resting-place of the faithful departed. How often is the pious Christian moved to pray for his deceased brother, when he sees graven on his tomb, - 'Of your charity pray for my soul'!"[30]

The churchyard at Alton was therefore planned with infinite care. A handsome churchyard cross, carved in stone after the medieval fashion, was placed close to the west door, while in the cemetery east of the church there is a large wooden Calvary under a tiled gable **(42)**. According to the Abbé Vandrival, who in 1847 visited S. John's in the company of Ambrose Phillipps, this crucifix was only the second of its kind to have been set up in England since the Reformation, the first being that at the Phillipps home at Grace Dieu[31].

Pugin's concern for the proper care of the dying and the dead is illustrated by a letter

41. Maria Theresa, Countess of Shrewsbury: likeness carved in stone, S. John's, Alton.

written to Lord Shrewsbury on Christmas Eve 1841, in which he mentions the death of Peter Bailey, of the local family of stonemasons. It also reflects the close relationship which Pugin had with many who worked for him on the buildings at Alton:

> "...As I arrived at Alton the other day the bell was tolling for poor Peter Bailey. He died very penitent & with all the Sacraments. I designed a stone cross to be placed on his grave. He is buried under the yew tree near the hospital with a simple inscription cut on the cross"[32]

In the margin of the letter Pugin drew a small sketch of the memorial. Peter Bailey was buried in the nearby parish churchyard of S. Peter's, for the cemetery at S. John's was not opened until 1843. The Burial Register gives the date of his funeral as December 15th, and his age as 47. A Mass would no doubt have been said for him at the Towers Chapel, but the actual interment was carried out by the Revd. J. Pike Jones, the Anglican vicar of Alton, who - in accordance with general practice - would have claimed the right to officiate at all interments in the parish churchyard, whether Anglican or not. This practice was a matter of some dispute between Pike Jones and the earl's chaplain, Dr. Rock. There is a very large yew by the wall closest to the hospital, but, alas,

Peter Bailey's memorial is no longer there. There are, however, many of this type at S. John's dating from 1843 onwards: small crosses of varied pattern cut in local stone, but standing no more than two feet tall, and with simple inscriptions in Pugin's characteristic modified Gothic which would have been taught to the local stonemasons. There are some of a more elaborate kind, such as the ledger-stone with a floriated cross which Pugin designed personally for the children of Richard Orrell, who kept the Shrewsbury Hotel by the Farley entrance to the Tower[33]. Thomas Kearns, the painter who decorated the interior of S. John's is also buried here, and although he died some years after Pugin, his memorial is exactly of the coped-slab variety commended in *The Present State,* thus showing that the standards set by Pugin continued at least into the later nineteenth century. As one progresses eastwards into the newer part of the burial ground - and into the twentieth century -

42. The Calvary, S. John's Churchyard.

43. Part of letter from Pugin to Lord Shrewsbury, 24th December 1841 (HLRO 339/17) with sketch of revised plan for east range of hospital buildings (marked a a), and sketch of proposed memorial to stonemason Peter Bailey.

the incidence of "Pray for the soul of......" diminishes, even in this most Catholic of surroundings, and gives way to the ubiquitous "In loving memory" sandblasted into slabs of foreign marble and granite.

The opening of the chapel and school in 1842 marked the completion of the first phase of the hospital buildings, i.e. the northern range as illustrated in Pugin's *Dublin Review* article. The precise shape and function of the remainder of the buildings was still uncertain. As originally conceived the eastern range was intended for the accommodation of twelve "poor brethren" in more commodious lodgings, no doubt, than those provided in the Middle Ages, for example at Browne's Hospital where the brethren slept dormitory-fashion in cubicles in the Infirmary Hall. It was also envisaged that chaplains serving the North Staffordshire missions might, as they became too old to serve, end their days at S. John's in relative comfort. This latter notion was developed out of a conversation which Pugin had with Dr Wiseman in December 1841, and it resulted in a change to the original scheme for the eastern side of the hospital buildings. Wiseman said that there was an endowment of £40 a year for each priest, but that they were presently lodged individually in farm houses all over the district. Pugin thought that if they could be accommodated at Alton they could live in community as a college of priests, and say the Offices together in the chapel. He urged Lord Shrewsbury to consider this, and included in his letter[34] a small plan indicating a new scheme for the east range of the hospital (**43**). This would consist of "a plain convent building .... with a common dining room and library for them...... It would be of immense service and become a foundation worthy of the old time". Under the revised scheme the poor brethren would be housed in the proposed south wing, and a single kitchen would serve both communities.

44. South-east view of Alton Castle.

Although Lord Shrewsbury was a most generous patron, Pugin knew from experience that he was not given to overspending on any one project, and that he expected the funds to be carefully managed. As if to anticipate any possible objection on the grounds of extra cost, Pugin pointed out that the most expensive part of the hospital was already complete. The rest would be very simple and could be finished in two years using the existing work-force. Lord Shrewsbury agreed with the idea of accommodating the "decayed priests", but over the next few months there were yet more changes. The popularity of the new school created a need for more space than could be provided in the existing schoolroom, i.e. the nave of the chapel. There was also talk of establishing a community of the Sisters of Providence. Meanwhile work had begun on S. Giles', Cheadle, a project that was to absorb an increasing amount of Pugin's time, and in the autumn of 1842 urgent and extensive building operations began at the Towers[35]. Denny's work-force was therefore stretched, and it is not surprising that work at the hospital slowed down. Discussions between Pugin and Lord Shrewsbury about the next stage of development appear to have resumed in the Spring of 1843, and they proved to be the most controversial: the rebuilding of the Castle.

With its dramatic location and pyramid-capped towers, Alton Castle (44) is one of the most romantic of Pugin's buildings, and it is also one of the most mysterious in that its purpose is not easy to determine and appears to have changed during the course of construction. The plan of the castle (fig.5) is approximately L-shaped, with two wings running west and south of the chapel which stands at the junction. The two wings are different in character, and the more one looks at them the more apparent It becomes that they were built for totally different purposes. Like the chapel, the southern wing is noble in style and ornament. On the first floor are two large rooms with carved stone chimneypieces (45), and the larger room has a pair of oriel windows. The chimneypieces,

45. Chimneypiece, Alton Castle.

Fig. 5 ALTON CASTLE (1989) *David Mansfield Associate, Knutsford; and author*

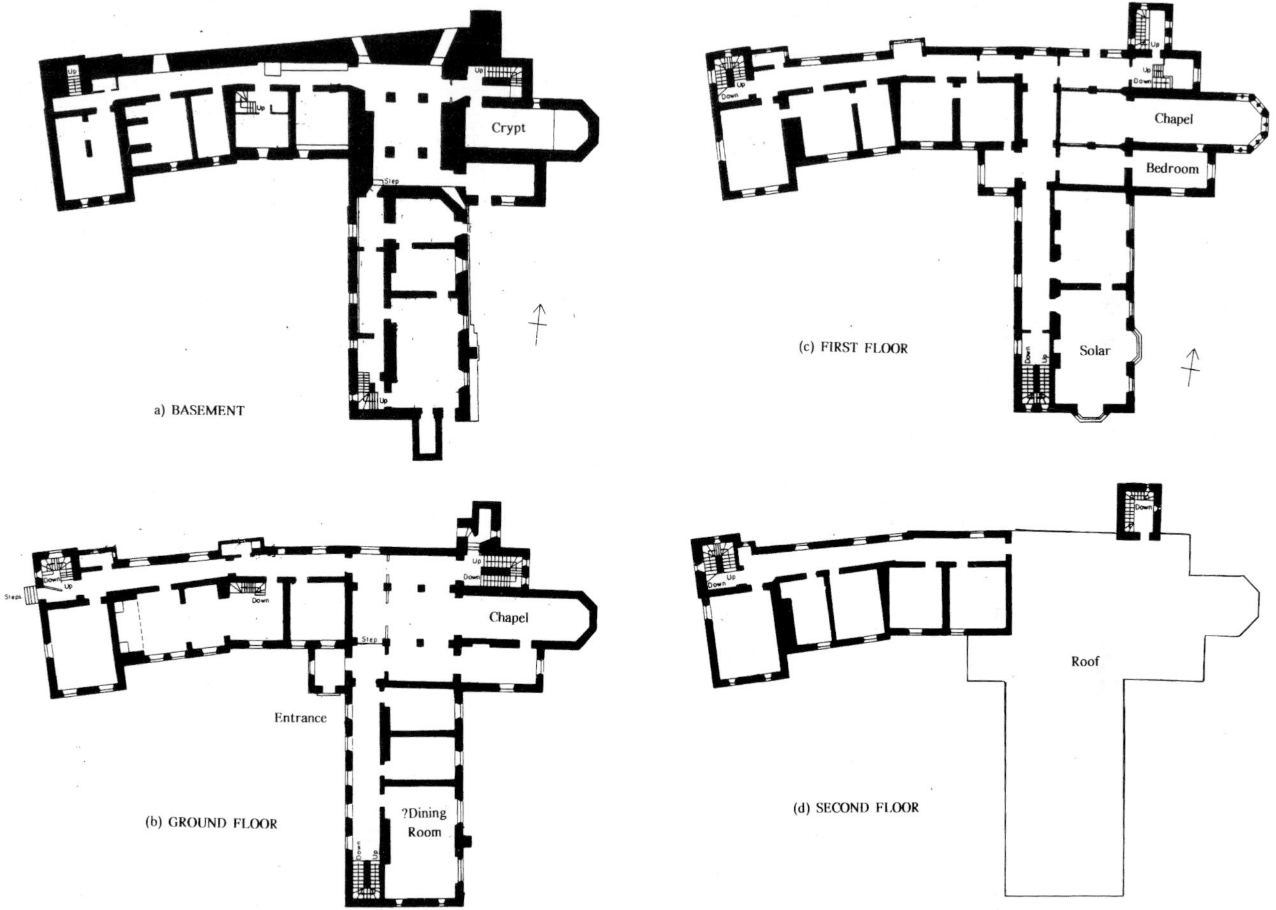
Crypt
Step
Up
a) BASEMENT
Chapel
Bedroom
Solar
Up
Down
(c) FIRST FLOOR
Chapel
Step
Entrance
?Dining
Room
Steps
Up
Down
(b) GROUND FLOOR
Roof
Down
Up
(d) SECOND FLOOR

the corbelled-out oriels with Pugin's trefoil trademark in the spandrels, and the cornice with its carved bosses, are almost identical with those added by Pugin to the south front of Alton Towers in 1849-51. As to its purpose, suggestions have been made that it was intended as a residence for the earl's cousin and heir Bertram who, as he approached his twenty-first birthday (1853), might be expected to set up an establishment of his own.

The castle might also have been intended ultimately as a dower-house for the countess, should the earl predecease her. Lady Shrewsbury most certainly had a great affection for S. John's and attended Mass there frequently when in residence at the Towers[36]. On the altarpiece, formerly in the Towers chapel and now in S. Peter's church at Bromsgrove, there is a detail which may be significant. Set in the frame designed by Pugin there are fanciful portrayals of the earl and countess in medieval dress of the time of the first Earl (d. 1453). Lady Shrewsbury is shown in her chamber kneeling at a prayer-desk, attended by her patron saint, the Blessed Virgin Mary. Through a window in the background is a view towards Alton Towers and the Flag Tower on the summit of the hill exactly as it is seen from the castle; i.e. the

46. Maria Theresa, Countess of Shrewsbury, as depicted on the Alton Towers altarpiece (S. Peter's Church, Bromsgrove). photo: Graham Miller

countess would appear to be in a room at the castle rather than at the Towers (**46**). Though the painting was done in about 1840 this detail may indicate that quite early on the castle was being thought of as the possible location of a future residence for her in what was already a favoured spot.

On the building itself there is nothing in the contemporary iconography to identify it specifically with either the countess or with Earl Bertram. The shields on the chimneypieces are blank, and the bosses on the cornice have only general Talbot emblems such as the letters S and T, lion-masks and Talbot dogs. These are, however, enough to delineate the southern wing of the castle quite clearly as an intended residence for a member of that family.

There is no such iconography in the west wing where the cornices are devoid of any ornament, and where there are no grand chimneypieces. The windows are plainer, with fewer cusps in the heads, and the "Puginian trefoil" is missing. Indeed the whole character of this part of the castle (**48**) is gaunt by comparison with the south wing; "institutional" rather than residential, rising to three storeys with a row of south-facing dormers in the roof, and rows of identical windows. Built on the very edge of the cliff above the River Churnet, it declines to the south-west part way along its length in order to follow the line of the bedrock. The cellars are partly cut into the bedrock and the walls at this level on the north side are enormously thick. The layout of the rooms is institutional too: pairs of identical rooms on the first and second storeys and a row of garrets in the roof. It is not difficult even now to visualise this part of the building as the residence for "decayed priests" which is what Lord Shrewsbury clearly had in mind for the castle in 1843.

By the summer of 1843 Lord Shrewsbury had decided to call a halt to the work at the hospital and to develop the castle site. For Pugin, the news that the hospital was to be left unfinished was bad enough, but the thought of building a castle for priests was also an affront to his "true principles". The design of a building must reflect it function, and priests do not live in castles. Pugin was

47. Alton Castle - the medieval crypt under the chapel.

in Ireland when he received the news, and in response he fired off two letters, one after the other, to the Earl. The first one, dated June 24th, reveals his anger, his disappointment, and his concern for the way in which the scheme could undermine his credibility as an architect of principle:

> "....I implore & entreat your Lordship if you do not wish to see me sink with misery to withdraw that dreadful idea about the alteration to the hospital. I would sooner jump off the rocks than build a castelated (sic) residence <u>for Priests</u>. I have been really ill since I read the letter. The hospital as designed would be a perfect building. What, no cloister, hall, gatehouse, after it has been engraved and everybody is looking forward to it. I can bear things as well as anyone, but I would almost as soon cut my throat as to cut that hospital to pieces. For heavens sake, my dear Lord Shrewsbury, abandon this suggestion which must be a device of the Devil to spoil so fair a design. Hence I say no more till I get to Alton, but I know it would spread disappointment on one side and derision on the other..."[37]

Of the second letter, written on the very next day, only a fragment has survived, but it reveals Pugin in an even darker mood:

> "This Castle at Alton has made me sick at heart after writing a book against mock Castles, a book dedicated to your Lordship[38], you call on me to violate every principle & build a Castle for Priests!!!! Moses broke the tables of the Law when he saw the Israelites dancing around the golden Calf, & after this ... I could burn everything I ever wrote or drew..... & turn fisherman".[39]

The immediate consequence of these letters is not known, except that Pugin did not of course part company with Lord Shrewsbury, or jump off the rocks, or turn fisherman.

48. Alton Castle - west wing.

There was too much to lose, especially Cheadle which, with good reason, he described as "my consolation in all my afflictions"[40]. He had indicated that he would be at Alton by the 10th August, and because his diary for 1843 is missing, one can only assume that he was; indeed it would have been a matter of some urgency. The long-term consequence appears to have been a compromise: the castle scheme would go ahead, and the hospital would also be completed eventually.

Preparatory work for the buildings at the castle appears to have begun in September 1843 when a Mr Horden was paid for "bricks for Alton Castle Chapel"[41]. This also indicates that the chapel was regarded as a priority. It was to be built directly over the crypt of the original medieval chapel **(47)**, which had been exposed during the clearing of the site, and other basement areas were cut into adjacent areas of solid rock. In 1844 Pugin was at Alton from the 19th July to the end of the month to supervise, amongst other things, the commencement of work at the castle, and he notes in his diary that the foundations were started on the 27th.

The earlier controversies were soon forgotten as Pugin became absorbed once more in the work at Alton and Cheadle, "the only jobs that give me real pleasure and satisfaction", he told the earl[42]. Cheadle was clearly the priority until after the opening in September 1846. Thereafter work at the castle gathered pace, but not without further disputes. The west wing - the intended residence for the priests - was progressing well in the summer of 1847 and would have been ready for roofing-in before the winter but for a change of plan by the earl himself. Lord Shrewsbury, it seems, wanted to incorporate some features from the derelict palace of Linlithgow, the birthplace of Mary, Queen of Scots[43], notably the addition of a high roof with dormers to a block which was already intended to be three storeys high. Pugin disagreed:

> "...There is no comparison between this building and Linlithgow; the latter is an immense pile with a gigantic hall, towers & turrets in every direction, while the castle building if carried up so high with dormers will look like the beginning of a row of houses. Nothing can be more dangerous than looking at points of buildings and trying to imitate bits of them. These architectural books are as bad as the scriptures in the hands of the protestants. If a high roof was to be added the 3rd storey could well have been dispensed with... "[44]

In the end Pugin had to concede, and the west wing was built to full three-storey height, complete with high roof, and the dormers on the south side. It is thus taller than the adjacent two-storey south wing, to which it is rather awkwardly joined **(48)**.

Well might Pugin have compared the picking and choosing of features of different buildings to the protestant habit of ransacking the Bible for handy proof-texts, yet he himself was responsible for other features which make Alton Castle something of a pastiche, albeit a very attractive one. The dramatic location of the medieval ruins, and the deep fosse which separated them from the hospital buildings, may well have called to mind the French Norman castles which Pugin had seen in his youth, and which were illustrated in Charles Nodier's *Voyages pittoresques et romantiques dans l'ancienne France* (1820)[45]. The apsidal chapel is very high and narrow, with tall windows and a vaulted roof, almost like a miniature *Sainte Chapelle,* and certainly very different in style from S. John's **(49)**. Externally the steep roof is covered with coloured tiles, an idea which may have come from the Hotel Dieu, a noted almshouse founded in the fifteenth century at

49. Alton Castle - the chapel interior, c.1980. (photo: courtesy Alton Castle)

Beaune in Burgundy. The roofs there have brightly-coloured tiles arranged in geometrical patterns. Pugin was travelling in this part of France, between Besançon and Dijon, in June 1847, and Beaune lies only a few miles off this route. It seems unlikely that the architect of a "perfect revival of a Catholic hospital of old time" would have missed the opportunity of seeing what was one of the best examples. Herbert Minton, the ceramics manufacturer, was asked to experiment with the production of coloured roofing tiles, and by the autumn of 1848 he had succeeded. "Minton has perfectly succeeded with the tiles", Pugin told the earl, "and I have ordered them for the chapel".[46] This is the only building in which he used coloured tiles to make a patterned roof.

Another hospital - Browne's Hospital at Stamford - was the source for the two-light openings set below the pyramid cap of what Pugin called the "look-out", the tower which stands at the south-west corner of the castle **(50)**. They were copied directly from the cloister-arches at Browne's **(51)**. Having visited Stamford for a second time, in August 1848, Pugin sent the drawings for this tower and gable-end for Lord Shrewsbury's approval[47]. The pyramid caps on the towers may seem like an

50. Alton Castle - the lookout tower.

71

51. Browne's Hospital, Stamford - the cloister arches.

innovation, but, as Pugin well knew, the towers of medieval churches and castles often had such caps, pyramidal, conical or polygonal, depending on the form of the tower. Their disappearance was generally the result of postmedieval decay, but there were some survivals, for example at Windsor castle; and not far from the Pugin family home was the ancient Kentish church at Reculver which, although ruined, still retained the framework of its tower-caps **(52)**. Significantly, perhaps, Pugin visited Reculver in July 1849 while making an extensive survey of medieval churches in north-east Kent. The dramatically tall caps on the twin towers of Southwell Minster (Notts.) had been removed some forty years before Pugin's visit there in September 1842, not to be replaced until 1880, but he would doubtless have known of them from earlier drawings[48].

The pyramid caps at Alton Castle, notably the one on the lookout tower, are of the Southwell type. The chapel tower was to have a more elaborate cap, as is indicated on a contemprorary drawing **(53)** indicating how it would look when completed, but it was never finished, and the tower remains flat-topped.

Actual building work at the castle seems to have progressed slowly, but Denny and his men were building elsewhere too. No sooner was S. Giles' finished (1846) than S. Wilfrid's and the other buildings at Cotton were started. When Cotton was finished (1848) attention turned to the great dining hall and other new rooms at the Towers. That was not, however, the only reason. "Fine jobs will always be slow", Pugin explained to the earl. "See how the finest trees grow and how long they last in comparison to the quick shooting sorts. Oak versus larch, so it is in building". "The work at the castle must be slow. It is impossible to construct so fine and solemn a building very fast".[49]

The chapel is easily the most fine and solemn part of the castle, as no doubt it was intended to be. At Alton Towers Pugin inherited a vast barn-like chapel which previous architects had built, and he had to

52. Reculver, Kent: nineteenth-century print.

53. Alton Castle from the valley: drawing as published in Ferrey, Recollections of A.N. Welby Pugin... *1861.*

content himself with improving the interior as best he could. At the castle he had the chance to show what the private chapel of a gentleman's residence ought really to look like when built from scratch by the master himself, and because the projected rebuilding of Garendon for Ambrose Phillipps never materialised, the chapel at Alton Castle is unique in Pugin's *oeuvre.*

In first place there is a narthex, or ante-chapel, which stands at the junction of the two wings of the building. It extends upwards through both storeys and is crowned with a pyramid-capped lantern. Galleries at first-floor level are carried on stone piers and segmental pointed arches, and there are matching piers and arches in the crypt below. At first-floor level the east wall of the narthex is pierced by an internal window with mullions and tracery which filters the view into the chapel itself **(54).** The galleries act as a kind of concourse at this level, with corridors leading from the south and west wings. One wonders if they might also have been intended as a tribune - as at the Towers chapel - from which the family of the house might hear Mass privately.

In the west gable-end of the chapel there is a curious feature, namely a spherical triangular window which, because of the form of the roof, is visible only on the outside of the building. It was the subject of a quarrel between Pugin and Denny who, it seems, made some remark to the effect that because it served no practical purpose it was merely a piece of gratuitous decoration, and therefore a breach of one of Pugin's basic principles. He may only have been joking, but Pugin was always extremely sensitive to comments of this kind, and in this instance it came from his own clerk-of-works, which he would have counted as disloyalty. The matter was resolved, and Denny was forgiven, but Pugin's subsequent letter to the earl shows how deeply to heart he had taken it:

54. Alton Castle - chapel; interior window at.gallery level.

".....I have forgiven Denny & written to him to that effect, as it appears he did not call my gable window a sham one, but I am sure your Lordship will admit that a more horrible charge could not be invented against the author of the *true Principles* than that of having introduced a sham window especially in such a building as Alton"[50].

The soaring lines of the chapel itself, and the surprising stone-vaulted roof, lift the eye heavenward. "It is a room which inspires worship", says Pevsner in BOE *Staffordshire*, but sadly it does so no longer. The stalls have been replaced with refectory tables and the chapel has been turned into a dining area for the use of the young people who now use the castle as a retreat centre. Old photographs of the interior **(55)** show furnishings - the altar especially - that cannot have dated from Pugin's time. They were almost certainly introduced by the French nuns who occupied the castle from 1904 to 1919. The old photographs reveal something else. The corbels from which the vaulting-shafts spring appear as unworked blocks of stone: they were carved into their present angel-forms only in 1948 in preparation for the Golden Jubilee celebrations of S. John's Preparatory School (formerly S. Aloysius' School for Little Boys) which had taken over the castle after the departure of the French nuns in 1919. The capitals of the shafts remain uncarved to this day. These details underline the fact that when the seventeenth earl died in 1856 much internal work was left unfinished. The glass in the windows is likewise of 1948, but it is of interest in that the lower lights form a kind of frieze telling the history of the castle and hospital, with reasonable likenesses of Lord Shrewsbury, Pugin, and Ambrose Phillipps.

With the exception of the cap for the chapel tower, the structural work at the castle - as distinct from masons' and carpenters' work on the inside - appears to have been completed by the Spring of 1852, when Lord Shrewsbury wrote to Pugin from Palermo:

"....I suppose Denny is now at the Hospital having finished the Castle which must be a beautiful object in the summer time - I long to see it again. What a deal will have to be done before our return!..... I want to finish the Hospital as a residence before the Castle, that Dr. Winter may get into his new quarters & the Sisters of Providence occupy his old ones, & that the whole yard may be completed & kept neat & trim. Surely the masonry will all be done this summer & autumn, including the gateway & wall - for he has no other job"[51].

The date of this letter is significant; 1st March 1852 - Pugin's fortieth birthday, and his last, for he was already in the grip of the final illness which took him to his grave six months later. Aware of Pugin's condition, the earl urged that he should leave immediately for Palermo and take an extended holiday with the Shrewsburys at their Villa Belmonte[52]. It is quite possible that the decision to switch attention from the castle to the hospital was taken in the hope that it would aid Pugin's recovery, for the earl knew just how much the project meant to him.

Apart from the gateway and the wall mentioned in the earl's letter, the structural work at the hospital was already complete by this time, leaving only the interiors to be finished "as a residence". The eastern range of buildings intended originally for the "poor brethren" is shown on a drawing of 1849[53]. The cross-gabled entrance with its corbelled-out oriel, and the dormers (56), make it far richer than the "plain convent building" which Pugin had in mind in 1841 and which is shown in the bird's-eye view

55. Alton Castle - postcard view of chapel interior, c.1920 (The Lewis Family Collection).

of 1842. It was here that the Sisters of Mercy were eventually lodged, but not until 1875, when Dr. Winter's successor, Fr. Anselm Gurden, moved into what was to have been the schoolmaster's house.

The southern range of buildings consists of the Guildhall (57), sturdily-buttressed,

56. S. John's Hospital, Alton - the eastern range.

and having windows with ogee tracery similar to those in the church at Brewood, with triple lights on the ground floor, and double ones above. The east end of this range is really a separate building, carried, on the south-facing side, by three open arches, and it has a lower roof level. This building forms the junction with the east range, and it was probably intended to accommodate the refectory

57. S. John's Hospital, Alton - the Guildhall.

and the kitchens which, Pugin had said, would serve both the poor brethren and the aged priests[54]. As eventually built, the Guildhall was to house the Upper School. The curious staircase tower at the west end, and the fact that the Guildhall range is different in style from the east range, have led some to doubt of they can be by A.W.N. Pugin at all, and to suggest that they might have been done after 1852 by his son Edward, or even by Fradgley of Uttoxeter[55]. The documentary evidence is, however, clear enough. First of all there is a letter written by Pugin in 1847 to accompany the working drawings:

> "I am now enabled to send your Lordship the working drawings of the school and guildhall. I have quite satisfied myself with the staircase tower, and have introduced provision for 3 clock faces which will give it a most picturesque effect..... I think altogether it will make a very substantial and picturesque building" [56].

Only the clock faces are missing from the circular openings set under gables projecting from the saddleback roof **(58)**. The top of the tower, with its pyramid-capped bellcote, is similar to those of the school and convent in Cheadle. The Guildhall must have been completed by the autumn of 1849 because - as stated below - it is known that social functions were taking place there in October of that year.

Pugin's consideration of the "picturesque effect" of his buildings and their environment extended beyond the precincts into the valley below, where any development could impinge upon the prospect of the castle and hospital

58. The Guildhall Tower.

as viewed from the wooded walks below the Towers or from the valley itself. In 1849 the railway arrived in Alton: a branch of the North Staffordshire Railway which linked the towns and villages of the Churnet valley with the main-line stations at Manchester and Derby. Pugin was enthusiastic about the railways. The great period of railway building coincided exactly with the years when he was most active professionally, giving him a degree of mobility that no previous architect or designer had enjoyed. The railway was thus a key factor in enabling him to undertake so many projects simultaneously in different parts of the country in a working life which spanned little more than fifteen years, and to supervise them personally.

The subject of railway architecture interested Pugin, and he included some illustrations in *An Apology for the Revival of Christian Architecture* (1843). It is tempting to think how his ideas might have developed if he had lived longer and had the chance to work with the engineer Isambard Kingdom Brunel (1806-1859) with whom he had much in common[57]. The closest Pugin came to being a railway architect, however, was at Alton where he viewed the arrival of the railway as a benefit and as a challenge, thinking that he might have the opportunity to design some bridges and stations. On hearing of the successful launch of the Churnet Valley Company, he wrote enthusiastically to Lord Shrewsbury, "This looks well. I hope it will be carried through & then we may get some model stations"[58]. He was most anxious that the earl's estates should be safeguarded against "vile erections and designs" on the part of the Railway Company, otherwise "the greatest horrors will be perpetrated under the very walls of the old castle & the whole place ruined"[59]. Clearly, he saw himself as the one to set the standard for railway architecture in this part of Staffordshire.

To begin with, Alton station had just a temporary platform, where Pugin first arrived by train in October 1849 - a fact which he noted in a letter to Lord Shrewsbury[60]. He produced some plans and elevations for a permanent station, to be built of brick with a stone trim: "I think it will make a picturesque building"[61]. When it came to producing detailed specifications of the work inside, however, and putting the designs out to tender - which is what the Company wanted - Pugin admitted that this was not his accustomed way of working, and it was possibly because of this that the Company eventually went elsewhere. The result was precisely the kind of "vile erection" that Pugin had most feared: Italianate in style, and thus totally at variance with the castle and with the Station Lodge. Perhaps a perverse spirit was at work, a view which gains credence when it is known that neighbouring stations such as Cheddleton, Oakamoor, Dove Bank and Rocester were all Gothic in style, with high gables, steep roofs, tall chimneys and mullioned windows, i.e. of the kind that Pugin would most certainly have built at Alton[62]. As it is, Alton station clashes so violently with Pugin's Station Lodge across the road that they could well have appeared side-by-side in a third edition of *Contrasts* under the heading of "Contrasted Station Buildings".

The Station Lodge is a very different building (**59**), and it was intended as the entrance to Alton Towers for visitors arriving by train who could then be conveyed by carriage directly up to the house rather than having to take the more circuitous route via the Farley or Quixhill entrances. There was already a building on the site known as Alton Cottage, which was the home of estate worker Joseph Jackson, his wife, and six children. They were

59. Station Lodge, Alton.

to be rehoused in the new building which Lord Shrewsbury wanted to call "Jackson's Lodge", until Pugin insisted that it be called Gatehouse[63]. Eventually it became known as Station Lodge or Tudor Lodge: a picturesque building, asymmetrical, with fine moulding to the entrance arch, and rich heraldry above it.

It was not just the physical appearance of the village which changed as the buildings took shape. The spiritual and social consequences were far-reaching too, as both earl and architect intended. The free education provided at the new school attracted non-Catholic families, and space for an upper school had eventually to be made in the Guildhall building. The activities of Dr Winter, who gave evening lectures on aspects of the Catholic Faith, and the charitable work of the Sisters and of the countess too when in residence at the Towers, also played their part. This was indeed the "Second Spring" of English Catholicisim following in the wake of the Emancipation Act. Even before S. John's was opened Pugin wrote, "It is quite wonderful what Dr Winter has done here. He received whole families into the Church at once. The chapel at the Towers is literally crammed and fresh converts are coming every day"[64]. By Christmas 1841 he was even more euphoric: "Nobody now dies a protestant at Alton," he quipped, "even if they do not all live catholics"[65].

The Baptism Register for S. John's (which also records baptisms at the Towers Chapel up to 1842) reflects this trend: a very sharp rise in numbers between 1841 and 1846. The social life of the village also found a focus at the Hospital, with the Guildhall functioning as a Mechanics' Institution - the Victorian equivalent of the Worker's Educational Association - and as a community centre. In October 1849 Pugin wrote home to his wife, "There are strange doings here at S. John's. Balls in the Guild Hall, dancing till 2 in the morning, the Rev. Dr. (Winter) playing the French Horn!!"[66]. Catholic England, as Pugin reminded his readers, was merry England.

Not everybody was inclined to be merry, least of all the Rev. John Pike-Jones, the vicar of S. Peter's. Pike-Jones was not an extreme protestant; indeed, he had been one of the few Anglican clergymen to have argued the case for Catholic Emancipation, and this was no doubt a factor in his appointment to the parish of Alton of which the Earl was the patron[67]. Nevertheless he accused Dr Winter of setting out deliberately to make converts in a much more vigorous way than his predecessor, Dr. Rock, had done, and a war of words ensued. The Abbé Vandrival's statement that in May 1847 Pike-Jones had a congregation of only five is almost certainly an understatement[68], but the parish registers of S. Peter's reveal a marked decline in the number of Anglican baptisms in the 1840s, corresponding to the increase at S. John's. When it came to the ecclesiastical census of 1851 Pike-Jones said - perhaps significantly - that he did not have sufficient data to give the numbers attending S. Peter's on census day, March 30th[69]. Attendance at morning Mass at S. John's totalled 300, with 104 scholars, while in the evening there were 200 and 104 respectively. The total population of Alton at this time was 2,326.

The death in 1856 of Bertram, the last Catholic Earl of Shrewsbury, and the eventual succession of the Chetwynd-Talbots to the titles (1858) and to the Alton estate (1860) had a profound effect upon the village. The estate accounts show that remaining work on the castle and hospital stopped abruptly, and of course the generous financial support hitherto given by the Talbots also ceased. Some villagers considered it prudent to abandon the Catholic faith so as to identify with their new landlord. It is said that one of them went to work wearing his coat inside-out, to indicate to the new earl that he would quite literally become a turncoat to keep his house and his job.

Thus the scheme which had begun with such optimism in 1840 never came to full fruition. No bedesmen were lodged at the hospital, no "decayed priests" came, and the castle was home to neither heir nor widow. Pugin, in characteristically self-critical mood, once said that he had spent his life thinking fine things and achieving only poor ones. He could not say that of Alton though. It was, along with Cheadle, something that he believed in passionately, and he believed in it right to the end, when he was trying to impress upon a somewhat impatient earl the virtues of progressing slowly with solid and substantial buildings. The quality of the work at Alton speaks for itself; and it speaks too of the skilled craftsmanship of John Denny and those who worked with him - Peter and John Bailey, Thomas Harris, Thomas Kearns, Thomas Roddis, and others whose names are recorded in the estate accounts. The fault, if there is any, lies not with Pugin, but in the failure of the Catholic Talbots to produce a male heir capable of continuing the line and maintaining the level of support for the Church given by Earls John and Bertram. Changes were afoot anyway. The restoration of the hierarchy in 1851 - which Earl John supported - diminished the importance of the seigneurial families whose role had been so vital in the years of persecution.

As for the use of the buildings, the schools - which had ever been a part of the scheme of things - flourished, and S. John's Junior School still occupies the Guildhall. The chapel of S. John formally became a parish church in 1930. The hospital became the residence of the Sisters of Mercy, who ran the preparatory school established in the castle in 1921, and when the Sisters left in 1993 the building was for a time used by a community of Benedictine monks. Finally the castle - which had lain empty since the closure of the Preparatory School in 1989 - was purchased in 1995 by the Archdiocese of Birmingham on behalf of the Catholic Youth Association, and it has been developed imaginatively as a residential centre for young people. The hospital now forms part of this complex. Thus the Church has been able gradually to assume responsibility for all of the buildings, and to fulfil at least some of the intentions of their architect and founder.

5 ALTON TOWERS

"...the mansions erected by our ancestors were not the passing whim of a moment, or mere show places raised at such an extravagant cost as impoverished some generations of heirs to the estates, but solid, dignified, and Christian structures.." A.W.N. Pugin, *True Principles.*

That Pugin should have carried out alterations and additions at the home of his wealthiest and most influential patron is hardly surprising. It is only recently, however, that the full extent of his contributions to this vast Gothic mansion **(60)** has been perceived, surveyed and recorded[1], and they were considerably more extensive and significant than was formerly thought to have been the case **(fig. 6)**. It is now known that they comprised the Talbot Gallery and the Talbot Passage linking the gallery to the West Wing (1839-40), the remodelling of the Octagon (1839-42), substantial fortifications on the north and east sides of the house (1842), kitchens and servants' accommodation (1841-49), the Doria Rooms (1843), new rooms over the Great Drawing Room and on the north front (1850-52), conservatories on the south side of the house, and other garden buildings (1846-48) the Counslow and Station Lodges (1841 & 1849), and the Great Dining Room (1849-51). Pugin completely altered the internal appearance of the chapel (1839-40 and 1851); and he redecorated the Great Drawing Room, Long Gallery, and several of the family rooms, as well as designing furniture for the West Wing, and stained glass, metalwork and woodwork for other existing rooms.

This catalogue of structural and decorative work reveals Pugin as the Romantic in his completion of the dramatic galleries, the ecclesiastical designer in his transformation of the chapel, the military engineer in his construction of the barbican and other defences, and the man of *The True Principles* in his masterly creation of the great dining room. "You will be greatly pleased with the works at Alton", he wrote to Ambrose Phillipps in 1851, "which have improved the house amazingly"[2]; and yet more was in hand at the time of his death.

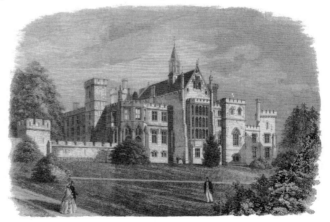

60. *Alton Towers: drawing by T.J. Rawlings,* Illustrated London News, *21st April 1860.*

Several architects had worked at Alton before Pugin arrived in 1837. These included Thomas Hopper (1776-1856), William Hollins (1763-1843) and Thomas Allason (1790-1852). Between them they transformed and extended a small Georgian house ("Alveton Lodge") into what was from 1811 to 1831 known as Alton Abbey in the romantic, but historically inaccurate, fashion of the time. The house was set in extensive grounds which included the famous valley gardens created out of a waterless rocky wilderness by the fifteenth earl of Shrewsbury and completed by the sixteenth. Following the fire which

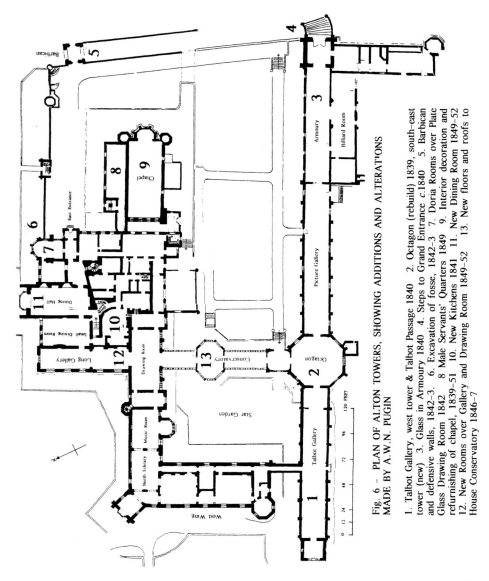

Fig. 6 – PLAN OF ALTON TOWERS, SHOWING ADDITIONS AND ALTERATIONS MADE BY A.W.N. PUGIN

1. Talbot Gallery, west tower & Talbot Passage 1840 2. Octagon (rebuild) 1839, south-east tower (new) 1840 3. Glass in Armoury 1840 4. Steps to Grand Entrance c.1840 5. Barbican and defensive walls, 1842-3. 6. Excavation of fosse, 1842-3 7. Doria Rooms over Plate Glass Drawing Room 1842 8 Male Servants' Quarters 1849 9. Interior decoration and refurnishing of chapel, 1839-51 10. New Kitchens 1841 11. New Dining Room 1849-52 12. New Rooms over Gallery and Drawing Room 1849-52 13. New floors and roofs to House Conservatory 1846-7

*61. S. Michael's Gallery, Fonthill Abbey: Rutter,
Delineations of Fonthill..., 1823.*

destroyed the Shrewsburys' principal residence at Heythrop (Oxfordshire) in 1831, a great west wing was added to Alton Abbey by a local builder-architect, Thomas Fradgley of Uttoxeter (1801-1883), and Fradgley, along with Joseph Potter of Lichfield, built the new chapel in 1832. It was at this time that the house was re-named Alton Towers.

One of the many extraordinary features of the Towers was the series of linked galleries on the south side of the house through which visitors would be conducted before entering the house itself. Passing under a formidable barbican, and along a gently rising driveway between two huge curtain-walls, they would arrive at the steps of a lofty entrance tower flanked by a pair of stone Talbots - the dogs associated with the family coat-of-arms at least since the days of the first Earl, "the Great Dogge Talbot" himself (c.1384-1453). At the top of the steps visitors would enter through a pair of immense doors, nailed on the outside, and emblazoned on the inside with the full armorial bearings of the Earl of Shrewsbury. A second pair, similarly embellished, led into the 120-foot-long Armoury filled with over three hundred items of arms and armour. Beyond was the Picture Gallery, its walls lined with paintings by celebrated artists of the Italian, French, Flemish and German schools. Another change of scene awaited in the Octagon hall, reminiscent of the chapter-house of Wells cathedral, with a central column and vaulted ceiling. Ahead lay the Talbot Gallery, the most splendid of all the galleries, the view into which was filtered by a glazed timber screen. Having caught a brief glimpse of the splendours beyond, visitors would - tantalisingly - be directed by a ninety-degree turn out of the Octagon into the House Conservatory filled with the colour and scent of exotic plants, and the songs of birds in gilded cages, before entering the house itself. Entrance Tower, Armoury, Picture Gallery, Octagon, Conservatory - over 150 yards of them - were no more than a prelude to the magnificent *enfilades* of richly decorated and furnished apartments which lay beyond.

The scale and richness of these Romantic Interiors exceeded even those of Fonthill Abbey (1796-1812) built by James Wyatt for millionaire-eccentric William Beckford. No documentary evidence survives to prove that Wyatt (1746-1813) had ever worked at Alton, and in any case the galleries were built a decade and more after his death. Yet Fonthill was undoubtedly the inspiration for the Alton galleries linked to a central Octagon; so much becomes clear by comparison with John Rutter's illustrations **(61)** to *The Delineations of Fonthill* (1823), while his account of how the glories of Fonthill were revealed little by little to the eye of the visitor could apply equally to Alton which, when the galleries were begun, was known as "The Abbey".

The similarities extended to small Romantic details. William Beckford kept a liveried dwarf in his entrance-hall to emphasise the height of the building; at Alton the Talbots had a blind Welsh harper, named in the 1841 census as Edward Jervis, who lived in the Harper's Cottage (subsequently called the Swiss Cottage) at the head of the valley-gardens. A drawing of the Armoury done at this time by Samuel Rayner **(62)** shows him sitting at the entrance, from where his gentle playing and singing would carry down the galleries and also out into the grounds, much to the delight of visitors.

62. Alton Towers: The Armoury; Pencil drawing by Samuel Rayner, c.1840 (The Potteries Museum and Art Gallery, Stoke-on-Trent).

It is a little ironic that soon after his arrival at Alton Pugin should have been given the task of completing a set of rooms so reminiscent of Wyatt, whom he was wont to describe as "the wretch" and "this monster of architectural depravity". Yet his work on the Alton galleries effected an even closer resemblance to Fonthill, principally through the addition, in 1839-40, of the Talbot Gallery **(63)** to the west side of the Octagon which thus became - as at Fonthill and as it was to be at the New Palace of Westminster - the central element of an axial system of linked chambers. A tall square tower was built at the west end of the new gallery to balance the entrance tower at the eastern extremity of the range.

The combined east-west length of the Alton Galleries and Octagon (480 feet) far exceeded that of the principal axis at Fonthill (280 feet). Every device of lighting, space, and rising levels was exploited to the full, and the view from the new Gallery through the entire range was breathtaking:

> " ... When the reader recollects that the whole of this vista is filled with works of art of the noblest character, or with the remains of antiquity of the most interesting kind, he may have some idea of the magnificent *coup d'oeil* which presents itself, and of the difficulty we find in giving anything like an

63. Alton Towers: The Talbot Gallery: pencil drawing by Samuel Rayner, c.1840 (The Potteries Museum and Art Gallery, Stoke-on-Trent).

adequate description of it"[3].

The construction of the Talbot Gallery - built on a level higher than that of the existing buildings - involved raising the walls of the adjoining Octagon by several feet. The central column had also to be raised[4]. Since the walls were not strong enough to support a stone vault, Pugin had to agree to the reinstatement of a plaster vault worthy of "the wretch" himself, and the retention of cast-iron screenwork at the Picture-gallery entrance. The new Gallery was furnished with two massive chimneypieces similar to the one in the Great Hall at Scarisbrick, and also surmounted by suits of armour. Willement painted over a hundred shields for the heraldic frieze, and Hardman supplied a set of eight sixteen-light *coronae* bearing the Talbot motto *Prest d'accomplir.* It was the *pièce de resistance* of the entire house. Visitors arriving by the Grand Entrance would catch glimpses of it through Pugin's openwork screen as they passed through the Octagon to the House Conservatory. Only when they had completed the tour of the house would they return, via the West Wing, to enter as the climax of their visit - what was described as "the last and noblest of the halls in Alton Towers"[5]

Even in the Talbot Gallery Pugin had to agree to install cast-iron skylights to match those of the 1820s Picture Gallery. Elsewhere he was involved in the creation of replica Talbot tombs cast in plaster (for the Octagon), and much time and energy were expended in finding suitable armour and a horse for an equestrian figure of the first Earl ("The Grand Talbot") to stand in the Armoury. It may be no coincidence that this work in the galleries was started in the year of the Eglinton Tournament[6]. The compromises, and the restrictions under which Pugin had to work in his earlier years at Alton, help to account for the "all-or-nothing" stance he adopted a decade later over the design of the new Dining Room.

Other additions by Pugin to the Armoury and entrance included a set of windows executed by William Warrington depicting William I and various Talbot ancestors, and the exterior steps with their attendant Talbot hounds. It was in the Octagon and Talbot Gallery that Pugin was able to make his boldest statements. At the Gallery entrance he set a glazed wooden screen Perpendicular style - and in the south wall of the Octagon a five-light window by Willement with figures of Talbot bishops. On the south side he built a square tower with pyramid-capped bartizans at the corners, much in the Scottish baronial style. This was probably intended as a look-out associated with the defences constructed in 1842.

It seems likely that Pugin's satire of "castellated architecture" in *The True Principles (1841)* was inspired by one of the many irritating features he found at Alton, where the fortified grand entrance led eventually to the State Rooms via the House Conservatory which was completely unprotected.

> "On one side of the house machicolated parapets, embrasures, bastions, and all the show of strong defence, and round the corner a conservatory leading to the principal apartments through which a whole company of horsemen might penetrate at one smash into the very heart of the mansion' - for who would hammer against nailed portals when he could kick his way through the greenhouse?"[7]

64. *Alton Towers: The Barbican.*

It was not just a matter of good taste, or of correcting the errors of his unenlightened predecessors, which led to the fortification of this side of the house in 1842. This was the year of widespread Chartist agitation, with mass meetings, demonstrations and riots in the Potteries towns, and in July there were disturbances and damage in the Cheadle district caused by colliers from North Staffordshire. Pugin's diary for 1842 shows that he was at Alton for several days in June-July, and that Lord Shrewsbury was also in residence at this time. While at Alton Pugin noted in his diary under July 18th "Home fortified against the colliers" which has been taken by some to refer to Pugin's own house, but this is unlikely since at this time his family home was in Cheyne Walk, Chelsea. It is much more likely that

65. East end of Alton Towers Chapel: pencil drawing by the author, based on pre-1950 photographs and other original sources.

he was referring to some provisional arrangements at the Towers. Pugin - always wary of radicals and revolutionaries - travelled through Stoke on July 22nd, calling on Herbert Minton whose workers, like those in other potteries, had struck in sympathy with the miners who were then marching towards Macclesfield. He wrote back anxiously to Lord Shrewsbury, "I do not perceive any immediate danger, but your Lordship should not by any means relax in vigilance and have all made fast at night till things are really settled. I have not yet got the brass guns as I have heard of a better market for them."[8]

Other sources make it clear that very substantial fortifications were being constructed at Alton in 1842 and into the following year. In the first place there is the Barbican gateway at the north-east corner of the house, which bears the date 1842 (**64**). Associated with it are the high walls which run southwards either side of the carriage-drive, and which gave protection to the hitherto vulnerable east side of the mansion, and the east terrace-wall which communicates with the Barbican at its upper levels. These were in themselves considerable feats of civil engineering carried out at some speed; added to which was the excavation of a deep fosse, or ditch, along the whole of the north front, under the very walls of the house itself. It caused Pugin some anxiety, and it was commented on by at least one foreign observer[9]. The Chartists never came, but the fortifications marked an important stage in Pugin's attempt to transform a Georgian mansion of the romantic "Abbey style" into something more serious.

Transformation of another kind took place in the chapel, a cavernous building erected in 1832-33 by Fradgley and Potter. Lined throughout with oak wainscot, and with an unpainted roof, the interior was somewhat sombre, while the abundant use of cast iron painted to look like wood was precisely the kind of sham which Pugin abhorred. His improvements were carried out in two stages. First of all, in 1840, he designed an elaborate triptych reredos for the altar, similar in style to the one at Oscott, and to complement this, all around the apse containing the altar, the entire east wall was covered with Gothic screenwork of carved timber, painted and gilded, and with figures of saints and angels in canopied niches (**65**). It was a most ambitious scheme, which Pugin never repeated elsewhere. To complement the dado in the apse - which was made from medieval panels brought from the chapel of Magdalen College, Oxford[10] - he placed panelling along the lower parts of the side walls, and this was decorated with stencilled patterns, thus introducing a degree of colour into the main body of the chapel.

The second phase of Pugin's work in the chapel was done in 1850. The ceiling was decorated with a pattern of stars and sunbursts on a blue ground

66. Alton Towers Chapel - the ceiling under restoration in 1993.

(66). The cast-iron corbels in the form of kneeling angels, painted originally to resemble wood, were now coloured and gilded, and the ceiling was given a rich frieze painted on canvas panels, and carrying the words of Psalm 113. A series of tall, narrow panels topped with crockets and pinnacles was placed along the walls below each of the angel-corbels, and some of the pictures were given new Gothic frames[11].

Even in its relatively unadorned state, before Pugin's additions and decorations, the chapel was described as "not surpassed in beauty and richness, we believe, by any other (private chapel) In England; perhaps not in Europe"[12]. The effects of Pugin's work were quite stunning, as is shown by the only known contemporary painting of the interior[13] and by contemporary descriptions of it[14]. Though the chapel was - shamefully - gutted in the 1950s, fragments of the screenwork and the frieze have survived, and the ceiling was restored in 1994 along with one of the frieze-panels. The altar and reredos had been removed to Grafton Manor, Bromsgrove, in 1860, to be transferred to the new Catholic church of S. Peter in the same town, where it may be seen today.

The Towers chapel was the scene of some spectacular celebrations such as the reception of Pugin's wife, Louisa, into the Catholic Church in May 1839[15], and visits by foreign royalty. It was also equipped with all the necessary furnishings, vestments and vessels for the correct performance of the revived medieval English liturgy as researched and promoted by Pugin and by Dr. Daniel Rock who was Lord Shrewsbury's chaplain from 1827 to 1840[16]. Thus the Towers chapel attracted the attention of both Catholics and Anglicans who were curious to observe how the liturgy should be performed In Pugin's revived Gothic settings. Being a private chapel, it was free from the restrictions - and censures - which hampered and frustrated Pugin elsewhere in his attempts to re-introduce the Old English vestments and ceremonial so alien to the Catholic Church of the time.

The central feature of the north front of "Alton Abbey" was the entrance hall, set transversely, and with a high gable and a large Gothic window (fig. 7). When the new Grand Entrance was built on the east side of the house, the original entrance hall was

Fig. 7

ALTON TOWERS – THE ENTRANCE HALL/GREAT DINING HALL

a) as built by Thomas Allason, c.1818   (b) as rebuilt by A.W.N. Pugin, 1851

converted into a state dining room, and the external doors were replaced with another window. It was an elegant room, with a lofty plaster-vaulted ceiling and much ornamental ironwork including a spiral staircase by which those arriving at the house would ascend to the principal rooms on the first floor. Following the conversion, guests would now descend by the same staircase into the dining room. It was not a particularly convenient arrangement, and in the early 1840s Lord Shrewsbury proposed to alter it by inserting a new floor ten feet above the level of the existing one, and thus raise the dining room to the same level as the state rooms. Pugin saw this as the opportunity to create something far more grand and ambitious, and it was the subject of a good deal of controversy between earl and architect, with Lord Shrewsbury arguing the case for a fairly simple alteration of the existing room, and Pugin pressing for what amounted to a complete rebuilding.

All of Pugin's schemes for great houses - executed and unexecuted - provided for a Great Hall in which he imagined that lord and tenant would feast together on great occasions as they had done in the Middle Ages[17] Alton was to have the grandest of them all, as befitted the home of England's premier earl; and, having compromised his principles again and again over matters such as the plaster vaulting and mock sarcophagi in the Octagon, cast-iron frames in the Talbot Gallery, and the theatrical horse and rider for the Armoury, Pugin was determined that this time the "True Principles" would prevail:

> "...I have nailed my colours to the mast: a bay window, high open roof, lantern, 2 grand fireplaces, a great sideboard, screen, minstrel gallery, all or none"[18].

What Pugin was pushing for - and what finally he got - was the reduction of the existing room to a shell, the insertion of the new floor as originally envisaged, and the corresponding raising of the walls by some ten feet. Only in the newly-created basement area were any significant traces of the old hall suffered to remain. Within this re-worked fabric, a completely new room was created, exactly as Pugin had planned.

"The great work", as Pugin called it, began in April 1849, and he entered a large drawing of the interior scheme for the Royal Academy exhibition later in the year[19]. The structural work involved much more than the internal reconstruction of the existing building. The east wall of the room was not of sufficient depth or strength to accommodate the two huge chimneypieces worked in Bath stone, so a brick reinforcement had to be provided on the far side of the wall. This meant closing off the rooms immediately to the east, with consequent disruption including a good deal of mess and noise - in what were the private quarters of the earl and countess. The raising of the walls by ten feet also created an imbalance in the appearance of the north front, and this could only be redressed by the addition of a fourth storey west of the dining room, involving yet more upheavals. It was not without good reason that the earl had tried to rein in Pugin's ambitions, although it has to be said that he and the countess were able to take refuge in Italy while most of this work was going on.

Pugin's Royal Academy drawing appears no longer to exist, but several of his drawings for the fittings of the dining room are extant in a private collection[20]. These include the great brass and crystal chandelier modelled on one in Nuremburg cathedral, and which is now in the Palace of Westminster; and details of grates and fire-irons. The two chimneypieces had Minton tiles set into the reveals; the lower parts of the walls were clad in carved oak panelling, while at the west end the screens passage and minstrels' gallery - also of carved oak - were fronted by a great sideboard made by J.G. Crace. This was made to display the fine array of plate specially made by Hardman, including a great dish 30" (76cm) in diameter. The drawings for most of these survive[21]. Finally, Pugin's stained glass designs for the north and south windows were executed by Hardman, the great oriel filled with heraldic devices, and the south window having as its central feature the figure of the first Earl of Shrewsbury - "The Grand Talbot". The hall was crowned by a high open timber roof, with arch-braces, wind-braces, and a central lantern from which the chandelier was suspended by a (still extant) chain (**67**). The roof is richly-decorated in a red, blue and gold pattern incorporating Talbot lions. Pugin estimated the total cost of this work at £2,271[22].

Neither Pugin nor Lord Shrewsbury lived long enough to see the "great work" completed, and it is clear from the 1857 Alton Towers Sale Catalogue, an inventory of 1869, and the Alton Estate Accounts, that work continued in the dining hall for many years while furnishings intended for it were stored in other parts of the house. Later photographs show that it was eventually finished according to Pugin's original scheme. Several items intended for the hall - the chandelier, the Great Talbot window, the sideboard and plate were displayed in the Medieval Court at the Great Exhibition of 1851 where the applications of Pugin's wide-ranging genius as a designer were shown in the work of Crace (wallpaper, fabrics and furniture), Hardman (metalwork and glass), Minton (ceramics) and Myers (carved woodwork and stone).

Alton Towers itself was a kind of permanent exhibition in which the full extent of Pugin's talents were displayed to distinguished visitors such as Sir Robert Peel, Charles Barry, and - later - Benjamin Disraeli who adapted it as the "Muriel Towers" of his romantic novel *Lothair* (1870). As early as 1841 Charles Barry told a Parliamentary Committee that the style of Pugin's decorations in the Chapel and the Talbot Gallery would apply equally well to the New Palace of Westminster[23]. Without doubt Barry's influence was crucial in securing for Pugin the work he carried out on the interiors of the Palace, and recent re-appraisal of Pugin's work at Alton leads one to the conclusion that his decorative and structural work there should rank equally[24]. This makes the gutting of Alton in 1952 the

NEW DINING ROOM at ALTON:1851

MF 2001

67. *Pugin's new Dining Room at Alton Towers: pencil drawing of interior by the author, based on 1890s photographs, and illustration of sideboard in* Illustrated London News, *20th September 1851.*

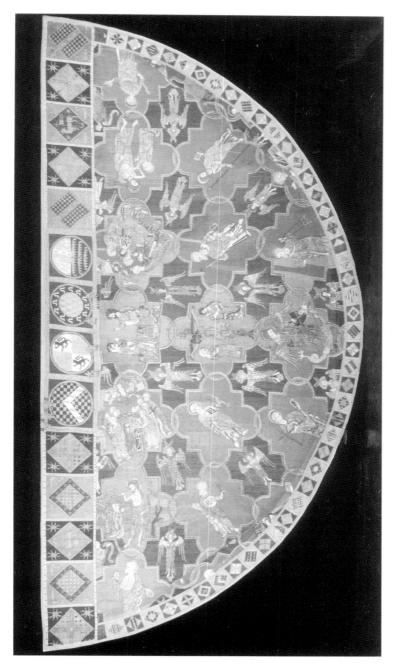

Plate 1. The Syon Cope (V&A Picture Library), *once part of Lord Shrewsbury's extensive collection of medieval eccelsiastical art.*

Plate 2. *S. John's Church, Alton: the chancel*
(photo: Graham Miller)

Plate 3. *S. John's Church, Alton:
detail of reredos carved by Thomas
Roddis.*

Plate 4. *Drawing together the many strands of Pugin's genius as an ecclesiastical designer: S. Gile's, Cheadle - the screen and chancel.*

Plate 5. S. Gile's, Cheadle: the Easter Sepulchre.

Plate 6. *Stained glass. Detail from the Works of Mercy window in the south aisle, S. Gile's, Cheadle. Pugin was particularly pleased with William Wailes' execution of his design for this window.*

Plate 7. *Encaustic tiles designed by Pugin for All Saint's Church, Leigh, and manufactured by Herbert Minton. The arms are of Richard Bagot, Bishop of Oxford.*

Plate 8. *Church metalwork: Gilt-brass monstrance designed by Pugin for S. Gile's, Cheadle, and made by Hardman* (photo: Graham Miller)

Plate 9. *Frontispiece designed by Pugin for John Masfen's* Views of the Church of St. Mary at Stafford, *published in 1852.*

Plate 10. *Church of the Holy Angels, Hoar Cross: the Rood Screen by G.F. Bodley, 1874.*

more regrettable, but even in their reduced state the chapel and the dining room bear eloquent testimony to Pugin's achievements as a domestic architect, while other structural features such as the oriel windows of the south front and of the Doria Rooms, the servants' quarters and the barbican gateway, speak as effectively as a page from *Contrasts* against the "mock" Gothic of his unenlightened predecessors. Though there was much at Alton that would have annoyed him as much as it was later to annoy William Morris (who dismissed the Towers as a "gimcrack palace"), Pugin spent long periods there, delighted in the Romantic North Staffordshire landscape, its rich Catholic history and medieval survivals; and he assured Lord Shrewsbury, "I am sure I do not need much inducement to stay, for I am nowhere so happy"[25].

6. S GILES', CHEADLE

"I will not let anything pass for Cheadle that is not the true thing. It must be perfection" - A.W.N. Pugin

Cheadle has two churches dedicated to S. Giles: J.P. Pritchett's Anglican church built in 1837-8 to replace its decayed medieval predecessor, and Pugin's Catholic S. Giles' begun just three years later. Placed side-by-side these two churches could well have come from a page of Pugin's *Contrasts,* for they give a striking illustration of the changes which took place over these years, thanks largely to Pugin, in the understanding and application of Gothic architecture **(68)**. Pritchett's church is admittedly of the better kind of the so-called "Commissioners' Gothic"[1]; its interior furnishings and decorations have been altered drastically, and it has gained a deep chancel. When opened, however, it had all the features which Pugin ridiculed: an embraced west tower, a box-like nave without a proper chancel, incorrect window tracery, galleries on three sides, and a three-decker pulpit obscuring the altar. In other words, it was basically a preaching-house overlaid with a veneer of quasi-Gothic ornament. It has to be said, of course, that these arrangements perfectly expressed the state of Anglican worship in the early nineteenth century when the emphasis was on the spoken word, not the performance of a grand liturgy, and when the irreducible minimum of ritual observances required by the 1662 Book of Common Prayer had in fact been reduced through decades of neglect. All this was about to change, and had the medieval S. Giles' managed to survive just a few years longer, the rebuilding might have been carried out in a very different way under the impact of Pugin's writings, the work of the Oxford and Cambridge architectural societies, and the close proximity of "the real thing": Pugin's S. Giles' to which the "Oxford Men" (as Pugin

S. Giles', Cheadle, by J.P. Pritchett
1837-8

S. Giles', Cheadle, as designed by
A.W.N. Pugin, 1841

CONTRASTED PARISH CHVRCHES

68. Contrasted Parish Churches - the churches of S. Giles in Cheadle, drawn by the author.

was wont to call them) and other Anglican scholars and architects were irresistibly drawn.

It was one of Pugin's frequently-voiced complaints that the English Catholic Church of his time was lacking in taste and propriety, that the church buildings were barely distinguishable in design from nonconformist chapels, that their furnishings were foreign and shabby, and that the liturgy was badly performed. The truth of the matter was that the English Catholic Church had only recently emerged, blinking and rubbing its eyes, into the daylight of Emancipation after 250 years of persecution when matters of architecture, furnishings and ritual were of little concern in comparison with the basic question of survival. Indeed, some of the dingy chapels and mass-houses were even revered as the places where the Faith had been nurtured during the Penal times, and on account of their association with some who had actually suffered persecution.

69. *S. Giles' from the south-east:* Illustrated London News, *9th January, 1847.*

At Uttoxeter Pugin had been able to demonstrate that a Catholic Church built according to the "true principles", and properly equipped, need be no more expensive than one which was not; so there was no financial reason for not doing things his way. Though originally conceived as something rather smaller and less ornate than it eventually became, S. Giles' was from the beginning intended to be a kind of text-book church in which everything would be done according to the principles set out in Pugin's key writings, with every part of the building designed to instruct, to inform, to have a definite purpose. Unlike the Uttoxeter church, it would have aisles, a tower and spire, and a porch (69). It was to be the practical outworking, in every detail, of the ideal of the medieval parish church as set out in *The True Principles of Pointed or Christian Architecture (1841) p.42:*

> "An old English parish church, as originally used for ancient worship, was one of the most beautiful and appropriate buildings that the mind of man could conceive; every portion of it answers both a useful and mystical purpose. There stood the tower ... terminated in a heaven-pointing spire surrounded by clusters of pinnacles, and forming a beautiful and instructive emblem of a Christian's brightest hopes. These towers served a double purpose, for in them hung the solemn sounding bells to summon the people to the offices of the church, and by their lofty elevation they served as

beacons to direct their footsteps to the sacred spot. Then the southern porch, destined for the performance of many rites, - the spacious nave and aisles for the faithful .... the impressive doom or judgment pictured over the great chancel arch, - the fretted screen and rood loft, - the mystical separation between the sacrifice and the people, with the emblem of redemption carried on high and surrounded with glory, - the great altar, rich in hangings, placed far from irreverent gaze, and with the brilliant east window terminating this long perspective..."

The key phrase here is, "..as originally used for ancient worship". Pugin intended S. Giles' to be the perfect setting for the revival of the Old English liturgy, namely the Sarum Rite which was being researched in depth by Lord Shrewsbury's chaplain, Dr. Rock. Though the Sarum Rite was little different in form from the Tridentine Mass which had been normative throughout the Western Church since 1570, it was accompanied by an elaborate ceremonial which by the nineteenth century had long been forgotten. It also required a range of medieval-style furnishings, vessels and vestments which had likewise been superseded or abandoned; and in matters of music a return to plainchant which, strictly speaking, was still the only officially-sanctioned form of music to be used in the liturgy. Pugin was determined that S. Giles' should have everything necessary - even though much of it would be alien to clergy and laity alike - for he believed it was as much a part of the heritage of England as the architecture itself. S. Giles' was to be a kind of flagship for *English* Catholicism. It is this which accounts for Pugin's passionate approach to S. Giles', his determination that everything should be perfect, and that nothing should be spoiled. "I will not let anything pass for Cheadle that is not the true thing," he told Lord Shrewsbury. "It must be perfection"[2]. And this rule applied as much to Lord Shrewsbury as to anyone else.

The style chosen for S. Giles' was the "middle-pointed" style of the early fourteenth-century, the period which Pugin had come to regard as the golden age of Christian architecture in England. "It will be a perfect revival of an English parish church of the time of Edward I", he told his *Dublin Review* readers in 1841. S. Giles' was Pugin's greatest opportunity to show the world what Catholic art could do; and whereas so many of his other buildings were starved because of shortage of money, Pugin had here a wealthy patron who was equally enthusiastic about the role of church buildings in propagating the Catholic Faith. He was determined to make the most of it:

> "I am quite willing to stake everything upon the success of Cheadle, and if I fail to produce a glorious effect there then, indeed, it will be time to think of the Roman style. Cheadle will have what none of my other buildings ever got, the means to carry out the work in a solid and finished manner........
> When I am annoyed I think of Cheadle and feel happy again"[3].

By the late 1830s there was a practical need for a new Catholic church in Cheadle. A mission had been established in the 1820s by Fr William Wareing (later Bishop of Northampton) as an offshoot of the Cresswell Mission. For a time he used an upstairs room of a private house - No. 4 Charles Street, but it soon proved inadequate. The fifteenth Earl of Shrewsbury (d. 1827) regularly attended the mission when he came to

Alton without his chaplain, and it was he who commissioned Fr. Wareing to look for larger premises. He eventually purchased a building in Charles Street which had been used as an armoury during the Napoleonic Wars, and the adjoining adjutant's house, and these were converted into a chapel and priest's house. The first resident priest was Fr. James Jeffries, appointed in 1827 and maintained by the sixteenth Earl of Shrewsbury who in that year succeeded his uncle to the titles and estates. By 1833 the number of communicants had risen to ninety, and a school had been established[4]. In the same year Fr. Jeffries was succeeded by Fr Francis Fairfax who was to be the first priest of the new S. Giles'. The dedication to S. Giles - a seventh-century French abbot - was chosen because he had been Cheadle's medieval patron. Indeed, he seems to have been quite popular in North Staffordshire, with other dedications at Newcastle-under-Lyme, Haughton, and the gate-chapel of Croxden Abbey only a few miles from Cheadle. Medieval iconography usually depicted him with a deer, a reference to the story of his being nourished with the milk of a hind while living as a hermit, and of his subsequent rescuing of the animal from the hunters.

Pugin's diary records a visit to Cheadle in October 1839, probably to inspect the site of the new church. In March 1840 he spent several days in Norfolk visiting and sketching medieval churches which he could use as "authorities", i.e. instances of medieval building practice and decoration on which he could draw for his own designs[5]. The preliminary drawings for Cheadle were completed by Christmas 1840. "I have taken great pains with them", Pugin wrote to Lord Shrewsbury. "It is the first really good thing I have done"[6]. Pugin used three of these drawings, and a ground-plan, to illustrate his first *Dublin Review* article in May 1841, thus ensuring that S. Giles' would attract immediate attention right from the start. The working drawings were complete by early January 1841. "It would do your heart & eye good to see them", Pugin wrote to his friend, J.R. Bloxam, "every detail of an old English Parish church is restored with scrupulous fidelity"[7]

The foundations of S. Giles' were laid early in 1841 - the year in which Pugin published *The True Principles*. Pugin promised the earl that he would stake out the plan himself to avoid there being any mistake in what he then envisaged as "a complete thing in its way as a small parish church"[8]. Existing structures, such as a beer-shop, were acquired and demolished so as to give the church the whole of the corner site fronting Bank Street and Chapel Street. The building was aligned so that the west end would be as close as possible to the street in order to make the biggest impact when approached from the Market Square via Cross Street. In respect of S. Giles', "west" and "east" have always to be understood in the ritual sense, for on account of the narrowness of the site the actual alignment is northwest-southeast. This detail is of some importance when considering the disposition of features such as windows. As at S. John's, Alton, the churchyard was planned with scrupulous care, with a large stone cross on the south side as the common memorial to all, as was the medieval custom.

There was no ceremonial stone-laying until the 24th February 1842 when Bishop Walsh came to lay a corner-stone, by which time the south side of the church was well-advanced[9]. Most of the stone was quarried locally, at Counslow hill between Cheadle and Alton, which yielded excellent sandstones of the "Hollington" type. Pugin wrote enthusiastically about the Counslow quarry and the masons' workshops which were built there:

> "The Counslow quarry is capital. I think there is as good a masons shed as any in England, they can work in it during the severest frost as it all shuts up, and the blocks of stone run into it on a sort of railway from the crane. 2 labourers sleep there to protect the tools and the men have a capital refectory, it is quite a settlement & they turn out a deal of work"[10].

So, in addition to his many other roles in the fields of architecture and design, Pugin appears to have assumed personal responsibility for the quarries, providing facilities for the masons to live together in a self-contained community, and ensuring that the production of worked stone could continue all the year round. The quarry-faces at Counslow can still be seen, along with the well from which the masons would have drawn their water **(70)**. Remains of the buildings mentioned by Pugin still exist, and portions of the paved wagonways by which stone was transported in one direction to Cheadle, and in the other to Alton where construction work was taking place at the Hospital of S. John, the Castle, and at Alton Towers. Not far from the quarry was a cottage which stood at the

70. Counslow - the quarry face, and the well.

entrance to the Earl's Drive, the main entrance to the Alton Towers estate from the Cheadle side. Pugin carried out improvements and additions to this cottage which was re-named Counslow Lodge. The alterations included the addition of a stone Talbot and various heraldic devices, and a massive chimney-breast and fireplace[11].

It appears that Lord Shrewsbury wanted S. Giles' to be as far as possible a local product constructed from local materials. Only when suitable material was not to be had locally did Pugin look elsewhere, for example Park stone which Pugin considered would be stronger for the nave piers, and close-grained white Banbury stone for the sedilia and Easter sepulchre because it would take the delicate carving better than Counslow sandstone[12]. Some of the statuary on the outside was carved from ochre-coloured local sandstone, which took fine detail, and was painted red afterwards to match the building-stone. Unfortunately some of this has weathered badly, revealing the base colour. The large statues of the four Latin doctors of the Church - SS Ambrose, Augustine, Gregory and Jerome - which stood under canopied niches at the base of the spire also crumbled, and they had, unfortunately, to be removed for reasons of safety.

Alabaster for the altars came from the Fauld quarry near Tutbury, and it was beautifully carved by Thomas Roddis whose work at S. John's, Alton, so delighted Pugin. Roddis also carved the pulpit, out of a single block of stone. It is in the form of an irregular hexagon with one very broad face on the north-west side which incorporates a sacrarium for the adjacent Lady-chapel altar, and it is entered via a doorway from the Rood stairs. The statuary includes S. John the Baptist (the earl's patron saint), and three noted friar-preachers: S. Francis, S. Anthony of Padua, and S. Bernardine of Siena. Pugin was especially pleased with the quality of Roddis's carving on the capitals of the nave piers - every one different - which he considered to be equal to those of York Minster[13]. George Myers, who undertook so much of Pugin's building and carving elsewhere was called in only for the sedilia and sepulchre. Timber for the roofs and benches in the nave came from the Alton estate, while the encaustic and printed tiles for the floors and walls were made by Minton of Stoke-on-Trent. Most of Pugin's metalwork - of which S. Giles' has one of the finest collections - was made in John Hardman's Birmingham workshops. To supervise the entire operation Pugin had the services of John Denny who was already in charge of the works at the Towers and S. John's. "Denny is constantly on the ground looking after the men,"

71. S. Giles' Cheadle: north aisle window with figures of SS Peter & Paul.

Pugin told Lord Shrewsbury. "He is indefatigable. I cannot speak of his conduct too highly. His heart is set on the work, and I can thoroughly rely on him"[14]. In the same letter he promised that all the work would be done by his own men, with the exception of Roddis. This shows that Pugin personally hand-picked the masons, carpenters and others for Cheadle, probably from amongst those who were already working for him at Alton and at the Towers and whom he had come to know well during his frequent visits. Nothing was to be left to chance.

For stained glass (71), Pugin had to go further afield, to William Wailes (1801-1881) of Newcastle-on-Tyne, having been disappointed at the quality and the price of work done at the Towers and at S. John's by Thomas Willement (1786-1871) and William Warrington (1796-1869). "The Glass painters will shorten my days", he told Lord Shrewsbury, "they are the greatest plagues I have"[15]. Much of the interior painting was done by the earl's glazier and decorator, Thomas Kearns, of Alton; but from 1844 some of the more complex work was done by the London decorating firm of J.G. Crace who worked extensively on many of Pugin's other buildings. Several of the designs which Pugin submitted to Crace for decorations in the chancel still exist[16].

Thus the combined efforts of local and nationally-renowned artists, craftsmen and manufacturers created at S. Giles' a stunning interior which brought together the many strands of Pugin's genius as a designer, so much so that some visitors to the church were

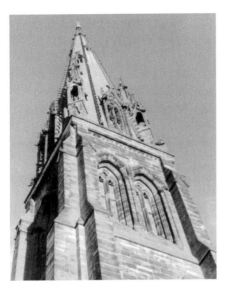

72. S. Giles' Cheadle - the "heaven-pointing" spire.

at a loss as to what to look at first. While the decorating was still in progress, Lord Shrewsbury wrote to Pugin about the visit of a Mr Warburton from Cheshire. Ecstatic at what he saw, he "pulled out his book to sketch, but as soon as he began one thing, his attention was drawn off to another & a better, & so on till at length he shut up his Book as blank as when he opened it"[17].

As work on S. Giles' progressed, the design of the building was altered; for example the overall height of the tower and spire was increased to 200 feet **(72)**. This was done as late as 1843. It amounted to a completely new design for the upper part of the tower and the lower part of the spire. "I have got a new collection to make it from", Pugin told Lord Shrewsbury[18]. The south aisle was extended eastwards by the addition of the Chapel of the Blessed Sacrament, a north porch was added, and the pillars and walls - shown on Pugin's earlier drawings **(73)** as quite plain - had coloured stencilling applied to them. So what had been planned originally as a fairly modest parish church grew into something far more grand and ambitious. The cost escalated too, from the £5,000 which Lord Shrewsbury originally agreed to spend, to a final budget of £40,000. Even the original sum was rather more than "modest" and it needs to be set in the context of other commissions. At Brewood, for example, Pugin was able to build an aisled church with a tower, spire and porch for £2,010. The sudden increase in the funding for S. Giles' meant, however, that for once in his life he experienced the exact opposite of what was so often the case elsewhere. Thus Cheadle - and Alton - provided him with a unique opportunity: "They are the only 2 buildings on which I can look with real satisfaction", he told Lord Shrewsbury in 1842, "....if I fail in this church may I never come within 20 miles of Alton again which would be the severest interdict I could receive"[19].

Pugin also referred to S. Giles' as "my consolation in all my afflictions"[20] and there is no doubt that by plunging himself heart and soul into this project he was able to work through the pain and anguish he felt following the death of his second wife, Louisa, in 1844, and the frustration of his plans to marry Mary Amherst as the third Mrs Pugin in 1846. Mary's mother was adamantly opposed to the marriage, and to stop it she went to the lengths of putting her daughter in a nunnery in Nottingham. "I suffer all the agony of despair", Pugin wrote to Lord Shrewsbury in April 1846[21]; but S. Giles' came to the rescue. A few days later he wrote, "I was at Alton and Cheadle Thursday and Friday, the sight of that glorious spire somewhat revives me"[22]

It needs to be remembered too that S. Giles' was not the only project on which Pugin was working. Aged only 29 when the foundations of S. Giles' were laid, Pugin already had major publications to his credit, he was working on a number of other buildings including four cathedrals and two country houses, and while he was occupied with these, more commissions came his way, including the interior designs for the New Palace of Westminster, and more publications flowed from his pen. When Lord Shrewsbury, impatient for results, once suggested that Pugin might not have enough to do, Pugin replied with characteristic indignation:

> "Your Lordship says I cannot have much to do. Now this is too bad to a man who has hardly time to dine. I never had so much to do. I have several plates to engrave, diverse articles to write, new churches at Newcastle, Birtley, London; finish buildings at Liverpool, London, Loughborough, Downside etc., all sorts of altars, stained windows, screens etc. I have not an instant to spare, nothing to do!!! I am obliged to work without ceasing, why Cheadle with all its details, tiles, stained windows etc. is almost one man's work. When buildings are carefully finished as mine are with every ornament varied the time they consume is enormous"[23].

The care and energy which the overworked Pugin put into S. Giles' are obvious from his writings and from the building itself, His *Dublin Review* article - later included in *The Present State of Ecclesiastical Architecture* - helped to ensure that large numbers of people came to see the church while it was being built and decorated. It seems that, notwithstanding his admiration of Pugin's work, the earl's chaplain, Dr. Rock, had doubted the wisdom of building such an ambitious church in a remote Moorlands market-town where few might see it[24], but he was proved wrong. "Cheadle ... excites immense interest", Pugin told the earl at the end of August 1841, "so far from nobody seeing it hundreds come already. It will do immense good".[25]

Not everything at Cheadle was plain sailing, and - surprising though it might seem - there were several differences of opinion between Pugin and Lord Shrewsbury over matters of structure, furnishing and decoration, particularly when the earl seems not to have had such a

73. S. Giles', Cheadle: interior as originally envisaged by Pugin and illustrated in the Dublin Review, *1841.*

74. S. Giles', Cheadle: the north aisle, 1846 (Illustrated London News, 9th January 1847).

thorough grasp of "The True Principles" as Pugin might have wished. It has sometimes been thought that the expansion of S. Giles' into something larger and more grand than had originally been intended was due entirely to Pugin's powers of persuasion over a sometimes hesitant earl, but that was not always the case. In March 1842, when the building was already well-advanced, it was Lord Shrewsbury who suggested that the nave be given a clerestory of quatrefoil-shaped windows, and Pugin was obliged to point out that to do so at this stage would mean changing the whole character of the building, raising the level of the nave walls, and altering the tower; so the matter was dropped[26].

It is a commonly-held fallacy that the prime function of the nave of a church is to hold as many people as can possibly be crammed in. The size of a church is often viewed in terms of seating capacity, as when visitors marvel at the vastness of some East Anglian church set in a tiny village, and wonder from where on earth the people came to fill it. But there were generally very few seats in medieval churches, and the nave and aisles were not an auditorium filled with a static body of people in fixed seats, but rather liturgical space in which there was movement and drama, for example the festal processions on high days and holy days, and the penitential processions in Lent. Aisles (by which we mean side-passages; *aile*=wing) were never intended to be cluttered-up with seats: they were passageways for processions. The size of the building and the size of the local population were not necessarily related. Fixed seating in the shape of box-pews (which Pugin denounced as "dozing-pens") came about only after the Reformation when the grand liturgy of previous centuries gave way to the hour-long sermon. Pugin was therefore horrified when Lord Shrewsbury proposed to fill S. Giles' with seats running the full width of the nave, without so much as a central passage.

"I have made a church on the effect of which I will stake all I possess ....
no-one but your Lordship in this present time could erect such a perfect

revival but do not mar it for heavens sake by any modern things. If I was to disposed (*sic*) the benches in one length I might as well pew it from one end to the other. I do not hesitate to say and I speak seriously and advisedly the interior of the church would be ruined spoilt utterly destroyed - now I bear all adversities, miseries, disappointments, bad debts everything with perfect resignation on the mere hope and delight of Cheadle but I shall sink into utter despondency if your Lordship proposes such dreadful things."[27]

In the end, the seating was arranged as Pugin wished: elm benches in the nave, with a central passage, and in the aisles - following medieval precedent - nothing more than a stone ledge along the walls. The benches presently in the aisles are of a later date; a woodcut of 1847 shows the north aisle as Pugin intended - clear liturgical space **(74)**.

Many of Lord Shrewsbury's ideas on church furnishings reflected current taste - or as Pugin would see it, lack of taste - in Catholic church buildings which in many respects were not unlike nonconformist meeting-houses with their pews and galleries. Not only did the earl want seats running the width of the nave at S. Giles, he also wanted a gallery at the west end to house the organ and singers. There was, after all, a west gallery at the Cresswell Mission, one for the organ and choir over the tribune in the Towers chapel, and one even at S. Chad's, Birmingham. Such a feature at Cheadle, Pugin argued, would completely destroy the view down the church from the west doors, and interrupt the lighting of the building from the great west window. This was an important point, because the abundance of stained glass and the absence of a clerestory meant that the principal source of clear light had to be from the west window. Pugin also had an eye to the likely reaction of visiting "Oxford men" to such an incongruous feature as a gallery, and the consequent damage to his reputation. Thus the idea of a west gallery - and the earl's determination to have it - provoked one of Pugin's most violent outbursts:

> "....I can only say that when it is erected I shall be almost induced to turn Johnathan (*sic*) Martin and set fire to the building. There are no less than 5 <u>protestant</u> archdeacons pulling down galleries of every kind, all the works of the Camden and Oxford Societies denounce them and now..... your Lordship proposes to erect a gallery in the <u>only perfect</u> revival that has been accomplished. What am I to say or do. The gallery would not hold 20 people if crammed full and it would ruin the church. All the learned men will flock to this church as a model and they will see this monstrosity. What a miserable fate awaits every architect of this wretched country. I have lived to see almost every building on which I have set my heart either upset or ruined, and now a gallery at Cheadle, <u>perfect</u> Cheadle. Cheadle my consolation in all my afflictions..... Pray my dear Lord Shrewsbury do not mar this great and good work by such a protestantism as a west gallery. All the sublime effect of the tower arch will be lost...."[28].

Instead of the west gallery, Pugin proposed an organ loft over the inner sacristy on the north side of the chancel, with a staircase on the outside to that the organist and singers could enter and leave without setting foot in the sanctuary. The provision of a fireplace

and flue would ensure that the organ would be kept free from damp. "Altogether it is an immense improvement at small expense", Pugin argued[29]. Lord Shrewsbury was persuaded, and the "odious" west gallery was abandoned in favour of Pugin's scheme which forms an interesting multi-gabled group, with tall chimneys, on the north side of the church, adding an element of asymmetricality. At the west end of the nave, the light from the large window is uninterrupted; there is no stained glass, and the walls are completely unadorned so as to allow the maximum amount of light to be reflected into the nave. There is no doubt that Pugin's scheme was the better one, but high in the south wall of the tower a blocked doorway marks the intended position of the west gallery, and indicates the seriousness of the earl's original intention.

The south porch was another source of controversy. Porches, as Pugin well understood, were not merely entrances to the church where people might leave their hats and umbrellas, and scrape their shoes.

75. S. Giles', Cheadle - holy-water stoup, and details of vaulting, south porch.

They had a definite liturgical function. Historically the first part of the baptismal rite took place in the porch, so did the reconciliation of penitents. The porch was the correct location of the holy-water stoup from which the faithful would sprinkle themselves before entering the nave, and so prepare themselves for worship and prayer. Following his study of church porches in East Anglia and elsewhere, Pugin was determined to give S. Giles' an exceptionally fine south porch, with a groined stone roof. Lord Shrewsbury thought that a timber roof would suffice, but Pugin argued passionately for a stone one, giving a list of medieval examples. "I have taken more pains with the south porch at Cheadle than anything I have ever done", he wrote[30], and one can well believe it. The porch repays careful study, with its massive angle-buttresses, and the rich carving in the vaulting of the roof and around the stoups which are set under ogee arches (**75**). Over the outer door is a statue of Our Lady and the Christ-child, flanked by censing angels, and a floriated cross on the gable. "The most glorious porch since the old time", was Pugin's own verdict when he saw it completed in November 1845[31]. The north porch - over which there seems to have been no controversy - is plainer in design, with a statue of Christ in majesty giving a blessing. It does not appear on the original plan. The floors of both porches are set with encaustic tiles carrying the text "We will go into the house of the Lord with gladness";

while those just inside the inner doors bid those entering to "pray for the good estate of John the XVI Earl of Shrewsbury of whose goods this church was built". Similar tiles were used for the floors of the nave and aisles which have the words *bene fundata est domus domini supra firmam petram* worked into the borders: "the house of the Lord is well founded upon a strong rock".

Naturally enough, the earl who provided the "goods" wanted some influence over how they were used, and although earl and architect were at one in most things, differences of opinion continued to arise over details, with Pugin - almost inevitably - winning the argument more often than not. There was, for example, a disagreement over the aisle windows. Following ancient precedent, Pugin wanted to make the windows in the south aisle larger than those in the north aisle, and he wanted to fill them with stained glass rather than plain. Because the south aisle actually faces south-west, Pugin referred to it in a letter

to Lord Shrewsbury as the *west* aisle, and, by reference to the glass in the west-facing state rooms at Alton Towers he reminded the earl that the most beautiful effect of stained glass is produced by light from the setting sun[32]. To reinforce the argument, Pugin protested that he had spent £30 of his own money on an expedition to see and sketch "the very cream of the Norfolk churches", and that he had then spent weeks on the working drawings for the windows. Once again, the earl gave way. In February 1844 Pugin visited William Wailes' workshop in Newcastle-on-Tyne to see the work in progress, and was delighted with the richness of the glass and with the standard of draughtsmanship[33]. There was the added advantage that Wailes' glass was up to sixty per cent cheaper than Willement's[34], a factor that would no doubt have helped in convincing Lord Shrewsbury.

The stained glass was not there simply to look beautiful. It had an instructional value too in its representation of Biblical characters, figures of saints, and the graphic representation and exposition of Christian doctrines. This "poor man's Bible" as it was sometimes called, was needed no less in the nineteenth century than it had been in the fourteenth, for as Pugin himself observed, "....while the children of this enlightened age are ignorant of the very saint by whom their country was converted to the Christian faith, they are well versed in the legends of Mother Goose and Puss in Boots!"[35] In the south aisle the windows are all of three lights each. The westernmost

76. S. Giles, Cheadle - south aisle window - figure of S. Giles which Pugin altered at his own expense (see p.115).

one has - appropriately for its location in the Baptistery - the figure of S. John the Baptist in the centre light, flanked by eight personified attributes of the baptised Christian, standing triumphantly on animal forms which represent the opposing vices. Moving eastwards, the next window has in its central light the figure of Our Lady with the moon and stars, and the inscription *pulchra ut luna* ("fair as the moon",). In the side lights are four seraphim, and titles of Our Lady from the Litany of Loreto in words and symbols: Mystic Rose, Tower of David, Morning Star, House of Gold. The next window has the figures of S. John the Evangelist, S. Giles **(76)** and S. Chad ; and finally, in the window by the entrance to the Blessed Sacrament chapel, the Sacred Heart of Jesus in the centre light, with petitions from the Litany of the Holy Name in the side-lights. All of this helps to illustrate the important function of stained glass as a stimulus to prayer and meditation. In the north aisle, the windows are of two lights each, except for the easternmost, which is of three. The westernmost is set with the heads of six Anglo-Saxon saints: Edmund, Edward the Martyr, Edward Confessor, Etheldreda, Ethelburga and Mildred. In the middle window there are canopied figures of SS Peter and Paul. Next to it is one which especially delighted Pugin when he visited Wailes' factory. It represents the Holy Spirit in the form of a dove, and the seven corporal acts of mercy: clothing the naked, visiting prisoners, giving drink to the thirsty, sheltering the homeless, feeding the hungry, visiting the sick and burying the dead **(Col. plate 6)**. Finally, in the Lady Chapel, a three-light window depicts Our Lady with the Christchild, and the Annunciation.

The original plan for S. Giles' **(fig. 8a)** shows that the nave was to have had three subdivisions marked off by parcloses: the Baptistery, and the chapels of S. John and of Our Lady at the east end of the north and south aisles respectively. Of these, only the Baptistery was constructed exactly as planned. Pugin lamented the fact that proper fonts were seldom to be found in modern Catholic churches where a jug and basin often sufficed, and in one instance the sacrament was administered out of an old medicine phial[36]. Its position just inside the south door, and its enclosure within parcloses emphasises the importance attached to the Sacrament of Holy Baptism as the means of entry into membership of the Church: according to ancient practice only the baptised may be allowed to approach the sanctuary. The font itself was given a towering pinnacled canopy based on the surviving medieval examples which Pugin had seen in several East Anglian churches **(77)**.

As regards the two chapels originally

77. S. Giles, Cheadle: the font-cover.

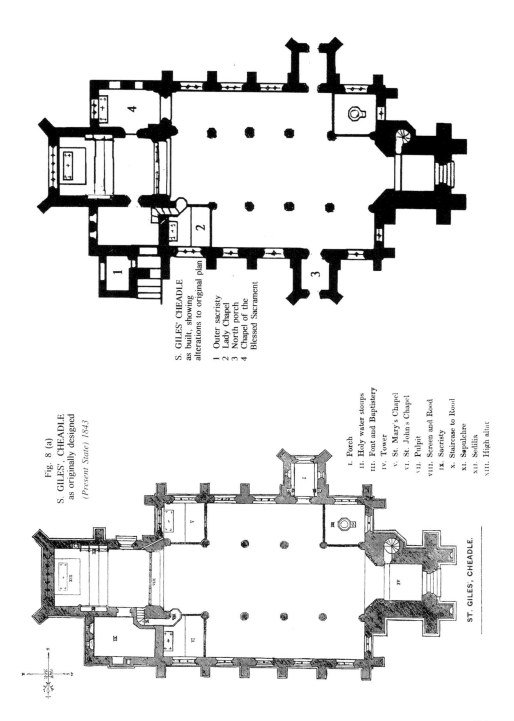

Fig. 8 (a)
S. GILES', CHEADLE
as originally designed

(*Present State*) *1843*

ST. GILES', CHEADLE.

I. Porch
II. Holy water stoups
III. Font and Baptistery
IV. Tower
V. St. Mary's Chapel
VI. St. John's Chapel
VII. Pulpit
VIII. Screen and Rood
IX. Sacristy
X. Staircase to Rood
XI. Sepulchre
XII. Sedilia
XIII. High altar

S. GILES' CHEADLE
as built, showing
alterations to original plan

1 Outer sacristy
2 Lady Chapel
3 North porch
4 Chapel of the
  Blessed Sacrament

78. S. Giles', Cheadle: the Lady Chapel

proposed for the east ends of the aisles, the Lady Chapel was moved over to the north side, while the south aisle was extended to form the Blessed Sacrament chapel as a distinct structure parallel to the chancel. It appears that Lord Shrewsbury then considered doing away with the chapel in the north aisle altogether, but Pugin protested that it had been provided for in the original estimate, that it would cost barely £100, and that without it the north aisle would look "like an aisle sacked by the calvinists"[37]. Pugin finally got his Lady Chapel **(78)** though minus the parclose screen. Only the base was constructed, forming a very low enclosure in the last bay of the aisle. The chapel was given a superb alabaster altar, carved by Thomas Roddis, with figures of angels holding M monograms, and, at the corners, angels with scrolls inscribed *Ave Maria.* Above the altar Pugin placed the fine early-sixteenth-century Flemish reredos of carved oak which Lord Shrewsbury had originally earmarked for S. John's, Alton, until Pugin objected that it would obscure part of the east window, so to Cheadle it came[38]. The circular window originally intended to terminate the north aisle had to be omitted when it was agreed to relocate the organ loft over the sacristy, so a bold feature was absolutely necessary to fill up what would otherwise have been a totally blank wall. The aisle walls were appropriately decorated with a tiled dado and rich stencilling above. In the north aisle the predominant colour is blue for Our Lady, while on the south side red and gold complement the décor of the Blessed Sacrament Chapel. The Stations of the Cross date from 1864.

At the east end of the nave the great Rood, with its attendant figures of Our Lady and S. John, was the focus of devotion for the people, while the fretted screen on which it was set was considered by Pugin to be an indispensable feature of an English parish church **(79)**. He wrote passionately about them, and at length, but in *The Present State of Ecclesiastical Architecture* (1843) he expressed most succinctly the prime function of the screen

> "...To mark the separation between the faithful and the sacrifice, the nave and chancel, emblematic of the Church militant and the Church triumphant, into which latter we can alone enter by merits of Christ's passion on the cross, whose image, as crucified for our sins, is affixed on high above the centre of the screen"[39]

Rood-screens were, of course, another revival, and as such they were unfamiliar to

English Catholics of the nineteenth century. Though Pugin and Ambrose Phillipps considered the screen to be essential from a liturgical and aesthetic point of view, others disagreed precisely because it acted as a division between the sacred and the secular, conflicting with the modern "all-seeing" principle; and the battle for screens dogged Pugin to the end of his life. At Cheadle, however, there was no such argument, and, armed with the sketches of surviving medieval screens done on his East Anglian tours, Pugin set about designing an exceptionally fine one. He was especially delighted with the painted and gilded decorations he saw in East Anglia in April 1844: "Such screens, exquisite painting. I shall have glorious authorities for Cheadle. I am delighted beyond measure to have seen them before we begin the decoration there"[40]. He made yet another visit to East Anglia in July 1845, and many of his sketches have survived[41].

It seems that the timber for the screen was sawn out on site, and by early 1844 the

79. S. Giles', Cheadle: the Rood-screen
(Illustrated London News, 9th January 1847).

fine carving was well under way. At this point the woodcarver left, and Lord Shrewsbury suggested that the carving could be finished more cheaply by local craftsman Thomas Harris than by engaging a new carver. Harris had already worked for the earl at Alton

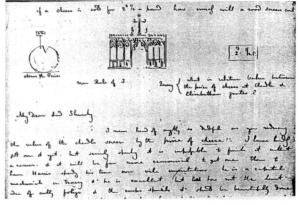

80. Part of the letter from Pugin to Lord Shrewsbury about the Cheadle screen (HLRO 339/47)

Towers and, significantly, on the screen at S. John's, Alton. In an extraordinary letter, Pugin remonstrated with the earl for running the risk of ruining the screen by practising false economy. The difference in rates of pay amounted to no more than the price of a pound of cheese in Cheadle market, and though an expert carver might charge more per hour, it would be more economical in the long run than "to have Harris spending time over vile

81. S. Giles', Cheadle - screen, pulpit and corona: postcard view of c.1905 (The Lewis Family Collection).

imitations. He is a capital mechanic in tracery and he is excellent, but he has not the least idea of cutting foliage"[42]. To reinforce the point, he illustrated the letter with drawings of a rood screen and a cheese **(80)**. That a young architect should have been able to address England's premier earl in such a forthright manner, accusing him of penny-pinching, suggests a relationship somewhat more personal than the purely professional one of architect and client, and so it was. Lord Shrewsbury seems to have taken Pugin's rebuff with a dose of good humour, and the quality of the carving on the screen **(81)** does suggest that another professional was called in. The capitals of the shafts, and the cusps of the tracery have very finely-carved flowers and leaves; there are angel-heads over the doorway, and there is a rich cornice of vine-scroll above the coving. The whole structure is raised on two steps which have Latin texts from the prophet Isaiah cut on the risers in modified Gothic letters: "The house of the Lord is built on the top of the mountains and exalted above the hills, and all peoples will come to it and say: Come, let us go up to the mountain of the Lord and the house of the God of Jacob" *(Isaiah 2: 2-3).*

The painting and gilding of the screen was probably done by Thomas Kearns. It is clear that Pugin intended the panels at the base of the screen to be decorated with figures of saints, like the medieval ones he had seen in the church at Castle Acre **(82)**[43], but - whether or not through lack of a sufficiently-skilled figure-painter - this was never carried out, and the panels remain blank. The main shafts have spiral decorations of the kind that Pugin called "barber's pole-work", and above the cornice runs the painted text, + *Christus factus est pro nobis obediens usque ad mortem, mortem autem crucis propter quod et Deus exaltavit illum et donavit illi nomen quod est super omne nomen* - "For us Jesus

108

became obedient to death, even death on the cross, therefore God has exalted him and given him the name which is above all others" - *(Philippians 2, vv 8-9)*. Thus the great Rood, occupying the central place in the church, draws together the whole of the Redemption history: the atoning death of Christ on the Cross, and his

82. Castle Acre, Norfolk - base of medieval screen.

universal sovereignty; while beyond the screen the eye is led onward into the sanctuary to a foretaste of the life of the world to come **(Col. plate 4)**. How perfectly it is all brought together by Pugin who knew his theology as well as his architecture: no wonder he was so passionate about screens.

Above the Rood is the "Doom" painting, representing the Last Judgement, another feature of many medieval churches which Pugin sought to revive. Pugin would have preferred to have followed medieval precedent by having the painting applied directly to the wall, but it was eventually painted on canvas by Hauser, a member of the German

83. S. Giles', Cheadle - postcard view of interior, c.1930

community of artists in Rome, and in fixing it Pugin had to take precautions against damp by allowing air to circulate behind it. Over the years a certain amount of undulation has appeared, confirming Pugin's worst fears that by using canvas for this kind of work the solid effect would be lost[44]. When it came to the painting in the chancel - which the earl also wanted to be done on canvas - Pugin took a much tougher line. A detail worth noticing on the Doom painting is the representation amongst the Blessed of Lady Gwendoline, the younger daughter of the earl and countess, who died in 1840 aged only 23. It is possible - although there is no documentary proof of it - that Lord Shrewsbury's sudden increase in expenditure on S. Giles' may have been intended as a local memorial to Gwendoline (who died and was buried in Rome), and that, like Pugin, he found in the building of this church a consolation in times of grief.

Other figure-painting in the nave includes the representation of ten Old Testament patriarchs and prophets, copied from Italian frescoes, and painted on thin discs of copper attached to the walls over the arcades. Above, the open roof - also richly painted - has wall-posts, open trusses with pierced tracery at the apex, and wind-braces. The outer roofs are of lead, with elaborate gilded iron cresting along the ridges.

Lighting in the nave was originally provided by a set of hanging *coronae,* or chandeliers in the shape of crowns, made in brass by Hardman. "There was scarcely a church in ancient times which was not provided with a *corona*, richer or plainer in design, according to the wealth or dignity of the foundation", said Pugin[45], so S. Giles' had a set of four. Each one held twenty-four tapers, and was inscribed *Domine da nobis lucem* (O Lord, give us light). Sadly, these were removed in the 1960s and replaced with the present wrought-iron ones, but they can be seen on old photographs **(83)**. Just to the east of the screen, hanging over the present working altar, is an exceptionally

84. S. Giles', Cheadle: fifteenth-century corona in the chancel.

beautiful hexagonal corona with lettering executed in pierced ironwork **(84)**. The text links it firmly with the Rood: *Tuam crucem /adoramus domine /gloriosam passionem /recolimus etiam /miserere nobis /qui passus es pro nobis* ("We adore your cross, O Lord, and we honour your glorious passion; have mercy upon us for whom you have suffered"). It is of fifteenth-century date, and was brought from Flanders - possibly by Pugin - in a badly-damaged condition. Repaired and restored, it was described by one contemporary observer as "one of the most beautiful pieces of church furniture in the country"[46].

At the heart of the Catholic liturgy there lies the breathtaking concept that for a few moments the veil between this world and the next is so very thin that a glimpse may be had of what lies beyond: the worship of the Church on earth united with that of the Church in heaven, through Christ who is adored on his throne of heavenly glory and upon earth in his sacramental presence upon the altar. Thus the altar is the focal point of the entire building, and its setting is supremely important. So the chancel is differentiated structurally from the nave by its lower roof-level, by the elaborate bell-cote on the east gable of the nave for the Sanctus bell,

85. S. Giles', Cheadle: the high altar and reredos.

by the extra mouldings to the windows, and by the statues and other sculptures which adorn the east wall. Internally the dominant theme is the Holy Angels - in the wallpaintings and cornices, on the roof-corbels, on the sedilia, and predominantly on the altar and reredos. All of this consciously echoes the words of the Preface to the Canon of the Mass: "Therefore with angels, and archangels, and with all the company of heaven..." On the altar itself. Thomas Roddis carved figures of angels holding musical instruments, ready, as it were, to accompany the singing of the *Sanctus* (**85**). Meanwhile, on the reredos, the angels hold censers and torches, ready - just like the thurifer and acolytes at Mass - to honour the Presence of Christ. The central panel depicts the Coronation of Our Lady, the last of the Mysteries of the Rosary and - significantly - the only one which takes place entirely in heaven. Above the reredos, the east window depicts the genealogy of Jesus[47], and either side of it are the figures of S. Giles and S. Chad. As the Mass reached its supreme moment, the Sanctus bell high on the gable would ring to signify to passers-by that the Holy Mysteries were being celebrated within; for the absent as well as for those present, and embracing too those whose bodies lay at rest in the churchyard beneath the heaven-pointing spire, the symbol of the Resurrection.

An altar is, by definition, a "high place", and so it is traditionally raised on a flight of three or more steps to give it prominence, and it is approached with due reverence. The sanctuary at S. Giles' rises through four levels, and the risers have appropriate Latin texts incised into them. On the bottom level is part of the invocation *super oblata* said by the priest at the preparation of the Oblations prior to the Canon of the Mass: *Veni sanctificator omnipotens aeterne Deus* ("Come, almighty and eternal God, the sanctifier......."). The ascent to the altar is then marked by the antiphon *Introibo ad altare Dei + ad Deum qui laetiticat iuventutem meam* ("I will go up to the altar of God, even to the God of my joy and gladness") and the verses of Psalm 43 which form part of the Preparation said by the priest and assistants below the altar steps before Mass, concluding with the *Gloria Patri*.

Each level of the chancel, and the adjoining chapel of the Blessed Sacrament, is paved with encaustic tiles manufactured by Herbert Minton to Pugin's designs. They are decorated with floriated crosses, *Agnus Dei, and Sanctus* motifs. Some tiles are made up of four colours, and are therefore richer - and more expensive - than those in the nave. Pugin was greatly excited to know that the Minton floors would be the first of their kind in Europe[48]. Lord Shrewsbury was concerned about possible damage to these expensive tiles caused through walking on them. Denny suggested that the priest and acolytes should wear cloth overshoes in the sanctuary. The earl agreed, and told Pugin, "You may then have your tiles, and we shall want no carpet"[49].

The furnishings of the sanctuary were designed for the celebration of Mass according to the revived Sarum Rite, and so - as at Uttoxeter and Alton - there were some significant departures from post-medieval practice. The most prominent feature of the north side of the chancel is the Easter Sepulchre, set under a richly-carved ogee arch **(Col. plate 5).** In the back is a painting of the Resurrection, and the front of the sepulchre has five quatrefoils. They are decorated with the emblems of the Passion on shields, exactly as they appear in *Pugin's Glossary of Ecclesiastical Ornament and Costume* (1844). Ornate sepulchres of this kind were still to be seen in many medieval churches, for example at Hawton

(Nottinghamshire) and Heckington (Lincolnshire), and Pugin drew on these as his "authorities". Historically, the sepulchre was used in the liturgy of Good Friday and Easter for the symbolic entombment of Christ in the form of the Sacred Host consecrated at the Maundy Thursday Mass. Then, early on Easter morning, came the liturgical drama known as *Quem Quaeritis?* when three clerics, representing the women who went to Jesus' tomb on the first Easter Day, approached the Easter Sepulchre to be greeted by a fourth person representing the angel who announced the good news of the Resurrection. Though these practices had been discontinued in England in the sixteenth century, and were unknown in current Catholic circles[50], Pugin hoped to revive them, and by providing such a splendid sepulchre at S. Giles' he ensured that there would be no excuse for not doing things properly.

The sedilia - seats for the priest, deacon and subdeacon - set into the wall

86. S. Giles', Cheadle: the sedilia.

on the opposite side of the chancel (86), are of the medieval prismatory type, i.e. in addition to the canopied seats there is also a sacrarium, consisting of a stone basin with a shelf above it, also set under a rich canopy. Pugin was able to cite many surviving medieval examples such as the ones in the cathedrals at Exeter, Lincoln and Salisbury, but again he was attempting to revive long-forgotten practices. The sacrarium (or piscina) was for the *lavabo,* the ritual washing of the priest's hands immediately before the Canon of the Mass, and for the ablution of the sacred vessels at the end, while the shelf above was for the wine and water cruets. Modern practice was to use a small jug and basin for the lavabo, the ablutions were normally consumed by the priest or deacon, while the cruets were generally placed, along with other vessels, on a credence table near the altar.

Similarly, instead of fixed sedilia of the architectural kind, modern Catholic churches usually had three movable seats, with the priest occupying the central one. Pugin wished to revert to the medieval custom of the priest occupying the seat closest to the altar, with the deacon and subdeacon sitting to his left, and on lower levels. So the sedilia at S. Giles' has its seats set on descending levels, and - as if to make doubly sure that everyone sat in the right place the seats are labelled *sacerdos, diaconus*, and *subdiaconus,* with the appropriate emblems of each order; chalice and paten for the priest, the Gospel-book for the deacon, and wine and water cruets for the subdeacon. There was, it seemed, a need for such instruction. Ambrose Phillipps observed that High Mass with deacon and sub-deacon was in any case a rarity outside London[51], and Pugin himself was only too painfully aware of the fact that even though better things were now readily available, many clergy clung stubbornly to the customs they had grown up with, and some were bitterly hostile to "revivals".

At Uttoxeter, Pugin had wanted to revive the medieval English custom of reserving the Blessed Sacrament in a hanging pyx above the altar, but had had to settle for a tower-shaped Tabernacle on the altar itself. The original drawing for the chancel of S. Giles' (87) makes no such provision. It shows an aumbry in the north wall just east of the sepulchre, from which it may be deduced that Pugin planned to use

87. S. Giles', Cheadle: Pugin's original scheme for the chancel, Dublin Review, *1841 and* Present State, *1843.*

88. S. Giles', Cheadle: the west doors.

this for Reservation, again following medieval precedent. By the time he came to build, however, he had had second thoughts, based on his recent experiment at S. John's, Alton, where a tiny chapel on the north side of the chancel was equipped with a Reservation altar. At Cheadle he developed this idea into a full-scale Chapel of the Blessed Sacrament, with all the appropriate furnishings and iconography. It appears to have been one of the earliest alterations to the original plan[52]. The chapel forms an extension to the south aisle, and it is denoted externally by its separate gable, an additional weathering, and - at the junction with the aisle - a large buttress with a niche containing a statute of the Risen Christ.

Internally the chapel is divided from the aisle and chancel by metalwork screens and gates, the ones at the entrance from the aisle being of brass by Hardman *(front cover picture).* They have Eucharistic motifs such as the chalice and Host, and the *Agnus Dei.* The walls are richly stencilled, e.g. with crosses and crowns, and fruiting vines. The alabaster altar, by Roddis, has figures of the six-winged seraphim, the guardians of the Sacred Presence, standing under crocketed canopies, and a cornice with *sanctus* which also runs all around the dado in identical lettering. The reredos is made up of two panels of richly-coloured Minton tiles with the chalice and Host as the dominant motif, and between them, behind the Tabernacle, a stencilled panel of fruiting vines. The window above is of three lights. The centre panel shows the Risen Christ, and in the side-lights the seraphim hold texts from Jesus' discourse on the Bread of Life *(John 6: 54-56).* The risers in the steps are lettered *panem coeli dedit eis* ("he gave them bread from heaven") and *panem angelorum manducavit homo* ("man has eaten the bread of angels"). The entrance-arches from the aisle and the chancel are inscribed with the antiphon to Psalm 117 as sung at Benediction: *Adoremus in aeternam sacramentum sanctissimum* ("Let us adore for ever the most holy Sacrament"). The chapel is altogether a perfect expression of Catholic Eucharistic theology. John Henry Newman was no Gothic enthusiast, and he had some harsh words to say about Pugin, but when he saw the Blessed Sacrament Chapel on his first visit to S. Giles' in July 1846 he could not help saying to himself, *Porta Coeli* - "Gate of Heaven"[53]

As one might expect in a church financed entirely by the Earl of Shrewsbury, a certain amount of Talbot iconography is woven into the decoration of S. Giles'. The boldest statement is on the west doors **(88)** where the gilded ironwork is elaborated into rampant lions with engrailed borders, taken directly from the family coat-of-arms. In the south-west angle of the tower, the kneeling figure of Lord Shrewsbury is depicted, with Christ standing behind giving a blessing. Otherwise the allusions are restrained and concentrated at the west end: the heraldic tiles already mentioned and the Talbot hounds on the label-stops of the west window.

The date fixed for the consecration of the church was, appropriately enough, September 1st 1846 - S. Giles' Day. In the Spring of that year Pugin became increasingly worried that it might not be ready in time, and he pleaded with the earl for sufficient money to keep the workforce up to strength and to take on extra carpenters, otherwise it might be necessary to defer the dedication for another year. "We have not a bench or a door made, no sacristy fittings...... We must finish the sacristy fittings or all the vestments and ornaments will be spoilt if there are not places to stow them away"[54]. He even advanced money of his own so that Denny could pay the men until such time as a decision had been reached. Unhappy about the figure of S. Giles in the south aisle window **(76)**, he wrote to Lord Shrewsbury in April to say that he was going to have it improved at his own expense, "for I cannot bear to see the present S. Giles"[55].

Amidst all the anxieties there were also some brighter moments, such as when the bells were heard for the first time in February 1846, to Pugin's great delight[56]. Cast by Thomas Mears of Whitechapel, four of the original six bells are inscribed with invocations of Our Lady, S. Francis, S. Chad, and S. Giles; a reminder that, like everything else in Pugin's scheme of things, church bells had a spiritual function as well as a practical one. The others have Biblical texts: *Laudate Dominum de caelis: laudate eum in excelsis* ("Praise the Lord of heaven; praise him in the height" - Psalm 148), and *Tu es Petrus et super hanc rupem aedificabo ecclesiam meam* ("You are Peter, and upon this rock I will build my Church" - Matthew 16:18). The bells were rung again on July 2nd when Lord Shrewsbury came to see the church as it neared completion, Pugin, of course, accompanying him[57].

The vestments about which Pugin was so anxious appear to have been made by Lonsdale and Tyler of London, and some are still in use **(89)**. The design of the chasuble shows a compromise between the very ample medieval form preferred by Pugin, and the drastically cut-down French and Italian variety. This reflects the earlier disputes over the revival of the full medieval chasuble which had been censured in 1839 by the *Propaganda Fidei* in Rome, and which was actually banned by Bishop Wiseman just before Pugin's death in 1852. Nowadays the Pope himself almost invariably wears one.

89. S. Giles', Cheadle: chasuble designed by Pugin, but subsequently altered..

S. Giles' has the most extensive collection

of liturgical metalwork of any Pugin church, but some of this was ordered late in the day and had to be taken from stock patterns. Even so, Lord Shrewsbury spent around £1400 which was equivalent to the cost of a complete small church[58]. The Hardman metalwork day-books[59] show that items were being dispatched throughout August, one of the last being a set of six brass candlesticks for the high altar, and a matching cross. A silver cross for the Lady Chapel, finished with blue enamel, was dispatched at the same time, at a cost of £26. For most of the items, however, Lord Shrewsbury stipulated plated base metal so as to make the most of his money. Even so, the standard of Hardman's workmanship is superb. Particularly noteworthy is the "sunburst" monstrance - the vessel used for the Exposition of the Blessed Sacrament, and for Benediction **(Col. Plate 8)**. It is made of gilt brass and Pugin designed it from medieval examples. His own preference was for Benediction to be given with an enclosed pyx, as it had widely been done in the Middle Ages, to preserve an element of mystery, and also to safeguard the Blessed Sacrament from "irreverent gaze". So to complement the monstrance, he designed for S. Giles' a standing pyx for the reservation of the Host. It has a tall stem to enable it to be used, if desired, for Benediction and processions of the Blessed Sacrament without Exposition. Appropriately, there is engraved on the front the opening words of S. Thomas Aquinas' eucharistic hymn, *Adoro te devote, latents deitas* ("O hidden Godhead, I adore thee"). To hang before the Tabernacle in the Blessed Sacrament Chapel, Pugin designed a beautiful lamp of enamelled silver, inscribed with the attributes ascribed to God: *Charitas, benedictio, fortitudo, virtus, honor, sapientia.*

The inner sacristy at S. Giles' was fitted-out with the necessary "almeries" for the proper storage of the vessels and vestments. Given the quantity and quality of these items, Pugin felt that - as at Alton - it was essential to appoint a sacristan who knew how to look after them, and who would keep the church clean and tidy. "Cheadle will be finished most perfectly", he told Lord Shrewsbury, "but unless there is a responsible person in the shape of a sacristan to look after the church the whole thing will be ruined. Any Catholic church takes the whole time of one man to keep it in a proper state. Such a person is as necessary as the priest"[60]. The sorry state of the sacristy in his new church at Derby, only two years after its opening, convinced Pugin that the clergy left a great deal to be desired when it came to caring for the buildings and their contents. Such a thing could not be allowed to happen at Cheadle. By the end of April 1846 he had found a Mr Wheelwright, "a most zealous, willing man", to take on the role of sacristan. Wheelwright was also an organist, and thus able to serve S. Giles' in a dual capacity[61]. The organ was a small single-manual instrument with about nine stops, built by Parsons of London, the firm who had built a much larger instrument for Alton Towers Chapel in the 1830s. It was quite adequate for accompanying the Gregorian chant which Pugin envisaged as the only music which would be allowed at S. Giles'. He wanted none of the florid operatic-style Mass settings that were in vogue elsewhere. The organ was later extended, and it has latterly been replaced altogether.

The consecration of S. Giles' took place on Monday 31st August 1846. It was essentially a private affair, conducted by Bishop Wiseman, with the Revd. George Talbot as deacon and Dr. Ennis as sub-deacon. Talbot, a member of the Anglican branch of the family, was a recent convert, and had been in training at Oscott. First there was a procession around the outside of church during which the Bishop aspersed the walls with holy water, using a bunch of hyssop as a sprinkler. Three circuits of the church were made, then, at the singing of Psalm 24, "Lift up your heads, O ye gates...", the west doors were opened, and the procession entered. The altars - completely bare and without ornaments at this stage - were consecrated in turn, the bishop tracing in holy water and holy oil the five crosses incised on each *mensa,* symbolic of the Five Wounds of Christ. The inner walls of the church were aspersed, likewise the floor, and each of the twelve consecration crosses around the walls was anointed in turn with the Oil of Chrism. Each of these crosses was provided with a candle bracket incorporating a Shrewsbury lion. The candles were to be lit for the consecration, and on each subsequent anniversary. Bishop Walsh consecrated the altar and tabernacle in the Blessed Sacrament Chapel. All of the altar-linen, vessels, vestments and ornaments were dedicated and put in their proper places, and in conclusion a High Mass was sung. It is not difficult to understand why the whole ceremony lasted some four hours, by which time all was ready for the first public service in the newly-consecrated church on the following day.

In the evening 54 distinguished guests sat down to dinner in the state dining room - as yet unaltered by Pugin - at Alton Towers, while the earl's blind harper, Edward Jervis, played and sang. Some of the company were accommodated at the Towers, while the remainder were lodged at the Shrewsbury Arms at Farley[62]. The list of guests indicates the national and international significance of S. Giles' in the history of nineteenth-century church building. Among them were the Austrian Ambassador, the French Gothic Revivalists Adolphe-Napoleon Didron and Henri Gerente, and the Catholic politician and historian the Comte Montalembert, who had added a long appendix to Pugin's second edition of *Contrasts* (1841). There was also Charles Barry, the architect of the New Palace of Westminster, and of course Pugin himself, although exhausted and in poor health. Clerical guests included Bishops Walsh and Wiseman, the Archbishop of Damascus, and John Polding, Archbishop of Sydney, for whom Pugin executed a number of designs for Australian churches and church furnishings[63]. Lord Shrewsbury's hospitality extended to two recent converts from amongst the "Oxford Men": Frederick Faber and John Henry Newman, the future cardinal.

On the morning of 1st September - S. Giles' Day - Lord and Lady Shrewsbury set out from Alton Towers with members of their family and distinguished guests, in a convoy of eight carriages, and in brilliant sunshine. Spectators from miles around gathered on the streets to see them arrive, and then to witness sights not seen in Cheadle since the Reformation. Heading the procession from the school to the church were the thurifer, crucifer and acolytes, one of whom was the earl's thirteen-year-old cousin and heir-presumptive, Bertram Talbot. Meanwhile, the choir - borrowed for the day from S. Chad's, Birmingham - sang Psalm 122: "I was glad when they said unto me: we will go into the house of the Lord", in plainsong as one would expect. Then came about twenty of the lower clergy wearing long surplices of the Old English pattern, the revival of which had involved Pugin in no less controversy than had the revival of the Gothic chasuble. Next in the procession were forty or more priests in full vestments, followed by eight bishops and the two archbishops in white-and-gold vestments and mitres. The bishops were Ullathorne (Bath), Riddell (Newcastle-on-Tyne), Sharples (Lancashire), Brown (Wales), Gillis (Edinburgh), Norris (London), Briggs (Yorkshire) and Wareing (Northampton) who in his days as a mission priest at Cresswell had established the Cheadle Mission in the 1820s. Last of all were Bishops Wiseman and Walsh. Wiseman sang the Mass, and Walsh, as Vicar Apostolic, presided *ex throno*. The church was packed to capacity, and the congregation included many non-Catholics. The preacher was Bishop Gillis, chosen, no doubt, because of the ancient dedication to S. Giles of the cathedral and city of Edinburgh. His sermon was based on Psalm 127: "If the Lord does not build the house, in vain do its builders labour". Much of what he had to say was in accord with the social concerns of Lord Shrewsbury and Pugin, looking back to the golden age of medieval Catholicism in which the poor were properly cared for, and urging the congregation to support the various works of Christian mercy. After the Mass a "sumptuous collation" was served in the large room above the school, and the celebrations were brought to a close with Vespers and Benediction at four o'clock. On the following morning many of the clergy and other guests went to Alton village to see the buildings under construction at the hospital and the castle.

The opening ceremonies were given wide attention by the press. In addition to the expected coverage in Catholic Journals, national and local newspapers carried reports. One of the most detailed of these appeared in the *Staffordshire Advertiser* on 5th September. Written by a correspondent who was evidently familiar with Catholic worship, and who knew S. Giles' at first hand, it includes a comprehensive description of the church and its ornaments, as well as an account of the opening ceremony. Likening the scene inside the church to a casket of jewels and gold illuminated by the tapers on the altar and above the screen, it contains the telling phrase:

> "We can scarcely imagine anything more calculated to make men forget
> that they were living in a Protestant country than the scene and circumstances
> now presented .... here was enough sight and sound to affect the dullest
> imagination, and make one almost fancy it a vision of past ages".

Pugin could not have wished for a more glowing testimony to his success in achieving exactly what he had set out to do. On January 9th 1847 the *Illustrated London News* carried a detailed and equally complimentary description of S. Giles', including seven illustrations **(69, 74, 79)**. "Probably so perfect a church was never erected in England before, as there is a *completeness* in the building which defies words to express, or representations to give an idea of".

Not every observer was so admiring. S. Giles' has been criticised for the over-intensity of its interior decoration, and for the overwhelming height of the steeple in comparison with the length and height of the church, but perhaps no critic was more forthright than Pugin himself in acknowledging the shortcomings. In answer to various criticisms levelled at him in a magazine called *The Rambler,* he pointed out that the building had been altered several times in mid course as Lord Shrewsbury's funding had increased, and that the colouring of the walls had been an afterthought on the earl's part. "There is a great anomaly between the simplicity of its walls and mouldings and the intricacy of its detail.....

Had we commenced on the same scale as we ended, a truly fine building might have been produced"[64]. Lord Shrewsbury expressed himself more prosaically. When Pugin's earlier approval of S. Giles' was quoted to him, he smiled and said, "He won't say that now, though; he abuses it as much as everything else that he has done"[65].

Yet S. Giles' is popularly known as "Pugin's Gem", a soubriquet first applied, so it would seem, by Lord Shrewsbury himself even before the church was finished. When in residence at Alton Towers he would take guests over to Cheadle, and in a letter to Pugin he spoke of the impending arrival of George Talbot from Oscott: "I wait for him to go and see the Gem, which we shall do on the first fine day"[66]. In

90. Title-page from Pugin's Glossary, *1844.*

the same letter the earl mentioned the recent visit to S. Giles' of the Anglican architect, George Gilbert Scott, to whom he referred as "the Stafford Church architect" on account of Scott's pioneering restoration in 1842-44 of S. Mary's church in Stafford[67]: "He admired everything <u>exceedingly</u>. The stencilling absolutely made the water run down both sides of his mouth - I expect, when finished, it will be a text book for all good people".

A text book it most certainly is. In 1844 Pugin published one of his most beautifully produced volumes, *The Glossary of Ecclesiastical Ornament and Costume,* illustrated with seventy-three chromolithographs of his designs for a wide range of vestments, altar frontals, borders, stencil patterns, emblems and monograms **(90)**. S. Giles' goes a stage further by showing how Pugin's designs were applied in practice to walls and woodwork, textiles, metalwork and ceramics. It is a three-dimensional *Glossary.* Foreign visitors in particular were amazed that such a comprehensive range of applied arts could have emanated from a single mind. At S. Giles' Pugin demonstrated a principle that was to surface again in the later nineteenth century with Norman Shaw and the Arts-and-Crafts Movement, namely that an architect should take responsibility not just for the design of the fabric of a church, but also for its furnishings, fittings and decoration. Pugin drew together not just a variety of art-forms, but also a multiplicity of sources. The breadth and depth of his knowledge of medieval antiquities were astonishing, and this nourished his great talent as a designer who could draw deeply upon the details of Gothic art and architecture which he had observed and accurately sketched. His scouring of East Anglian churches for

91. S. Giles' School, Cheadle, and churchyard cross.

"authorities" has already been noted, but he went abroad too. The colouration of the walls and pillars seems to have been influenced by polychrome decoration of the Sainte Chapelle in Paris which was undergoing restoration at this time, and which Pugin visited in 1844 in the company of A.N. Didron[68]. Details for some of the windows came from glass which he had seen at Antwerp and Louvain in the summer of 1843[69], while the brass mounts of the altar-missal were copied from those of a medieval hymnal in Mainz cathedral.

Diverse though the influences may have been, Pugin drew them together into a coherent whole, and the key unifying factors were his deep understanding of Catholic doctrine and liturgy, and his overwhelming desire to express them through the media of "Christian" (i.e. Gothic) art and design. It is with these factors in mind that we can understand his passionate resolve that for Cheadle nothing less than perfection would do, and his intermittent battles with the earl to ensure that it would be in every respect a "True Principles" church. S. Giles' is therefore as much a theological text-book as an artistic one, and whatever might, with the aid of hindsight, be said about the proportions of the building or the density of its colouring, it is a brilliant outworking of Pugin's vision of what a parish church should be, and how it should instruct the faithful: *"Perfect* Cheadle" indeed!

The social dimension of the Catholic Faith, stressed by Bishop Gillis at the opening of S. Giles, found its expression in the nearby school and the convent of S. Joseph, both designed by Pugin. The school was finished before the church[70]. It is of brick with stone trim, "L" shaped in plan, with a tower and pyramid-capped belfry at the angle (**91**). The main building is similar in design to the Guildhall at Alton, which also accommodated a school. It has large brick buttresses and an upper floor running the length of the building, and this was used for a time for worship until the new

92. S. Joseph's Convent, Cheadle.

church was ready. The convent, finished in 1848, is also brick-built **(92)**. It has a tall tower with a saddleback roof and belfry (restored 2000). It was furnished with its own chapel, and it has a cloister - constructed largely of timber enclosing a small garden and with a direct access into the churchyard. There is a window set with Hardman glass in the north-west corner. The convent was occupied from 1848 to 1875 by a community of the Sisters of Mercy who came over from Carlow, Ireland, and who worked in the schools and in the parish at large. A third domestic building - the presbytery - was built in Chapel Street, opposite the church **(93)**. It has high gables with stone crosses, large chimneys, and mullioned windows. Both the presbytery and the convent are now (2001) in private ownership, and some excellent restoration work has been carried out on the convent belfry.

The death of the last Catholic Earl of Shrewsbury in 1856, and the failure of his executors to keep the titles and estates in Catholic hands, deprived the church, school and convent of the financial and moral support they had hitherto enjoyed from the Talbot family. "Pugin's Gem" was therefore something of a mixed blessing to the local Catholic community, which was not wealthy. From 1856 it was left to the parish priest to arrange for the upkeep of the church. Canon F.J. Jones (1855-1860) sold his books and his piano to raise funds[71], while Fr. Stuart Bathurst (1861-1871), though a man of independent means, gave away most of what he had to the poor. It may have been through Bathurst's influence that in 1866 the Anglican 18th Earl of Shrewsbury contributed £1500 towards the fabric of S. Giles'[72], thus acknowledging its wider architectural importance.

It is difficult to know for certain if the ritual arrangements of the Sarum Rite were ever fully observed at S. Giles', or if features such as the sedilia, sacrarium and sepulchre were redundant from the beginning. There is no doubt, however, that churches such as S. Giles' did much to raise the standards of Catholic worship, and inculcate a better sense of reverence. Old photographs show that the Tabernacle was for a time removed from the Blessed Sacrament Chapel to the High Altar, and the superb brass screen likewise disappeared. Both have since been restored to their proper places. The removal of the *coronae* from the nave has already been noted. Otherwise, S. Giles' has suffered to a far lesser degree than most of Pugin's other churches from the actions of those who - particularly in the wake of the Second Vatican Council - were given to large-scale "reordering" as the Tridentine Rite was itself superseded. The Rood-screen at S. Chad's cathedral in Birmingham, controversial even in Pugin's own

93. The former Presbytery, Cheadle.

time, was notoriously removed, along with much else, by Archbishop Dwyer, in 1967. The screen at S. Giles' has survived intact, and although Mass is generally said facing the people, the present working altar (a finely-carved alabaster one brought from S. Wilfrid's, Cotton) stands east of the screen, thus preserving something of Pugin's concept of the essential separation between "the faithful, and the sacrifice, the nave and the chancel". A Latin High Mass is still occasionally celebrated, and on such occasions it is tempting to imagine that at any moment Pugin himself might appear, vested in his cassock and full English surplice, ready to assist at the altar: "I assure you", he once wrote, "you would hardly know me when issuing from the sacristy door in full canonicals"[73]

7 S. WILFRID'S. COTTON

"A wild and beautiful solitude among the hills of
Staffordshire" - F.W. Faber

Cotton lies about two miles north of Alton Towers; a village of scattered houses and farms set in a wooded valley, with the spire of S. Wilfrid's church and the now-derelict college buildings appearing above the trees. Its remoteness and the small number of inhabitants belie the significant place which this village holds in the history of the Catholic Revival. Cotton is important for three reasons. S. Wilfrid's was the last church of the Pugin-Shrewsbury partnership, and it is different in style from those at Alton and Cheadle. It brought Pugin and Lord Shrewsbury into close contact with the converts who embraced Roman Catholicism as a result of the ferment caused in the Anglican Church by the Oxford Movement, and it also brought them into conflict with the people who were to be Pugin's greatest opponents on matters of architectural and liturgical style - the Oratorians.

Pugin's buildings at Alton and Cheadle were greatly admired by members of the Church of England who came to see them. It was not just a matter of aesthetics and architectural taste. There were the "Oxford Men", as Pugin called them. Some of them belonged to the Oxford Society for Promoting the Study of Gothic Architecture, founded in 1839. Their activities, along with those of the Cambridge-based Camden Society encouraged the restoration of old churches and the building and furnishing of new ones in "correct" Gothic form. They stressed the continuity of the Anglican Church with the Medieval Church, and the revival of art and architecture led inevitably to the revival of ornaments and ritual practices of a more Catholic kind, based on their interpretation of the Ornaments Rubric in the 1662 *Book of Common Prayer* which stated that such ornaments and vestments as were in use in 1549 should "be retained, and be in use". Other Oxford men were less concerned with matters of architecture and ritual, and operated on a more theological plane; men like John Henry Newman (1801-1890), John Keble (1792-1866) and Edward Pusey (1800-1882), whose aim was the renewal of the Church of England on an inward and spiritual level, as a divine institution rather than as an arm of the state. It was they who published the series of controversial papers, *Tracts for the Times*, which earned them the name of Tractarians.

In *Contrasts* and in *The Present State of Ecclesiastical Architecture in England,* Pugin attempted to demolish the notion – much loved by the "Oxford Men" – that the Catholic character of the Church of England had been preserved under Elizabeth I and that the real damage had been done in the 1640's by Cromwell. He drew attention to the wholesale destruction of altars, ornaments and vestments under the "female demon" Elizabeth as evidence to the contrary. Nevertheless, Pugin was fascinated by the awakening of a Catholic spirit in nineteenth-century Oxford. In about 1840 he encountered John Rouse Bloxam

(1807-1891), a Fellow of Magdalen College, who thereafter was Pugin's closest link with the Oxford Movement, a term which came to embrace both the theological and architectural dimensions. By the early 1840s the impact of the Movement was being felt in the parishes of England through the activities of young clergymen who while at Oxford had fallen under its spell; men like Michael Watts Russell (1815-1875) and Frederick William Faber (1814-1863). Michael Watts Russell was the second son of Jesse Watts Russell of Ilam Hall near Ashbourne, and was therefore a near-neighbour of Lord Shrewsbury. He went up to Oxford in 1833 - the year of Keble's Assize Sermon which triggered the Oxford Movement - and subsequently became Rector of Benefield in Northamptonshire. Faber was a contemporary of Watts Russell at Oxford, where he remained after graduation as a Fellow of University College before, eventually, becoming Rector of Elton, Huntingdonshire.

In spite of the animosity which Pugin, as a young convert to Catholicism, had earlier felt towards the Church of England, he was fascinated by the activities of the "Oxford men" both inside and outside the university, and their enthusiasm for what he was writing contrasted with the criticisms received from many within his own Church. "The number of Oxford men who come is quite surprising," he told Lord Shrewsbury in August 1841. "They bow reverently to the altar in the chapel at Alton, speak in whispers & Mrs Winter has been asked by them before entering if the blessed Sacrament was in the chapel that they might pay their proper devotions"[1].

The ferment caused by the Oxford Movement fostered in the minds of some the hope that the Church of England might be "catholicised" to the point at which re-union with Rome might become a real possibility. Ambrose Phillipps - himself a convert - certainly believed it, and Dr Wiseman was broadly sympathetic. In March 1841 Pugin wrote enthusiastically to Lord Shrewsbury, "....These Oxford men do more good in one week than we do in a whole year towards Catholicising England...... Some great result must shortly attend their labours for it is impossible the church of England can go long in its present position"[2]. Lord Shrewsbury was not entirely convinced. He was one of the "Old Catholic" school who were mystified at the sight of Anglicans embracing Catholic doctrines which their forebears had rejected and condemned, and for which so many English Catholics had suffered torture and martyrdom. Yet they did not take what to Catholics seemed the logical step - submission to Rome - and therefore they could be seen as a hindrance. Thus Lord Shrewsbury was suspicious of Newman, and he denounced Pusey as both deluded and insincere[3]. Meanwhile, individual conversions took place including, famously, that of Newman himself in 1845. It was this which precipitated the conversion of Watts-Russell and Faber, and a stream of converts followed them, both clerical and lay.

For many who "came over" there was a heavy price to pay. Having resigned their livings, clerical converts such as Faber suddenly found themselves without an income, and some had wives and children to support. Michael Watts Russell was married, so for him and for others in his situation there was then no prospect of ordination into the Roman priesthood. Such men found themselves vilified by former friends and colleagues whom they had left behind, and suspected and mistrusted by many in their new Church. At this time the principal centre for converts was Birmingham; it was not far from Oxford, Wiseman was there to give support and encouragement, and there was the pro-cathedral of S.

Chad's and the new Oscott College. At Wiseman's instigation, Newman and five of his friends set up an informal community at Old Oscott which he renamed Maryvale. Meanwhile, in May 1846, Faber and his companions took over Michael Watts Russell's house in Colmore Terrace where they adopted the name of the Brothers of the Will of God under the patronage of the Anglo-Saxon Saint Wilfrid (d. 709) to whom Faber had a particular devotion, Faber himself adopting the name of Brother Wilfrid (**94**).

94. F.W. Faber (1814-1863): photograph from Bernard Ward, Sequel, *vol.II.*

In spite of his earlier misgivings, once Newman, Faber and others had actually been received into the Church, Lord Shrewsbury gave them his friendship and support. In 1846 he suggested that the Wilfridians should move from Birmingham to Cheadle. He had bought a piece of land adjoining S. Giles' on which a monastery could be built. He had also, in 1843, bought Cotton Hall which he now offered to the Wilfridians as a rural retreat. Faber was given the choice of accepting either or both. He was present at the consecration of S. Giles' on September 1st, and it seems that the question of the move was discussed during the subsequent celebrations at Alton Towers. Faber decided to accept Cotton Hall rather than build anew at Cheadle, and the move took place almost immediately. A temporary chapel was provided within the house pending the completion of a new church, the foundations of which were blessed on October 12th - S. Wilfrid's Day - by Bishop Walsh. The architect was, of course, Pugin. He vowed that S. Wilfrid's would be "the only perfect chancel in England and with an east window he could die for...."[4]. Considerable alterations and additions had to be made to the house, which was basically Georgian but with some seventeenth-century survivals. Pugin added two new ranges, one of stone (**95**), and a more utilitarian brick one. On the same day that the foundations of S. Wilfrid's were blessed, Bishop Walsh admitted Faber and two other Wilfridian brothers to minor orders in the Towers chapel. Faber then prepared for ordination to the priesthood which took place at Easter 1847. Meanwhile, the Wilfridians undertook a systematic programme of proselytising, which may well have been in Lord Shrewsbury's mind when he first invited them to Cotton, despite the controversies that similar activities had already aroused in Alton.

Ambrose Phillipps had achieved remarkable success in winning converts in the Leicestershire villages around Garendon, and in addition to the monastery at Mount Saint Bernard he was able to provide missions in the area. Among these was his own chapel at

Grace Dieu which Pugin enlarged and re-furnished; and a new church at Shepshed - also by Pugin - to which Lord Shrewsbury made a generous contribution. Phillipps staffed these missions by bringing over from Italy members of the Order of Charity like Father Gentili, and of the Passionists such as Father Dominic Barberi. In 1842 Fr. Dominic settled at Stone, five miles north of Stafford. Wiseman had found a suitable house for the Passionists on the outskirts - Aston Hall, where a mission had already been established and where the relics of S. Chad had been discovered in 1839. In 1843 he was able to build a school-chapel in the town itself. Designed by Pugin and dedicated to S. Anne, this simple little chapel still stands in what are now the grounds of a new and much larger church and convent which were built ten years later and which testify to the success of Fr Dominic's work.

To begin with, Lord Shrewsbury was not entirely convinced of the wisdom of using Italian missionary priests whose English was not good, and who might only serve to reinforce popular notions that Catholicism was foreign. "We must have a new race of zealous English Missionaries, such as we are now bringing up at Oscott, under the good Bishop (Wiseman) and Pugin"[5]. The Oxford converts arriving at Maryvale and Cotton in the mid-1840s were ideally suited: Englishmen who from their personal experience and conviction could argue the case for Catholicism amongst their fellow-countrymen. Those who had held livings as Anglican clergy brought with them the practical experience of pastoral work. This was especially true of Frederick Faber, who had transformed his Huntingdonshire parish of Elton by his enthusiastic leadership, teaching and visiting. Among the converts was Edward Caswall, who, like Michael Watts Russell, was married and therefore could not join the community. Nevertheless he was befriended by Lord Shrewsbury and he visited Alton Towers and S. Wilfrid's where he made his own contribution in the

95. S. Wilfrid's, Cotton: the cloister and domestic buildings by A.W.N. Pugin. The tower formerly had a truncated pyramid roof and a belfry similar to Cheadle School (see pl.91).

form of a crucifix which he carved on a rock between Cotton and Alton Towers. His wife, Louise, seems to have had a particular fondness for S. Wilfrid's, for she was buried there in 1849. Her memorial is under the trees on the north side of the church: a ledger-stone with a cross on the top, and unmistakably Puginian in style. Following her death, Caswall joined the Oratory, but he is best remembered as a translator of Latin and German hymns, including *Bethlehem, of noblest cities*, and *When morning gilds the skies*.

It was Faber's original intention that Cotton should be a retreat at which the Brothers would prepare for missionary work in the large towns; but there was a change of direction as it was realised that there was much to be achieved locally. Faber found that some preparatory work had already been done by Fr. Kennedy - himself a convert from Anglicanism - who from 1845 had been chaplain to the previous tenant of Cotton Hall, John Campbell-Smith, and who remained for a time because Faber was not yet in priest's orders. The Wilfridians soon organised things on a systematic basis. Districts of the locality were assigned to individual brothers who spent a good part of the day making house-calls. Instruction of converts was undertaken by a First Confession Brother, a First Communion Brother and a Further Instruction Brother; there was a Confraternity of the Precious Blood, and a brass band[6]. During the summer of 1847 Faber preached outdoors because the chapel in the Hall was too cramped, and Pugin's church had not yet been completed. The Abbé Vandrival, who visited in May 1847, wrote that the outdoor sermons took place each Sunday when 300 people would fill the courtyard, and 150 came on Thursdays[7]. Stations of the Cross were set up in the garden, and large wooden crosses on the hills either side of the valley. Faber also placed a statue of Our Lady (whom he affectionately called "Mamma") and the Holy Child in front of the Hall. Lady Shrewsbury paid for the building of a school to which the earl gave a £65 per annum endowment in addition to the £2,300 he had already contributed to the church and the extensions at the Hall. The result of all this was an impressive number of converts from the immediate neighbourhood and from the nearby village of Oakamoor. Faber's description of the welcome he received on returning from his ordination on Holy Saturday 1847 shows that work at S. Wilfrid's had a momentum all of its own:

> ".... We arrived from Oscott about 9 at night; about three-quarters of a mile from St. Wilfrid's two guns were fired to our no little astonishment, and then the carriage was stopped by a huge crowd of peasants and labourers .This crowd, composed almost all of *Protestants,* took the horses from the carriage and dragged us home amid volleys of guns and fireworks and a brass band; a series of really most tasteful triumphal arches were reared along the road with illuminations and crosses on them; under each of these we stopped, for cheering and music. The poor Protestant minister had to pass to his chapel under the triumphal arches; he had only seven to preach to…"[8]

The "poor Protestant minister" was the Revd. Mr. Hendrickson, whose Regency-gothic church of S. John stood almost within the grounds of Cotton Hall, and who viewed with dismay the erosion of his congregation. A war of words ensued, not unlike the one between Dr. Winter and the Revd. John Pike-Jones at Alton. There were also brushes with the Primitive Methodists, as for example when one of their ministers pushed his way into a house demanding to hear what a dying man said to Faber in confessions.[9] Such activities only proved to be counter-productive according to Faber who wrote an open letter to his adversaries, concluding that

> "... You and yours are far more effective Catholic missionaries than we are; and I assure you, hardly a week passes without some one or more stragglers being driven into the bosom of the Holy Roman Church, declaring themselves fairly wearied out by the incessant curses fulminated against them from the pulpits of the State Church, and humbly echoed back with fury even wilder still, from the Dissenters' chapel and camp meeting, and desirous to seek refuge where they hear only of Almighty God, of the love of Jesus, and of duty, charity, peace, and kindly affection towards all, whether Catholic or Protestant......" [10]

There was another cloud on the horizon. Though the zeal and the achievements of the Wilfridians were impressive, their relationship to the wider Church was undefined, and Wiseman thought that they should be more regularised. Meanwhile Newman had been in Rome seeking guidance on what form of religious association would be best for him and

his colleagues, and the result was the Congregation of the Oratory, set up initially at Maryvale under the auspices of Wiseman. Faber was induced to join forces with it, and so in February 1848 he and his companions were received into the Oratorian Order. Since the Oratorians were committed to working in the large towns, Cotton was out of the question as the principal house. Faber and the former Wilfridians left in April 1849 to establish the London Oratory, leaving Newman and the remainder to find an alternative use for Cotton before transferring themselves to Birmingham. It was a grave disappointment to Lord Shrewsbury, for not only had he provided the premises and considerable funds; he had also seen the spiritual and social benefits of having a regular order

96. Cotton: the Faber School.

like the Wilfridians at work in the area. Eventually, in December 1850, the Passionists took over Cotton as a House of Studies for their English Province. This at least fulfilled the earl's intention that S. Wilfrid's should be in the hands of a religious community, and he gave an annual subsidy of £155 for the upkeep of the church and the school **(96)** which still retains Faber's name.[11]

The church of S. Wilfrid which Pugin built next to the hall was opened on Easter Tuesday 1848 amid uncertainties about its future. Wiseman sang the Mass, and Newman preached. Built of local sandstone, the church is asymmetrical in plan **(fig. 9)**, consisting of a nave, south aisle, chancel, sacristy, and at the south-west corner a tower with a broach spire **(97)**. The aisle has a pitched roof rather then the lean-to variety which Pugin had used at Cheadle and Brewood. The tower is entered by an external staircase and door on the north side, and the church is attached to

97. S. Wilfrid's. Cotton, from the east.

the hall by a cloister on the south side. All of these features contribute to the asymmetrical nature of S. Wilfrid's. Pugin had lauded the Ecclesiologists for their astute observation that symmetry and uniformity were not among the "true principles of ecclesiastical architecture", and that this applied particularly to the position of the tower[12]. S. Wilfrid's is therefore typical of Pugin's later churches where - in contrast to Cheadle (begun in 1841)

98. S. Wilfrid's, Cotton: the interior (2001)

and Brewood (1842) - the tower is not placed in the centre of the west front, but to one side.

Internally S. Wilfrid's presents a somewhat confusing picture on account of the alterations carried out at various times after 1848 **(98)**. The nave arcade is now of eight bays, but the piers are of two different types. The first six bays have round columns with rich leaf-carving on the capitals, the one exception being pier no. 4 which is square in section. Here the arch mouldings are carried

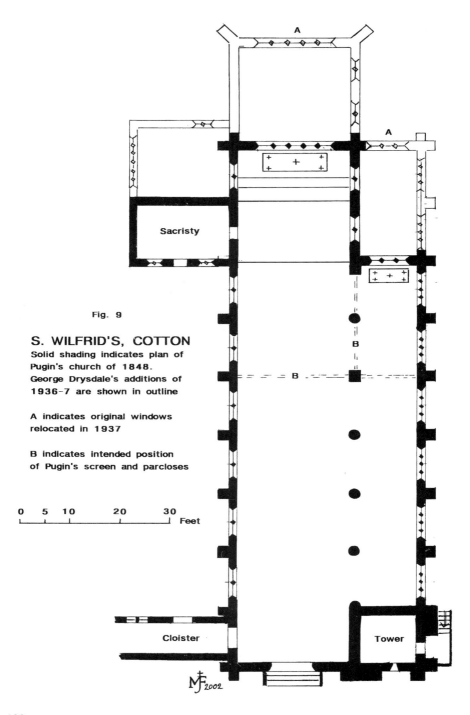

A

A

Sacristy

Fig. 9

S. WILFRID'S, COTTON
Solid shading indicates plan of
Pugin's church of 1848.
George Drysdale's additions of
1936-7 are shown in outline

A indicates original windows
relocated in 1937

B indicates intended position
of Pugin's screen and parcloses

B

B

0   5   10   20   30
⊢——⊢——⊢———————⊢———————⊢ Feet

Cloister

Tower

M⳨2002

99. S. Wilfrid's, Cotton: photograph of interior, c.1920.

down to floor-level without a break. This marks the intended position of the rood-screen and it was originally the only structural division between the nave and chancel which, until George Drysdale's alterations of 1936, were comprised under one roof: an unusual arrangement for Pugin who liked the nave and chancel to be delineated by different roof-levels[13]. Drysdale extended the chancel and Lady-chapel by creating two new bays, introducing a chancel arch, and enlarging two side windows to continue the arcade eastwards. The additional piers - like the one at the intended position of the screen - are rectangular in section, and the arch-mouldings continue down to floor level.

Pre-1936 photographs (**99 & 100**) show coloured wall-decorations in the sanctuary, and stencilled patterns around the windows, but S. Wilfrid's was never as intensely coloured as Cheadle, and such colouring as there was disappeared a long time ago. Minton tiles in the nave bear the expected Talbot iconography. In 1936 the stonework of the five-light east window which Pugin said he would die for was re-used in the new chancel, but the original glass was not. Only the figures of S. Etheldreda, S. Wilfrid, S. Chad and S. Hilda have survived, re-set in the west window. At this time the high altar and reredos were removed. The old photographs show that it had as its central feature a Tabernacle and Benediction throne surmounted by an exceedingly tall openwork spire of the kind that Pugin installed in some of his later churches such as S. George's, Southwark and S. Cuthbert's, Ushaw. The one at S. Wilfrid's was not, however, by Pugin, but an addition made as late as 1900 by J. Alphonse Pippett (d. 1904), one of the chief designers for

100. S. Wilfrid's, Cotton: postcard view of south aisle, c.1900.

Hardmans. Some fragments are preserved in the aisle: painted figures of saints under wooden Gothic canopies. The alabaster altar survives, in a reduced form, at S. Giles', Cheadle. The original Lady-chapel altar and reredos have also been replaced.

The tower contains two bells cast by Mears of Whitechapel, and their inscriptions reflect the changes which took place at Cotton at this time. The smaller one, cast in 1847, is dedicated to S. Wilfrid, whereas the larger one, cast a year later, invokes the patron saint of the Oratory - S. Philip Neri. The figure of S. Wilfrid - along with Faber clad in cassock and biretta - also appears in a south-aisle window, the only original glass in this part of the church, but it is no longer in its original location over the Lady-chapel altar. The interior of S. Wilfrid's has thus changed more radically than those of Cheadle and Alton, but it never did receive its full complement of Pugin furnishings and it was the subject of some controversy.

Soon after his conversion, Faber had visited Rome, where he immediately acquired a fondness for exuberant Italian devotions, and he brought back a large store of Italian rosaries, medals, crucifixes and other devotional aids. The Oratorians were given even more to Italian devotions which were not particularly liked by the "old Catholics", who viewed them as too exotic and flamboyant for their taste. Pugin and Ambrose Phillipps saw something far more sinister at work, namely the subversion of their cherished belief that Gothic was the only truly Christian style of architecture. So began the great Rood Screen controversy, the opening shots of which were fired in a conversation which took place when Pugin and Phillipps visited Cotton in May 1848. When Phillipps asked why there was no screen at S. Wilfrid's, Faber replied that it interfered with the modern rites of Exposition of the Blessed Sacrament. He denounced the screen at Cheadle, and said that if he had his way all the surviving sixteenth-century screens would be pulled down and burnt[14].

The issue of screens became a major one, with heated public debate on either side including, famously, Pugin's last major publication, the *Treatise on Chancel Screens and*

Rood Lofts (1851). That such controversy should have raged over this single item of church furniture might seem absurd, but the real point at issue was whether Renaissance Italian or Medieval English ideas were to prevail in the Catholic Church in England[15], and Pugin believed that in fighting for screens he was fighting for the whole Gothic principle. He was further incensed by the fact that among the leading Oratorians were former "Oxford Men"

101. Cotton College: buildings by E.W. Pugin, 1874-5

who had been admirers of the revived Gothic and who therefore ought to have known better. A middle course was suggested by Newman, who was by no means anti-Gothic and who readily acknowledged Pugin's genius. Could Gothic not be adapted to suit the needs of the Oratorians who were, after all, a post-medieval Order?[16] Had Pugin been prepared to compromise over what Newman regarded as "details" - and these would almost certainly have included screens - the outcome might have been different. Instead his "all-or-nothing" attitude helped to ensure that when the Brompton Oratory was built in 1878 it was Roman Baroque rather than English Gothic.

The Oratorians got their way at Cotton too, for when the church was opened in 1848 there was no screen. Three years later Pugin was glad to see them leave, and in August 1851 he wrote triumphantly, "...I am to turn out of St. Wilfrid's all the trash the Oratorians set up which is delightful, & the Passionists will have the screens up. Things have taken a wonderful turn in a few days......"[17]. Pugin did indeed design a rood-screen for S. Wilfrid's, and the drawings for it survive[18] but there is no evidence of its ever having been installed. The later screenwork, which now runs across the east end of the chancel behind the modern working altar, formerly enclosed the Lady chapel, and it was moved to its present position as part of the re-ordering of 1987[19].

The Passionists left Cotton in 1856 following the deaths of the sixteenth and seventeenth earls of Shrewsbury whose financial support had been crucial. The mission was then handed over to the Alton priests, and S. Wilfrid's was virtually closed until 1868 when it was reopened at the inauguration of what became known as Cotton College, the Preparatory School for Sedgley Park, an historic Catholic Boys' School near Wolverhampton. Additions were made to the College buildings in 1874-5 by E.W. Pugin **(101)**, and also in 1886-7 and 1931-2, but sadly these buildings are currently (2001) derelict following the closure of the college in 1987. The church continues to function as a parish church, under the aegis of S. Giles', Cheadle.

Faber's lasting memorial is undoubtedly the Brompton Oratory of which he was the Founder and Superior, rather than the Gothic S. Wilfrid's. Yet he had loved Cotton too. Like Edward Caswall, he was a hymn-writer, and some of his hymns - including *Faith of Our Fathers* - were written during his time at S. Wilfrid's and are still popular today. Moreover, the results of his labours as a pastor and teacher are still discernible some 150 years later in the number of local families who have kept the faith in sufficient numbers to support both the Faber School and the church which, through the generosity of Lord Shrewsbury, he was able to establish in this "wild and beautiful solitude among the hills of Staffordshire"[20].

8 S. MARY'S, BREWOOD

"if this little church can be raised it will be the means of saving the remnant of the old faith that remains, and of laying the foundations of better things" - A.W.N. Pugin

The market-town of Brewood (pronounced "Brood") stands about seven miles north-west of Wolverhampton, close to the Shropshire border. Though less thickly wooded than in former days - it once formed part of a Royal Forest - the area retains the essentially rural character which charmed Pugin in the 1840s. It is particularly rich in Catholic history. A return made in 1767 to the House of Lords giving the numbers of Catholics in England and Wales showed that of just under 3,000 in Staffordshire, no less than 389 lived in and around Brewood, second only to Wolverhampton with its 491[1]. A number of landed Catholic families resided in the area. The most important were the Giffards of Chillington Hall. whose ancestors had come to England with the Conqueror and held high positions of state in medieval England. Following the Reformation the Giffards remained firm Catholics, yet continued to be buried in the parish church at Brewood where fine alabaster tombs of Elizabethan and Jacobean date stand prominently in the chancel. Needless to say, most of their tenants were Catholics too, and when in 1688 Pope Innocent XI divided England into four districts each with a bishop styled "Vicar Apostolic", he appointed Bonaventure Giffard - a member of the Wolverhampton branch of the family - as first Vicar Apostolic of the Midland District.

Other Catholic landowners in the area included the Fitzherberts of White Ladies and Boscobel, the Whitgreaves of Moseley, and also the Talbot Earls of Shrewsbury, four of whom were buried at Albrighton, five miles south-west of Brewood[2]. Peperhill, near Albrighton, was for much of the seventeenth century a favourite residence of the Talbots, until George, the fourteenth earl (1743-1787) developed Heythrop (Oxfordshire) as the family's principal seat. The Albrighton estate was, of course, retained along with the title of High Steward. Bishop Thomas Talbot, a brother of the fourteenth Earl, was Vicar Apostolic of the Midland District from 1778 to 1795, and lived at Brewood.

The area is rich, too, in historic sites evocative of its Catholic past. Close to Brewood are the remains of two religious houses: Black Ladies, a Benedictine nunnery founded c.1140, and the slightly later White Ladies, properly the Priory of St. Leonard at Brewood. A house built on the Black Ladies site was in Giffard hands, and for a short period in the eighteenth century the relics of S. Chad of Lichfield were kept there[3]. The Giffards built a Catholic chapel at Black Ladies in about 1790[4].

Four miles from Brewood is Boscobel House, built by the Giffards in about 1630, possibly as a place of concealment for priests. It is well-equipped with secret hiding-places or "priest-holes", and in the grounds is the celebrated "royal oak" where Charles II hid after the Battle of Worcester in 1651[5]. Charles had, in fact, been sheltered at nearby White Ladies, a substantial timber-framed house attached to the ruins of the priory, yet another Giffard property. White Ladies and Boscobel subsequently passed into the hands of the Catholic Fitzherberts[6] who held them until 1812. The ruins of the Priory Church were used as a Catholic burial-ground until 1844.

In addition to the chapel at Black Ladies there was a centre for Catholic worship at Longbirch House. The chapel there was used for public worship from at least 1779 and it had its own priest-in-charge. Among those who served in this capacity was Thomas Walsh, who became Vicar Apostolic of the Midland District in 1825, and who later gave great encouragement and support to the Gothic building-schemes of Pugin and Lord Shrewsbury. Longbirch was used as the residence of the Vicars Apostolic until 1804 when the residence was removed to Giffard House, Wolverhampton.

Given all these circumstances, to say nothing of an influx of Irish immigrants, and the 1829 Catholic Emancipation Act, the Catholic cause in Brewood appeared to be in a flourishing state in the early nineteenth century. By 1837 west and south galleries had been built in the chapel at Black Ladies, and the chapel at Longbirch had been enlarged. It would seem that the provision of a new Catholic church in Brewood itself to replace these chapels was only a matter of time, but there were clouds on the horizon too. The Fitzherberts had already parted with the bulk of the White Ladies estate including Boscobel (though not the site of the priory itself), and the incoming Evans family were not Catholic. Meanwhile the Giffards, who had so staunchly upheld the Catholic cause during the years of persecution, were gradually becoming distanced from it. Thomas Joseph Giffard, who held Chillington at the beginning of the nineteenth century, had married an Anglican, the Hon. Charlotte Courtenay, in 1788. He died in 1823. Of their children only the eldest, Thomas William, continued in the faith of his fathers until his death in 1861. Waiting in the wings as heir and successor was his brother Walter who, along with all the female members of the family, was a member of the Church of England[7]. Sooner or later, therefore, the estates would pass out of Catholic hands, and the future of the chapels at Longbirch and Black Ladies was to say the least uncertain. By the early 1840s this prospect was causing considerable anxiety to both priest and people, and it further highlighted the need for a parish church in its own right.

The leading figure in the scheme for a new church was the Revd. Robert Richmond, who had served at Brewood from 1808 to 1811 and

102. S. Mary's. Brewood, from the south-east.

again from 1819 to 1821. He returned to Longbirch in 1838, having been Professor of Divinity and Vice-principal of Oscott College. His nephew, Henry Richmond, became chaplain at Black Ladies at the same time.

Robert Richmond was at Oscott when Pugin burst upon the scene there in 1837, aged only twenty-five, a convert of barely two years' standing, yet brimful of ideas for a revived Gothic England. Richmond would have witnessed at first hand the beginnings of the spectacular rise of Pugin, for whom Oscott was a prime launch-pad in his career as architect, designer, and Professor of Ecclesiastical Antiquities[8]. Pugin had a high regard for Richmond, and the location of Brewood in an "Old Catholic" area which appeared to be under threat appealed to him too. A statement needed to be made, and he approached the task with a mixture of delight and passion. His proposed design for S. Mary's appeared in the frontispiece of *An Apology for the Revival of Christian Architecture in England* (1843) where it is shown as a modest-sized building consisting of nave, chancel, aisles, and a west tower with a broach spire, i.e. very much as it was actually built in 1844 **(102)**. Pugin's diary for 1843 is alas missing, and there are no references to Brewood in his earlier diaries. However, a particularly important letter written by Pugin to Lord Shrewsbury about the church has survived. Though undated, this letter was almost certainly written in 1843[9]. It contains a detailed account of what appears to have been Pugin's first visit to Brewood, and he was clearly impressed with the area and the visible reminders of its Catholic past. He visited the church at Albrighton, where he saw the alabaster tomb of Lord Shrewsbury's ancestor, Sir John Talbot **(103)**. He thought it would be worth making a cast of it - probably to add to the two replica tombs of Talbot ancestors he had already installed in the Octagon Gallery at Alton Towers. Pugin also visited the ruins of White Ladies Priory **(104)** where he was thrilled to see the Catholic cemetery with 16th, 17th, and 18th-century tombs inscribed *pray for the soul of....*

103. Tomb of Sir John Talbot at Albrighton.

> "No protestant has ever polluted the consecrated ground", he wrote, "and this in England. Delightful. We said the *De Profundis* in the middle of the old ruined church. How could Fitzherbert sell such a property?"[10]

"We" indicates that Pugin was not alone on this occasion. His companion could well have been Robert Richmond of whom he wrote warmly:

> "... Mr Richmond is a most holy man, a real old parish Priest of venerable aspect, and if you saw his grief and anxiety for the Catholic population over

which he is pastor, your Lordship would feel as I do. I will serve him from my heart for the love of God and blessed S. Chad...."

Fr Richmond's main problem was raising sufficient funds to build the church. In March 1843 he wrote to Thomas Giffard that only £340 had been raised through subscriptions. Bishop Walsh had viewed the plans, but had told Richmond that he was unable to donate any money[11]. The scheme was clearly in jeopardy, and Pugin's letter to Lord Shrewsbury reflects a desire to enlist the earl as a major benefactor:

> ".... this seems to me a cause of the greatest importance, it is one of which the loss of souls is involved. I mean to do everything in my power for it, and I implore of your Lordship not altogether to turn away from this matter for it is urgent beyond any I know. This is the only means of keeping up religion among your Lordship's tenants in the Albrighton estate, and if you would only build enough of an aile (sic) to hold these poor people it would be a right good service....... It is heartrending to think of three fine estates thus lost to the church and cause, but if this little church can be raised it will be the means of saving the remnant of the old faith that remains, and of laying the foundations of better things."

However warmly Pugin may have felt towards Fr. Richmond's ministry at Brewood, Richmond's opinion of Pugin's buildings was by no means unequivocal. In a letter to his brother written in January 1844 he expressed the view that Pugin's churches were generally too dark, and he thought that the lych-gate at Brewood was ugly[12]. There seems nevertheless to have been no serious doubt as to who the architect of the new church would be, and – as stated earlier – Shrewsbury's financial support of church-building projects was conditional upon the employment of Pugin. The earl promised to donate £100, and in July 1843 Pugin wrote asking him to send the money soon after Christmas; "...I have advanced it as they were hard up"[13]. By 1843 Thomas Giffard had been prevailed upon to pay for the land for S. Mary's. It cost him the not inconsiderable sum of £486 and probably represents the Giffard family's last benefaction to the Catholic Church[14]. Among the other benefactors were Bishop Wiseman and the Revd. George Spencer who made donations in the name of the clergy. Henry Whitgreave of Moseley Hall, and Pugin himself, gave money for stained-glass windows, and Mrs Hardman gave £12

104. Ruins of White Ladies Priory.

for the Tabernacle[15].

In view of Lord Shrewsbury's involvement in church-building schemes elsewhere, and his ownership of tenanted properties in the Brewood area, Pugin may even have considered him to be the eventual successor to the Giffards in the seigneurial role, and the one to secure the future of the church at Brewood.

Pugin pointed out in his earlier letter to Lord Shrewsbury that there was sand (for mortar) on the site, and plenty of freestone and rubble close by, so S. Mary's was built largely of local materials, chiefly red sandstone. The setting of the church amid trees on the edge of the village also pleased him greatly:

> "... The church can stand due East and West with the south porch to the road, and a church in such a situation for an old Catholic population is most interesting".

Pevsner[16] observed that St. Mary's is "not as starved as most of Pugin's churches", a reminder that financial constraints often resulted in Pugin's buildings being rather less grand in reality than they appeared in his drawings. Brewood was an exception, remarkably so given all the circumstances. It was therefore possible to complete it in one build, just as Pugin had planned it, by the summer of 1844 **(fig. 10)**. The building contract was given to George Myers, who was paid £2,010 for the church, presbytery and school[17]. As at Alton and Cheadle, the building of a school would have been considered especially important in providing for the future of Catholic families in the area.

Pugin's diary for 1844 records a visit to S. Mary's during its construction, at the

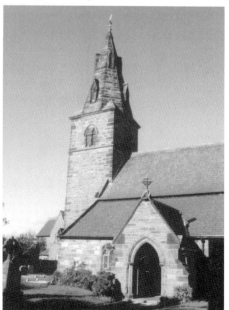

beginning of March. The consecration on June 13th was carried out by Bishop Wiseman, at that time President of Oscott, with twelve or more priests of the district assisting. Pugin's diary records that he was at Nottingham that day with Lord Shrewsbury, doubtless involved with discussions about the progress of S. Barnabas' church (later the cathedral) which was to be opened in August. Pugin would have been pleased to know that the consecration of S. Mary's was properly done within the context of a High Mass *Coram Episcopo* sung by the officiating priest, Fr. B. Ivers, with the choir from S. Chad's, Birmingham, singing a setting by Palestrina[18]. Sadly, Fr. Richmond died just a week after the opening of the church which, without his devotion and tenacity, might never have been built. The inscription on

105. S. Mary's, Brewood: the spire and porch.   his monument rightly describes him as the

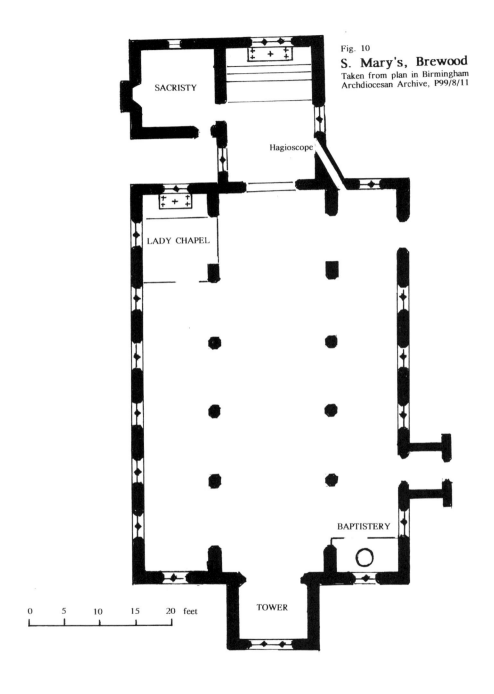

Fig. 10
S. Mary's, Brewood
Taken from plan in Birmingham
Archdiocesan Archive, P99/8/11

SACRISTY

Hagioscope

LADY CHAPEL

BAPTISTERY

TOWER

0   5   10   15   20   feet

founder, as well as the first rector, of S. Mary's. He was succeeded by his nephew, William Richmond, who died in 1848.

Built largely of coursed sandstone rubble, S. Mary's has a centrally-placed west tower, and a broach-spire with two tiers of lucarnes **(105)**. There is a south porch with stone benches and a stoup. Outside the porch is a medieval pillar-stoup reputed to have come from White Ladies. The nave has north and south aisles, but no clerestory. The aisles have two-light windows with ogee tracery. The chancel has a three-light east window with geometrical tracery in the head, and there is a sacristy on the north side. All the elements of the building are thus clearly-defined externally as Pugin believed they should be.

106. S. Mary's Brewood: the nave looking east (2001).

Inside there is an impressively tall tower arch, with double-chamfered mouldings which continue down the jambs, i.e. without capitals. The nave is of five bays: low

107. S. Mary's, Brewood: postcard view of interior with original furnishings and decorations, c.1920.

108. S. Mary's, Brewood: the high altar.

octagonal piers carrying tall double-chamfered arches **(106)**. The easternmost piers are elongated, and the mouldings of the eastern arches are continued downwards, i.e. like those of the tower arch. Was this done to demarcate the east ends of the aisles as side-chapels? The south aisle has a hagioscope giving a view of the high altar. The nave has an open timber roof with purlins and collar-beams; the chancel roof has closely-set scissor-trusses. Minton floor-tiles adorn both the chancel and the north aisle.

As in many of Pugin's other churches, the interior fittings and decorations have undergone considerable changes, although old photographs **(107)** record what there once was. The original seating ran right across the nave, leaving passageways only down the aisles - an arrangement which Pugin would have abhorred, but which was necessary in order to seat 400 people[19]. Gone too is the rood-screen from under the chancel arch. It had three single-light divisions either side of the door. The hanging crucifix is the only survival from it. The walls of the nave and chancel were enriched with coloured stencilling, but this has been whitewashed-over. The original stone altar survives **(108)**. It has three deep quatrefoils in the front, containing the *Agnus Dei* flanked by censing angels, and there is a simple stone reredos flanked by angels kneeling on brackets. In the south wall is a single stone sedilium with an adjacent piscina. Set in the floor of the chancel are two fine memorial brasses by Hardman commemorating the priests Robert and William Richmond: full figures in vestments under Gothic canopies.

The south aisle contains a plain tub-shaped font with a folding hinged lid and padlock. It has been moved from its original position, which was at the west end, just inside the door. Nearby is a large seventeenth-century crucifix which came from Black Ladies[20], and also a large statue in painted and gilded wood of the Virgin and Child. This would appear to be of fifteenth-century date, and is probably Flemish. One would like to know how it came to be at Brewood. Was it perhaps a gift from Pugin out of his large collection of medieval artefacts?

The north aisle/Lady Chapel was refurbished in the 1880s. At this time a stone altar was placed at the east end, while in the north wall a fine Hardman brass to members of the Whitgreave family suggests that it was they who became the principal benefactors of the church following the secession of the Giffards. Kneeling on one side of a large floriated crucifix is Henry Whitgreave (1816-1881) and his two sons, George (1842-1871) and Thomas (1849-1876); while on the other side are his two wives, Henrietta Clifford and Mary Selby, along with the children of his second marriage, Walter who died in infancy, and Alice who survived him.

Over the Lady-chapel altar, and set in an alabaster shrine of twentieth-century date, is one of the most interesting - and controversial - items in the church, namely the statue of the Virgin and Child known as "Our Lady of Brewood" **(109)**. It is made of wood, partly painted. Tradition has it that this statue was kept at White Ladies until the ransacking of the building in 1651 by Parliamentary troops in their search for Charles II. The gash in the lower part of the statue - which still "weeps" - was allegedly made by a soldier's sword. It would appear that from White Ladies the statue was taken to Chillington Hall, and eventually to the chapel at Black Ladies, where it remained for some time after the opening of S. Mary's, for in his account of Black Ladies (1867) James

109. "Our Lady of Brewood".

Hicks Smith makes mention of "a ponderous little statue of the Blessed Virgin, carved in wood", continuing to occupy the place of the altarpiece[21]. The statue was presumably removed to S. Mary's when the Black Ladies chapel was finally demolished in 1872.

The presbytery and school **(110)** lie immediately to the north-west of the church. Like

110. Brewood: the presbytery and school.

the ones at Cheadle, they are built of brick with stone trim. The school was intended to promote not just the survival of the Catholic Faith in Brewood, but its growth; as Pugin put it, "laying the foundation of better things". Fr. Richmond was well-pleased with the early success of the project; in June 1845 he wrote to his brother, George, that in the previous two weeks 156 people had been confirmed and there had been twenty conditional baptisms[22].

The story of the building of S. Mary's highlights one of the weaknesses of the "seigneurial system" of church patronage which had been so significant in upholding the Catholic cause during the times of persecution: there was no guarantee that a landed family would remain Catholic. The case of Brewood is especially ironic in that the Giffards, who had remained loyal to the faith - and at some personal cost - throughout the days of the Penal Laws should have seceded just as Catholicism was enjoying its "Second Spring". The Shrewsburys' patronage of the Catholic Church was set to suffer a similar fate, and with devastating consequences, when their titles and estates passed into Protestant hands in 1858.

9 UNFINISHED BUSINESS

In the autumn of 1852 the deaths of Pugin and Lord Shrewsbury left a considerable amount of unfinished business in "Pugin-land" and elsewhere to be taken up by their teenage heirs and successors. The new earl, Bertram, was nineteen, and Pugin's eldest son, Edward, only eighteen. One of Edward's first commissions was to undertake the arrangements for the late earl's funeral, only seven weeks after his own father's obsequies at Ramsgate. Having been brought back from Naples, where he had died on 9th November, the earl's body lay in state first at S. George's, Southwark, and then in the Talbot Gallery at Alton Towers, while the Towers Chapel was prepared for the funeral on 14th December[1]. The Pugin-Hardman partnership, with Edward now at the helm, swung into action with the production of an elaborate Gothic herse and catafalque to stand in the chapel **(19)**. Edward also directed the decoration of the chapel with funerary drapes and a Requiem altar, and arranged for the making of a splendid pall to cover the coffin. This - along with one of the copes made for the occasion - is presently kept at S. Chad's cathedral Birmingham **(111)**.

Bertram Arthur, seventeenth Earl of Shrewsbury, had been educated almost entirely by private tutors at Alton Towers, and had also accompanied the late Earl and Countess on their travels abroad. He was described as "a person of singularly mild and gentle disposition and of refined and elegant tastes; and an accomplished scholar, especially in modern languages,"[2]. It was upon Bertram that the fortunes of the senior, Catholic, line of the Talbot family depended, for he was the last male heir.

Edward Pugin was keen to continue his family's association with the Shrewsburys, and to complete any outstanding work. For his part, the new earl wrote to Edward assuring him that the Shrewsbury patronage would continue, but reminding him also that until he came of age in December 1853, the estate and all other assets inherited from his uncle were held in trust[3]. One particular concern was the cathedral at Shrewsbury which A.W. Pugin and Earl John had planned to mark the restoration of the hierarchy. They had corresponded about it early in 1852[4], and Pugin had done a sketch on the back of one of his drawings for the Palace of Westminster[5]. It shows an ambitious

111. Hood of cope made for the funeral of the 16th Earl of Shrewsbury (S. Chad's Cathedral, Birmingham).

building with a south-west tower and spire, and other features which E.W. Pugin developed into the water-colour which he produced later that year[6]. The cathedral was subsequently built, between 1853 and 1856, though in a reduced form. Meanwhile, at Alton Towers, Edward Pugin inherited the unfinished Great Dining Room and the "New Rooms" above the Drawing Room. The estate accounts show that masons, joiners and painters were still working in these areas of the house in 1855[7]. At least one new panelled ceiling was emblazoned with Bertram's initials[8]. Work was also continuing at the Castle.

Edward Pugin carried out some significant work elsewhere in North Staffordshire, and most of it grew out of contacts which his father had already made, or commissions already in prospect at the time of his death. In 1854 the nuns moved from

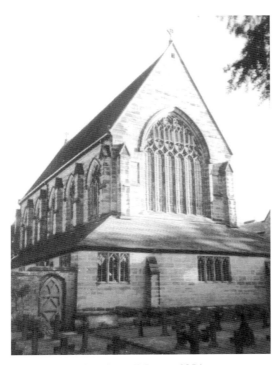

112. Oulton Abbey, by E.W. Pugin, 1854.

Caverswall Castle into new abbey buildings at Oulton, near Stone. E.W. Pugin was chosen as the architect, no doubt because of the alterations and additions his father had carried out at Caverswall in the 1840s. Oulton Abbey has an impressively large chapel (**112**) in the Decorated and Perpendicular styles. It is an early work, and therefore lacks the fussiness of some of Edward Pugin's later buildings. It nonetheless reveals some originality, for example in the tracery of the west window, and in the internal treatment of the roofs. Whereas A.W.N. Pugin would have insisted on open roofs, exposing all the structures, his son hid them with a coved ceiling. There is Hardman glass, including representations of six English abbesses in the west window, an ironwork chancel screen, and a richly-carved Benediction altar. Some domestic buildings connected to the east end of the chapel are also by Pugin junior.

The Lane End Mission in Longton was an offshoot of Caverswall established in 1819. The building was extended in 1835 and again in 1850, and in 1868-9 a new church dedicated to S. Gregory was built adjacent to the existing building which thereafter served as a parish hall. E. W. Pugin was the architect, and the new church - built of red brick with bands of blue brick, and stone dressings - consisted of an aisled nave with clerestories, a vestibule at the west end, and a high vaulted chancel (**113**). The east end terminated in a polygonal apse, roofed in a series of small gables with statues in between. There was a large rose-window at the west end[9]. S. Gregory's was considered by some to have been the best of

Edward Pugin's churches in the diocese[10], and therefore its demolition in 1970, on account of mining subsidence, is all the more to be regretted.

One of E.W. Pugin's last commissions before his death in 1875 was an extension to Cotton College for the Sedgeley Park Preparatory School which had moved in from Wolverhampton in 1868 under the name of S. Wilfrid's College. His principal addition was a wing set at right-angles to old Cotton Hall. It is of stone, two storeys tall, and two-light windows with tracery. The steep roof has dormers (101), and at the south-east angle there is a polygonal tower with a truncated spire-cap.

One major North Staffordshire commission which did not come Pugin's way was the Convent and Church of the Immaculate Conception and S. Dominic in Stone. A.W.N. Pugin had already built a small church here in 1843 for Fr. Dominic Barberi and the Passionists based at Aston Hall[11]. William Ullathorne, who at the Restoration of the Hierarchy became the first Bishop of Birmingham, favoured a local Catholic architect, Charles

113. S. Gregory's, Longton, by E.W. Pugin, 1869 (demolished 1970): postcard view of chancel, c.1910 (The Lewis Family Collection).

Hansom (1817-1888), and it was probably for this reason that Hansom was chosen in preference to E.W. Pugin to design the new convent, and the church where Ullathorne was eventually buried.

Edward Pugin was more fortunate in and around Stafford, where his father had made contacts in 1837. The most important of these was George Jerningham, who in 1824 successfully established his claim to the Barony of Stafford. The new Lord Stafford's brother, Edward Jerningham, was something of an amateur architect. Not only did he start to rebuild Stafford Castle to help strengthen George's claim to the title: at the same time (1817-19) he built the second church of S. Austin incorporating part of the original chapel of 1791. This was the church which A.W.N. Pugin visited in August 1837, and for which he later supplied furnishings. These included a new font with a pinnacled canopy - one of three which Pugin instanced in 1841 as examples of the medieval-style font which he was seeking to reintroduce[12]. Pre-1958 photographs of the third S. Austin's (114) show two Pugin-Hardman coronae hanging in the sanctuary; survivals, no doubt, from the second S. Austin's. Following the death of Edward Jerningham in 1849, his widow, Marianne, commissioned from Pugin a handsome silver-plated corona incorporating a sanctuary

114. S. Austin's, Stafford, by E.W. Pugin, 1862: postcard view of interior, c.1905, showing altar and reredos by P.P. Pugin.

lamp **(115)**. The inscription makes it clear that this corona was intended as an in memoriam gift, and was intended to hang before the Blessed Sacrament[13].

It was, therefore, hardly surprising that when the new S. Austin's was planned in the late 1850s, Edward Pugin was brought in as the architect. The parish priest from 1856 to 1858 was Francis Kerril Amherst (1819-1883) of the Warwickshire family for whom A.W. Pugin had built the church of S. Augustine at Kenilworth in 1841. He left Stafford in 1858 to become Bishop of Northampton. Edward Pugin was already well-acquainted with one of the benefactors of S. Austin's, Francis Whitgreave, who had engaged him to design his new house at Burton Manor, on the outskirts of Stafford, in 1854.

Edward Pugin's original design for the new S. Austin's[14] was quite ambitious, including a tall tower and spire **(116)**, but - as at Shrewsbury cathedral - the scheme had to be modified on grounds of cost **(117)**. The base of the tower was built, but for a time it had only a framework turret to contain the bell given by Mrs Anna Marie Masfen in thanksgiving for the conversion of herself and her four sons in 1861. Mrs Masfen was the sister of Edward Bellasis, a Serjeant-at-Law, and a former Tractarian who, after becoming a Catholic in 1850, had been a friend of the seventeenth Earl of Shrewsbury and an executor of his Will. As an Anglican, Mrs Masfen had earlier commissioned A.W.N. Pugin to design a memorial window to her deceased son, John, in S. Mary's church, Stafford[15].

The nave of S. Austin's is of six bays, with polished marble columns, and it has a wide, open chancel terminating in a polygonal apse. The battle for Rood Screens had ended abruptly with the death

115. The Stafford-Jerningham corona
(photo: James Joll)

of their champion in 1852, and S. Austin's, like most of Edward Pugin's churches, was built on the "all-seeing" principle which his father had so vigorously opposed. The church was opened in July 1862. In 1884 Edward's younger brother, Peter Paul Pugin (1851-1904), added a new high altar and a carved stone reredos, and he was also responsible for the altars in the Lady Chapel (1884) and the Sacred Heart Chapel (1894). The reredos of the high altar was demolished in 1958, when other original features - including wall decorations and the nave roof - were either obscured or removed. Extensive restorations carried out in 1998 have done much to restore the Puginian character of the interior, and the truncated tower has been given a lead-covered spirelet[16].

116. S. Austin's Stafford: one of E.W. Pugin's original designs.BAA P255/5/1

Amongst the benefactors of S. Austin's was Francis Whitgreave (1819-1896), a direct descendant of Thomas Whitgreave "the Preserver" who had played a leading role in the escape of Charles II after the Battle of Worcester in September 1651. The Whitgreaves' home was at Moseley, near Wolverhampton, and not far from Boscobel where the King famously hid in the oak-tree. Their roots, however, lay in the village of Whitgreave, just north of Stafford, and amongst their former properties was the site of a moated manor-house - Burton Manor - on the south-west side of Stafford. The manor itself had been demolished in 1606-7[17], but in about 1850 Francis Whitgreave, second son of George Whitgreave of Moseley Court, acquired the site with the intention of building a new home there. He was an antiquary, with a deep interest in his family's history, and was also the last lay student to be admitted to the English College in Rome, where English Catholic priests had been trained since the Reformation. He eventually became a barrister.

A.W. Pugin was most certainly acquainted with the Whitgreaves. As one of the leading Catholic families of the area they contributed to the building of Pugin's church at Brewood. Francis Whitgreave was a friend of Francis Amherst whom Pugin also knew well, and a certificate written by Pugin in respect of S. Augustine's, Kenilworth, somehow found its way into his possession[18]. In the summer of 1844 they were joined by George Talbot on an extended visit to Germany and Austria. Pugin also joined them for the first part of the journey, having dined with Amherst – and probably the others too – on the

117. S. Austin's, Stafford as built.

evening before they set sail. Whitgreave recalled that Pugin was "as usual most interesting and amusing during the voyage, full of life and spirit"[19]. Francis Whitgreave had an appetite for adventure that would have appealed to Pugin. In 1847 he and Amherst went on a pilgrimage to the Holy Land, first taking ship to Cairo, then travelling overland by camel[20]. Pugin followed this expedition with some interest, and in a letter to Lord Shrewsbury he expressed concern for the safety of the voyagers[21]. Two years later Francis' father, George Whitgreave, embarked on an adventure of another kind when he took as his third wife an Irish girl called Anne Sandford. He was more than old enough to be her grandfather. "Old Mr Whitgreave (age 70) has married a 19 year old girl in Ireland", Pugin wrote to

his wife Jane in the autumn of 1849[22].

Francis Whitgreave's name and address appear in the front end-papers of Pugin's diary for 1848. Whitgreave re-purchased the site of Burton Manor before 1851[23] and it is not unlikely that the building of a new house there was discussed before Pugin's death in the autumn of 1852. In the event, it was Edward Pugin who built the house, but his father's influence is much in evidence throughout, and there are some very remarkable similarities to the Pugin family home - S. Augustine's Grange - in Ramsgate, built in 1843-44. It seems very likely that Francis had visited the Grange, admired it, and decided that he wanted something very similar

118. Burton Manor, Stafford, by E.W. Pugin, 1855.

for his own family which included, ultimately, four children. Burton Manor is one of the most interesting - and least well-known - of E.W. Pugin's private, and secular, commissions **(118)**.

The design of Burton Manor was governed to an extent by its site. Although nothing remained of the original house, the location was marked by the medieval dry moat which Francis Whitgreave wished to retain. The moat was therefore bridged by a brick arch

119. Burton Manor - the vestibule over the moat.

carrying an elongated glazed porch - similar to the one at Ramsgate - leading to the front door **(119)**. Set on the gable of the porch is a stone cross presumed by some to be the

120. Burton Manor from the east: photo of c.1890 (courtesy Stafford Grammar School).

121. Burton Manor - entrance hall.

medieval one found at the site of the Franciscan Friary at Foregate, Stafford[24], while over the outer door is a stone plaque carved with the Whitgreave coat-of-arms and the motto *Regem defendere victum* ("to defend the vanquished king") - adopted no doubt after the exploits of Thomas Whitgreave "The Preserver". The house is of red brick with stone trim. It has bands of polychrome brickwork, crosses, and the intitials FW and TW, the latter signifying Francis' wife, Teresa. The fenestration is irregular: stone-framed windows of two, three, and four lights with trefoiled heads, and transoms. There are canted bays to the library, and to the drawing room and principal bedroom. The plan of the house is "T" shaped, with the drawing room, library, and the principal bedrooms above them set transversely to the main block. The service-rooms west of the main block are defined by lower roof-levels, and there is an octagonal stair-turret at the north-west angle.

The Whitgreaves gave up Burton Manor in the 1920s, and it was then bought by the firm of British Reinforced Concrete as a sports and social club. In 1930 the moat on the east side of the house was filled in, and a hall and other club facilities were built over it. A late nineteenth-century photograph shows the north side of the house as it was originally **(120)**, The turret then had an elaborate polygonal spirelet which no longer exists, and other features which have subsequently disappeared include bargeboards, ridge-crests, and chimney-stacks. The Manor is now part of Stafford Grammar School.

Internally, the layout of Burton Manor closely resembles that of the Grange at Ramsgate. First there is the entrance hall **(121)**, rising through both storeys, with a wood-panelled dado, and with banisters to the stairs and landings absolutely identical to those at Ramsgate.

The newels once carried brass antelopes (adapted from the Whitgreave crest), but these

122. Burton Manor - Dining-room chimneypiece.

have been removed for reasons of safety and they are now displayed on the upper walls. As at the Grange, there is a stone chimneypiece facing the entrance. The ceiling of the stair-well and landings retains its original stencilled wallpaper. There was, apparently, much more original wallpaper in situ before the building was adapted to its present use as a school[25]. The disposition of the principal ground-floor rooms - dining room, drawing room, and library mirrors Ramsgate too, and there is similarity in details such as the dining-room chimneypiece which is clearly copied from the one in Pugin's dining room at the Grange **(122)**. This, like the ones in the entrance-hall and dining room, has Minton tiles inset. There is another carved chimneypiece in the library. The ceilings of the drawing room and dining room are wood-panelled, and the panels have shields blazoned with various religious emblems and coats-of-arms.

123. S. John's Church, Alton - Memorial brass to 16th Earl of Shrewsbury. The inscription to the Countess is fixed on the wall behind.

Having set up home at Burton Manor, the Whitgreaves joined the congregation of S. Austin's, Stafford, and Francis may have had some influence over the appointment of his friend, Francis Amherst, to S. Austin's in 1856. In that same year, however, the Catholic cause in Staffordshire - and indeed much further afield - was shaken by the deaths of Maria, the Dowager Countess of Shrewsbury, and of the seventeenth Earl himself. The funeral of the countess took place at Alton on June 14th, and she was buried in Earl John's grave on the north side of the altar **(123)**. The Latin inscription on the simple brass memorial plate tells its own story. In translation it reads, "So united were their hearts whilst living that it semed fitting that their bodies should be placed in the same tomb where they await the mercy of the same Redeemer". Only a few weeks later, on August 10th, Earl Bertram died in Lisbon, and his body was brought back to England for burial on the south side of the altar in S. John's **(124)**. Aged only twenty-three and unmarried, Bertram was the last of the senior line of the Talbot family. A lengthy and widely-reported lawsuit then took place over the succession to the Shrewsbury titles and estates. Foreseeing the problems that might one day arise, both the sixteenth and seventeenth earls had laid plans whereby they hoped to keep the inheritance in Catholic hands. Meanwhile, the Anglican Henry Chetwynd Talbot (1803-1868), the third Earl Talbot of Ingestre Hall, had declared his intention to claim the titles and properties. Like Earls John and Bertram, he could claim lineal descent from the first Earl of Shrewsbury (d.1453), but the line was complex, and there were other claimants including Lord Edmund Howard (1855-1947), the infant second

124. S. John's Church, Alton: detail of Brass to Bertram, 17th Earl of Shrewsbury.

son of the Catholic Duke of Norfolk. The claim advanced on behalf of Lord Edmund was based on his descent from the first line of the Talbot family, through Alathea, sole heiress of Gilbert, the seventh and last earl in the senior line who died in 1616. She had married Thomas Howard, Earl of Arundel and Surrey.

Lord Edmund's trustees, and the executors of Earl Bertram's will, took immediate action to secure the properties and to contest Earl Talbot's claims. The Alton estate was administered on their behalf by a resident agent, assisted by loyal servants such as John Denny, the clerk-of works, and James Whittaker, the Head Gardener. In January 1857 the Duke of Norfolk himself visited the Towers along with the trustees - Serjeant Bellasis and James Hope-Scott - to address the principal tenants, and to entertain them to dinner in the new Banqueting Hall[26].

Though the succession to the earldom and the estates was in dispute, there was nothing to prevent the moveable properties being disposed of in accordance with Earl Bertram's will. Some important items were removed from Alton Towers by the Duke of Norfolk and taken to Arundel Castle. These included a quantity of maps, plans, and other papers relating to the Alton estate, and some articles from the cabinets in the chapel corridor. Amongst these were a silver bell and other relics from the former nunnery at Syon House, and a collection of crucifixes and other devotional items[27]. Significantly, the contents of the chapel, and family portraits, do not appear in the catalogue of the great sale which took place at the Towers in July 1857. The rest of "the magnificent contents of Alton Towers" - as the catalogue describes them - were auctioned in some 4,000 lots over a period of thirty days, and the sale attracted a good deal of attention in the local and national press[28].

The reason for the sale, so it was said, was to defray considerable costs incurred by Lord Edmund's trustees in contesting Henry Chetwynd Talbot's claim to the earldom. The Peerage Case was finally settled in June 1858 when the House of Lords ruled in favour of Earl Talbot who thereafter took his seat as the eighteenth Earl of Shrewsbury. The legal battle over the estates continued for another year, with the new Earl fighting now to establish that they were inalienable from the titles and that the provisions of the late Earl's will regarding them were therefore invalid. The Alton estate continued for the time being to be managed on behalf of Lord Edmund Howard, and although the house was now virtually empty, a few staff were retained, and Mass continued to be said in the Towers

Chapel. There was however an atmosphere of provisionality and uncertainty which was noted and brilliantly recorded by Mary Howitt of Uttoxeter, who visited the Towers in June 1859:

> ".... Passing into a vast court, we noticed on a lofty tower the tattered hatchment flapping in the wind. We entered, through an arched doorway, the gorgeous Catholic chapel, and were led onward by a pale-faced young man, with an anxious, depressed countenance, and who could not speak without sighs........"

The un-named young man turned out to be an organist, and he took Mary Howitt and her companion up into the gallery, lamenting the fact that the fine three-manual organ was very rarely played. When asked if Mass was still celebrated in the chapel, he replied mournfully, "Only Low Mass,and therefore no music". He then agreed to play if Mary and her friend would pump the bellows.

> ".... The next moment after commencing, the lofty chapel, from the highest centre of its roof to the lowest level of its floor, seemed throbbing and heaving with tempestuous swell of the most wonderful melody..... No longer dim-eyed, dreaming, and melancholy, he sat there an inspired musician, with flushed and upturned eye .... I wished from my heart that the Catholic heirs might come into possession, the old faith and worship be maintained, and he be chosen organist"[29].

It was a forlorn hope: on the very day of Mary Howitt's visit to the Towers, the news broke that Henry Chetwynd Talbot's claim to the Shrewsbury estates had been upheld, and on 13th April 1860 he took possession of Alton Towers. The consequences were serious not just for the Catholic Church locally, but for the whole Diocese of Birmingham which was in considerable financial difficulty. The character of the Catholic Church in England was also beginning to change following the Restoration of the Hierarchy as the clergy sought to free themselves from the kind of lay domination which Lord Shrewsbury had represented, and which was a relic of the days of persecution. In 1857 George Montgomery, a convert priest in the Midlands, well expressed the changing climate: "I am not one who would join in any cry to any earthly patron *oculi omnium in te sperant Domine*[30] as we seemed lately to cry to Lord Shrewsbury: but I do not despise the aid of the worldly great, and would do what I could without flunkeyism to secure it"[31].

The conclusion of the Shrewsbury Peerage Case, and the expenses incurred, meant that those who had stood to benefit under the contingency provisions of Earl John's will - notably Ambrose Phillipps and Charles Scott Murray - received only a fraction of what had been willed to them[32]. There was, however, an interesting epilogue to this story of Catholic Revival emanating from the heart of Staffordshire's "Pugin-Land". In the summer of 1927 - three years after the departure of the Chetwynd Talbots - Alton Towers was the scene of a gathering of many thousands of Catholics at which Dr. Barrett, Bishop Auxiliary of Birmingham, and his assistant clergy, officiated in the famous Shrewsbury cloth-of-gold vestments borrowed for the occasion from Oscott College[33]. Though emptied - for the second time - of furnishings and paintings, the house and chapel retained their fine woodwork, sumptuous wallcoverings, and radiant stained-glass windows. Amongst the thousands of people present on this occasion there may well have been a fewscore octogenarians for whom it evoked powerful childhood memories of Catholic celebrations of yesteryear, and of the Alton they had known and loved in the days of "Good Earl John".

10 THE ANGLICAN DIMENSION

"..... even in its present position, by its own existing canons and rubrics, the Anglican Church is bound, consistently, to work exclusively on the principles of Christian architecture, and to renounce all pagan adaptations whatsoever" - A.W.N. Pugin, Apology

North Staffordshire's fine array of Pugin buildings is complemented by some outstanding examples of the work of other Victorian architects who were greatly influenced by Pugin: George Gilbert Scott at S. Mary's, Stafford; George Edmund Street at All Saints', Denstone; George Frederick Bodley at the Holy Angels, Hoar Cross; and Richard Norman Shaw at All Saints', Leek. All of these are Anglican churches, and they all reflect the impact of the revival of Catholicism within the Church of England from the 1840s onwards. In its

125 Highnam Church, Gloucestershire - the Baptistry.

architectural aspect, this revival owed much to the writings of A.W.N. Pugin which were avidly read by members of the Oxford and Cambridge architectural societies. These were the "Ecclesiologists" who in the 1840s were attempting to restore the beauty of holiness through the restoration and re-furnishing of old churches and the building of new ones in a Gothic style based on proper understanding of architectural principles, and thorough research. Impressed by the Catholic spirit of the pamphlets which the Cambridge Camden Society were publishing for the benefit of Anglican churchwardens and church-builders, Pugin commented on them in some detail and recommended that they should be studied also by English Catholics who, "owing to their long exclusion from the sacred buildings raised by their ancestors in the faith, have woefully departed from the principles which influenced them in the erection of their religious buildings"[1].

Praise from a Catholic propagandist such as Pugin could, however, be embarrassing. John Ruskin tried to rid Gothic of its Catholic associations in order to make it more widely acceptable, and in the process was most unkind to Pugin. The Camden Society broke with him when in 1846 it published a derogatory article entitled *The Artistic Merit of Mr Pugin*. The author of this attack was Alexander Beresford Hope, an ardent ecclesiologist, who concluded that "Mr. Pugin, clever and enthusiastic as he is, has not answered the expectations that were formed of him"[2]. Yet nothing speaks more clearly or more succinctly of the practical impact of Pugin's ideas outside the Roman Catholic Church than the church of the Holy Innocents at Highnam, Gloucestershire, begun by Henry Woodyer (1816-1896), a few months after the opening of S. Giles', Cheadle. Its plan, its tall spire, its alabaster reredos, and font with pinnacled cover **(125)**, are clearly inspired by S. Giles'. The rich polychrome interior, complete with Doom painting over the chancel arch, was the work of the benefactor, Thomas Gambier Parry (1816-1888), and reflects his careful study of the interior of Cheadle. Completed in 1851, it is as "Puginesque" as it was then possible for an Anglican church to be.

When Pugin first visited Staffordshire in 1834 he saw Lichfield Cathedral as restored some thirty years previously by James Wyatt (1746-1813) and local architect Joseph Potter (1756-1842) who was still working there. Wyatt had re-ordered the east end of the cathedral by demolishing the altar-screen so as to join together the Choir and Lady Chapel, a favourite device of his. Pews had been introduced into the Choir, the choir-aisles had been walled-off, and a glazed screen erected to separate the whole of the east end from the nave. Pugin's reaction to Wyatt's treatment of the cathedral was fairly predictable:

> "... Yes - this monster of architectural depravity, this pest of Cathedral architecture, has been here. need I say more… The man I am sorry to say - who executes the repairs of the building was a pupil of the Wretch himself and has imbibed all the vicious propensies of his accursed tutor without one spark of even practical ability to atone for his misdeeds…"[3]

Had Pugin lived long enough to have returned to Lichfield some forty years later he would have seen the results of the restoration work carried out from 1857 onwards by George Gilbert Scott (1811-1878), and he would have been delighted to see the undoing of the misdeeds committed by "the Wretch", the restoration of the Lady Chapel to its proper function, the High Altar replaced and correctly furnished, and the stonework and statuary of the building restored in true Gothic style. Yet none of this could have happened without Pugin, for it was the "thunder" of Pugin's writings which enlightened and excited the young Scott almost to frenzy, to the extent of wishing that all his previous work could be burnt down. "I suddenly found myself like a person awakened from a long feverish dream. I was in fact a new man"[4].

S. Mary's church in Stafford was the first to be restored by Gilbert Scott following his "awakening". The work began in 1842 - the year of Pugin's *Dublin Review* article which had so excited him - and was completed by the end of 1844. The church is a large one, with a vast chancel and transepts which, until 1548, had housed a prebendal college. By 1840 it was in a dilapidated condition; the chancel and transepts were rarely used, and the nave was filled with an assortment of box-pews which faced westwards towards a huge gallery containing the pulpit and organ. Jesse Watts Russell of Ilam Hall contributed £5,000 for the restoration of the interior along the lines advocated by the Camden Society[5]. It was an impressive amount of money, enough to finance a whole new church, and it excited Ambrose

Phillipps to comment on the likely benefits to church-building within the Catholic Church consequent upon the re-union of Rome and Canterbury for which he hoped. "This as a specimen, when they are still in schism, may serve to show what the Anglicans will do when the reunion shall once be fairly accomplished"[6].

Watts Russell's generosity made it possible for S. Mary's to be furnished in grand style. The nave was equipped with finely-carved "poppy-head" benches, and the chancel (126) with cathedral-style choir-stalls. An elaborately-carved sedilia was set on the south side of the altar which was raised on three steps and furnished with tall candlesticks and a coloured altar-frontal worked by Jesse Watts Russell's daughters, standing beneath an east window glowing with stained glass. The entire east end of the church was paved with encaustic tiles by Minton, those of the sanctuary being the gift of Herbert Minton himself. They comprise an

*126. S. Mary's Church, Stafford: the chancel, 1844. Lithograph of drawing by John Masfen (*Views of the Church of St Mary at Stafford, *1852)*

exceedingly rich pavement of differing patterns on each of the four rising levels, and a dado with sacred emblems for the east wall, two years before those at S. Giles', Cheadle. Thus the internal appearance of the building was transformed almost beyond recognition, yet none of these "advanced" ritual arrangements seems to have provoked the kind of adverse reaction that was experienced elsewhere. It was after all completed a year before the furore raised by Newman's conversion to Rome, and the consequent growth in suspicion of all things savouring of "popery". The only controversy was over the external appearance of the south transept of S. Mary's, which Scott - backed by both the Oxford and Cambridge Societies - insisted on "restoring" to its original thirteenth-century form.

It was restorations along these lines which impressed Pugin, and persuaded him that all was not yet lost within the Church of England. It is known that he visited S. Mary's and pronounced it to be "the best restoration which has been effected in modern times"[7]. Nor was that all. When John Masfen, a brilliant young artist who had drawn a set of very fine illustrations of the restoration, died in 1846 at the age of nineteen, his mother commissioned Pugin to design a memorial window for the north aisle of S. Mary's. It shows the figure of

S. John the Evangelist under a Gothic canopy. Mrs Masfen later arranged for the publication of her son's drawings, with a detailed account of the restoration written by Scott himself[8], for which Pugin designed an elaborate frontispiece showing the memorial window flanked by angels, and views of S. Mary's and Stafford Castle **(Col. plate 9)**.

Among the leading Anglican families of North Staffordshire were the Bagots of Blithfield Hall, who, in the early nineteenth century, boasted a number of clerics amongst their younger sons. In 1829 Richard (1782-1854), a younger son of the first Baron Bagot, became Bishop of Oxford, a position which he held through the upheavals caused by the Tractarian Movement, before being translated to Bath and Wells in 1845. Pugin wrote in praise of Bishop Bagot for his refusal to condemn the *Tracts for the Times* in general, or the infamous *Tract XC* in particular[9]. The Bishop's younger son, Lewis, was at Christ Church along with his cousin Hervey - second son of the second Baron. Both graduated in 1834, were subsequently ordained, and eventually returned to home ground; Hervey to be Rector of Blithfield, and Lewis to be Rector of the neighbouring parish of Leigh, where the Bagots built a new church in 1845-46.

It is almost certain that Pugin was introduced to the Bagots by Lord Shrewsbury, who had stayed at Blithfield as plain John Talbot in 1822. After succeeding to the earldom, he and the countess were invited to archery parties and other social gatherings at the Hall[10]. Hervey Bagot's address appears in the end-papers of Pugin's diary for 1844. On the 3rd October 1845 he visited the new church at Leigh and on the same day he met Lord Bagot, possibly at Blithfield[11]. All Saints', Leigh, is a quite remarkable church, cruciform in plan, and with all the archaeological accuracy advocated by Pugin, Scott, and the Camdenians[12]. The architect was the little-known Thomas Johnson of Lichfield. Pugin was brought in to design encaustic tiles for the chancel, the fabric of which was paid for by Bishop Bagot who had himself been Rector of Leigh from 1807 and had continued to hold the living in plurality with his bishopric from 1829 to 1846. The tiles are as rich as any to be seen in the

buildings that Pugin designed himself, and they include the arms of Richard Bagot, with mitres worked into the border **(Col. Plate 7)**. They were, apparently, donated to the church by Minton himself[13]. Since Hervey Bagot was amongst the distinguished guests at the re-opening of S. Mary's church, Stafford, in December 1844, he would have seen the vast array of

127. S. Leonard's Church, Blithfield: window by A.W.N. Pugin.

160

Minton tiles in the chancel there.

In 1851 Pugin was working at S. Leonard's church, adjacent to Blithfield Hall; a church which retained an almost complete set of medieval bench-ends, a rood-screen, and some fine grisaille glass. Pugin designed glass for a window in the south clerestory (**127**) with figures of SS. Peter, James and John[14]. Some glass in the north aisle may also be by him: figures of the Evangelists Matthew and Mark which, like other glass on this side of the church, suffered damage from bombs dropped in the vicinity during the Second World War. The figures of Luke and John were completely destroyed. Pugin's

128. S. Leonard's Church, Blithfield: the chancel restored by Pugin, 1851.

work at Blithfield included the restoration (**128**) of the dilapidated chancel. The tradition is that he reproduced faithfully what was already there, but a water-colour done just before the restoration tells a different story. Though Pugin retained significant items such as the sedilia and piscina, and a fine array of Bagot memorials, he replaced the Perpendicular flat roof with a pitched one, and replaced the three-light east window with one of five lights and intersecting tracery[15]. The glass in this window was replaced in 1965; an unfortunate period for Victorian art generally.

John Ruskin (1819-1900) is credited with having "discovered" the Italian Gothic forms which became popular during the High Victorian period, following the publication of *The Stones of Venice* (1851-53), but Pugin was already well aware of them when, in 1847, he visited Florence and wrote back enthusiastically to Lord Shrewsbury that it was a perfect mine of Gothic art. "I have seen 3 of the finest altars in Christendom, and one of silver about 12 feet long .... the sacristies are full of Gothic shrines, reliquaries, chalices etc..... Rome is certainly a miserable place, but Italy is yet the richest country for true Christian art & I do not despair of S. Peter's being rebuilt in a better style"[16]. Had Pugin lived longer there is little doubt that he would have used Italian Gothic forms, including structural polychromy. In the decade following his death other continental sources came into fashion, particularly the Romanesque and robust early Gothic forms which, combined with polychromy and the use of coloured marble, produced the "muscular" churches of the High Victorian period. The leading exponents included George Edmund Street (1824-1881) who in 1862 built one of his very best churches of this type within a few hundred yards of what was then the principal entrance to Alton Towers: All Saints' Church, Denstone[17].

Pugin's basic church model, which became popular with builders both in Britain and overseas, is typified by the churches at Uttoxeter and Alton: a nave, chancel, bell-cote,

129. All Saints' Chruch, Denstone, by G.E. Street, 1862.

and perhaps a porch. In the interests of economy, aisles could be dispensed with. Denstone church is of this variety. It has a nave without aisles, a porch on the south side, a chancel, and a bell-turret; each element delineated by a different roof-level as Pugin said it ought to be done **(129)**. It is how Street handles these features that makes Denstone such an interesting building, and takes us beyond Pugin. The polygonal-ended chancel is taller than the nave, and the importance of the chancel is emphasized by the downward slope of the ground at the east end. The bell-cote, instead of being set on a gable, takes the form of a round turret with a conical roof, set at the junction of the nave and chancel on the north side. The windows on the north side are very different from those on the south. It is deliberately asymmetrical, as many of Pugin's later churches were. The treatment of the churchyard is not unlike that at Alton: a large churchyard cross, and, in the older part of the burial ground, small memorials of local stone with crosses instead of the "pagan" urns, inverted torches, cherubs, broken pillars and obelisks which Pugin believed should have no place in a Christian cemetery. There is also a lych-gate, timber-framed with a tiled roof.

Unlike Pugin's churches, in which internal space is compartmentalised, and where the view of the sanctuary is filtered through a fretted screen, Denstone is open from end to end, in accordance with the Tractarian belief that the altar should be visible from all parts of the building. The font, pulpit **(130)** and reredos are all made of alabaster and coloured marble, with rich sculpture and inlaid work. The Italian influence is seen most strongly in the design of the font. The square alabaster bowl has angels at the corners in the style of Niccola and Giovanni Pisano, thirteenth-century sculptors whose work Street greatly admired.

Street's patron at Denstone was Thomas

130. All Saints' Church, Denstone: the pulpit.

Percival Heywood, a member of a Manchester banking family, who lived in the village. He was Anglo-Catholic like Street who, it should be remembered, was for a time churchwarden at the Ecclesiologists' model church, All Saints', Margaret Street. Together they created at Denstone the kind of "Anglo-Catholic watering place" that fellow-Ecclesiologist A.J. Beresford Hope had intended to establish in the North Staffordshire village of Sheen a decade earlier[18]. Significantly, one of the windows in the apse shows an Anglican priest wearing full Mass vestments. Choral services were quickly established at which plainsong, the *Missa de Angelis,* and settings by Merbecke and Helmore were used. Visiting preachers included the celebrated "martyr of ritualism", Alexander Heriot Mackonochie of S. Alban's, Holborn, while the North Staffordshire Railway made Denstone a more accessible "watering-place" than Sheen could ever have become[19]. Denstone typifies the radical and widespread changes that, influenced strongly by Pugin, the Ecclesiologists had wrought on the setting of Anglican worship in little more than two decades. Gone is the "preaching house" style of box-shaped buildings overlaid with a veneer of Gothic ornament; galleries, box-pews, and dominant pulpit. In their place are solid, well-defined churches like Denstone, with well-ordered interiors in which the focus is unmistakably the altar. There was a strong philanthropic side too. All Saints' was very much a church for the rural poor. The inscription, "Every seat in this church is free" is cut into the stonework just inside the door, a reference to the odious system of pew-rents by which those who could afford it could reserve their

own seats. Street would have none of it at All Saints', Margaret Street, nor would Percival Heywood countenance it at Denstone. A village school was built to Street's design to the south of the church, six years before the more famous Woodard School - "Denstone College" - just outside the village.

Twelve miles south of Denstone, between Uttoxeter and Burton-on-Trent, is the tiny village of Hoar Cross, the scene of one of the most spectacular achievements of the Gothic Revival to be seen anywhere in England: the Church of the Holy Angels **(131)**. When, in 1872, Emily Charlotte Meynell-Ingram commissioned George Frederick Bodley (1827-1907) to build this church, neither could have foreseen the long-term

131. Church of the Holy Angels, Hoar Cross, by G.F. Bodley, 1874-6.

consequences of what they were doing. Emily's immediate concern was to build a memorial to her husband Hugo who had died tragically in 1870; but it became a project which absorbed her energies well beyond the opening of the church in 1876 as alterations and additions continued until her own death in 1904.

Just as Lord Shrewsbury's generosity allowed Pugin to build his "perfect Cheadle", so here Mrs Meynell-Ingram's wealth and generosity enabled Bodley to show what heights of perfection and refinement could be reached within the rubrics of that fourteenth-century English style which had so captivated Pugin and which was chosen for Hoar Cross. This church exemplifies the reaction against the muscularity of the High Victorian, and the move towards the elegance and refinement of the late-Victorian age, and thus it is very different from Denstone. Bodley's own career reflects this change of taste. Many of his earlier churches - e.g. S. Michael's, Brighton (1858-63) and S. Martin, Scarborough (1861-63) are similar to those of Street and Butterfield: robust and with polychrome decoration showing the influence of thirteenth-century Burgundian and Italian Gothic. As Pugin had reverted from the intense colouration of Cheadle to the more refined three-dimensional stonework of his own church at Ramsgate, so Bodley moved away from polychromy and

muscularity in his churches at Cambridge (All Saints', 1863-70) and Liverpool (S. John's, Tuebrook, 1868-70), and the *Ecclesiologist* noted with some satisfaction that "Mr Bodley has restricted himself to pure English forms .... The time for reaction from exclusively French or Italian types has at length arrived"[20].

Hoar Cross could not be more "English". The decoration is lavish, but it is of the three-dimensional moulded and sculpted type. No expense was spared, either on the fabric executed principally in sandstones from Alton and Runcorn - or on the furnishings. How Pugin would have loved this church, with its dimly-lit nave, soaring font-cover, and glorious rood-screen; the rich sanctuary with its legions of stone angels and saints; the founder's tomb and the chantries - just about everything that, as he had said back in the 1840s, there ought to be in an English Catholic Church, and all of the most exquisite workmanship. There is much about the interior of the nave (**132**) especially that

132. Hoar Cross - interior view from a painting by H. Axel-Haig (1835-1921).

is reminiscent of S. Augustine's, Ramsgate, which is also cruciform in plan, with a central tower (133). Latin texts and inscriptions executed in impeccable black-letter make visitors ask, "Can this really be an Anglican church?" It is altogether "more Pugin than Pugin", and thus it demonstrates a strange paradox, namely that those who paid most attention to Pugin's visions of a Catholic country filled once more with soaring towers and spires, stained glass, twinkling candles, gorgeous vestments and incense-laden ritual were members not of the Church of Rome but of the Church of England.

Emily Meynell-Ingram's brother was the second Viscount Halifax, President of the most influential of the Anglo-Catholic societies, the English Church Union; and like Pugin and Ambrose Phillipps before him, he looked towards the eventual reconciliation of the Church of England with Rome[21]. The reunion never came, for although Anglo-Catholicism emerged as a powerful force, it failed to convert sufficient of the Anglican hierarchy, while at grassroots level the majority remained stubbornly protestant, and churches like Hoar Cross were the exception rather than the rule. They nevertheless provoked some violent opposition, notably John Kensit's Protestant Truth Society (1890) whose activities included vandalism and the noisy interruption of "ritualist" services. Fearful that the Kensitites might visit Hoar Cross, Emily Meynell-Ingram had her four gamekeepers sit near the church door on a Sunday morning, with instructions to carry off any troublemakers to a ducking in the nearby pond[22].

Pugin complained often, and loudly, that the Catholic clergy did not know how to use

133. S. Augustine's, Ramsgate: watercolour by A.W.N. Pugin. (S. Augustine's Abbey, Ramsgate; photo by Michael Blaker)

his buildings and ornaments properly, in spite of the detailed explanations given in publications such as the *Glossary of Ecclesiastical Ornament* (1844) and Dr. Rock's scholarly expositions of the old English liturgy which they both sought to revive. Anglicans too needed instructions to supplement the meagre rubrics of Book of Common Prayer if churches like Hoar Cross were to be used as their designers and founders intended. The pioneer in this respect was Pugin's Oxford friend, J.R. Bloxam, whose *Hierurgia Anglicana* (1848) prepared the ground for the revival of ceremonial on English medieval lines. Ten years later John Purchas issued a handbook of directions for clergy at the altar under the title of *Directorium Anglicanum*, including the celebration of High Mass with a priest, deacon and sub-deacon (134). Its illustrations and descriptions of vestments and ornaments bear a striking resemblance to those in

134. An Anglo-Catholic High Mass, frontispiece to John Purchas, Directorium Anglicanum, *1858.*

Pugin's *Glossary*, and indeed it drew on some of the same sources; but it drew also on a source which Pugin had studiously avoided, namely Joseph Baldeschi's *Ceremoniario della Basilica Vaticana* (1839) which described the modern (i.e. Tridentine) Roman Rite as celebrated in the Vatican. Thus liturgical scholarship among the more "advanced" Anglicans mirrored the dichotomy within the Roman Catholic Church in England, some following the Puginian line by emphasising continuity with the medieval English Church, and others wishing to keep abreast of post-Reformation developments in Western Europe.

Among those present at Ramsgate on September 21st 1852 for the funeral of A.W.N. Pugin was Richard Norman Shaw (1831-1912), a pupil of G.E. Street, and representative of a new generation of British architects who built on Pugin's achievements. Better-known perhaps as the architect of domestic and public buildings such as the great Northumbrian mansion, Cragside (1869-1883) and New Scotland Yard (1887-90), Shaw designed sixteen churches, the largest and grandest of which was All Saints', Leek (1885-87). He described it as "the best and most satisfactory piece of work I have ever had done"[23], and it represents the full flowering of Shaw's ideas, developed over several years, of what he believed a church should be[24]. As one might expect from a pupil of Street, All Saints' **(135)** is open and spacious with an uninterrupted west-east view towards the altar, and Shaw treats the crossing under the tower in a novel and daring fashion, with broad arches pitched high so as not to impair the view into the chancel, and flying-buttresses cleverly incorporated into the aisle walls and roofs. Many of the details are, however, clearly derivative in style, the motifs of the window-tracery being generally Decorated/Perpendicular in character. The tracery of the east window was copied from the north transept of S. Oswald's, Ashbourne, while that of the west window is much more original. Thus Norman Shaw produced a remarkable synthesis. To visit Bodley's church at Hoar Cross is almost like entering a fourteenth-century time-warp; one cannot do that at All Saints'. Built on the "all-seeing" principle, it is exactly the kind of church that would have answered the needs of the Oratorians had Pugin then been willing to do as Newman suggested and broaden his vision of Gothic as a style capable of adaptation and development.

All Saints' is remarkable for other reasons too. The internal decor and furnishings make it a significant landmark in the early history of the Arts-and-Crafts Movement of the late nineteenth century, for two of Shaw's pupils and assistants, William Richard Lethaby (1857-1931) and Gerald Horsley (1862-1917), became leading members of that movement, and both had significant role at All Saints'. Horsley decorated the walls

135. All Saints', Leek, by R.N. Shaw, 1885-7.

and ceiling of the chancel, which are as intensely-coloured as S. Giles', Cheadle, and Lethaby designed the frame for the huge triptych altarpiece, along with the pulpit and font. All of these show highly original interpretations of traditional forms. The re-integration of the visual arts with architecture was something in which Shaw ardently believed, and it echoes Pugin's conviction that an architect should be responsible for both. All Saints' is also very much a North Staffordshire church in that it has a rugged, gritty, rock-faced exterior which accords with its natural surroundings, and which also belies the refinements within. The materials chosen were the sandstones and gritstones to be found in nearby quarries, and Shaw was fortunate in having as builder and local clerk-of-works a man who knew his quarries and materials[25]. Here is another parallel with Pugin, who likewise preferred local materials and was concerned that architecture should harmonize with its natural surroundings:

> "........ so well did the ancient builders adapt their edifices to localities, that they seemed as if they formed a portion of nature itself, grappling and growing from the sites in which they are placed .... The rubble stones and flinty beach furnish stones as rich for the natural architect, as the limestone quarry or granite rock.."[26]

Pugin had demonstrated this principle at Cheadle, with the infinite care he had shown over the Counslow quarry, while his own church at Ramsgate - S. Augustine's - is very much a Kentish church, built largely of stones from the nearby "flinty beach". Norman Shaw visited Ramsgate again in 1892, by then a mature architect, and arguably the dominant figure in English architecture. After the visit he wrote:

> "There is a charming little church here (Roman Catholic), built by the great Pugin, some forty-five years ago, for himself. He designed and paid for the whole thing, and it is full of interest all through........ a most delightful and interesting work, and done so long ago. I am afraid we have not advanced much. Such work makes one feel small, very small"[27].

All Saints' is not the only noteworthy Gothic building in Leek. On the southern approach to the town from Cheadle Road the skyline is broken by no fewer than six towers and spires. The spires are those of the cemetery chapels (by W. Sugden), the Congregational church (also by Sugden, 1863), and the Roman Catholic Church of S. Mary (by Albert Vicars, 1886) which is more prominent than the others on account of its size and the fact that it is built of Bath stone rather than the darker local stones. Pugin would have done it very differently had Lord Shrewsbury's intention to give Leek a new Catholic Church been fulfilled in his lifetime[28]. In addition to the squat tower of All Saints' there is the remarkably tall one of S. Luke's (by F. & H. Francis, 1848) with its stair-turret and pierced parapet, and finally the pinnacled tower of Leek's medieval parish church of S. Edward Confessor, which has a High Victorian chancel by Street, with much fine carving in marble and alabaster.

Apart from All Saints' the most remarkable of all of these is, in its way, the Congregational church (now United Reformed/Methodist) in Derby Street (136). It is the work of William Sugden (d.1892) who, along with his son and partner, William Larner Sugden, virtually monopolised public and private building in Leek between about 1860 and 1900. The Sugdens were versatile architects who could work in a variety of styles, from Gothic to the Old English and Queen Anne styles favoured by Norman Shaw. What is extraordinary about the Congregational church is that it is in the Decorated Gothic style, with a 130-foot high tower and slender spire set at the (ritual) north-west corner of the building. Pugin might well have considered Gothic and Nonconformist to be mutually exclusive, and Nonconformists were generally suspicious of Gothic as smacking of Romanism. This is nevertheless a successful adaptation of Gothic to the requirements of Nonconformist worship. As one might expect of a Congregational church, it lacks aisles and a chancel, but the window-tracery is extremely fine, and the buttresses and weatherings are convincing too. Though by no means unique in this respect, Leek exhibits well the diverse applications of Gothic Revival architecture: Roman-Catholic, Anglican, Nonconformist, and - in the case of the cemetery chapels, Municipal. It is all serious too: gone

136. Congregational Church, Derby Street, Leek, by W. Sugden, 1863: ink drawing by A. Mosley, 1891.

168

are the plaster shams, false ceilings, flimsy pillars and wiry tracery of the early years of the nineteenth century, and the credit for that lies with the pioneering work of A.W.N. Pugin.

In the nineteenth century Leek was a prosperous textile-manufacturing town specialising in the production of silk. In this lies the unique and magnificent contribution made by this moorland town to the Gothic Revival - the ecclesiastical embroideries worked from the 1860s onwards by Elizabeth Wardle and the ladies of the Leek Embroidery Society.

The revival of Gothic architecture and furnishings necessarily involved textiles; the production, for example, of vestments and altar-frontals. In the Middle Ages the manufacture of ecclesiastical textiles had given England an international reputation, with the name *opus anglicanum* ("English work") being universally applied to the superb embroideries done in silk and in silver and gold thread, mainly in London workshops, and by men. Then came the Reformation, which witnessed the wholesale confiscation and destruction of ecclesiastical art in all its forms. Such examples of *opus anglicanum* as survived were safeguarded in Catholic families for occasional clandestine use, or in Catholic Europe where some items were held in sufficiently high esteem to ensure their preservation. It was to these surviving examples, and to illustrations in medieval illuminated manuscripts and on old memorial brasses, that leaders of the Gothic Revival turned when seeking to recover a long-lost art. Lord Shrewsbury's role as a collector of medieval textiles has already been noted, and in particular his ownership of the Syon Cope, one of the most magnificent pieces of *opus anglicanum* to have survived; and it was to examples such as these that Pugin directed those who, he hoped, might revive this important art-form.

In *The Present State of Ecclesiastical Architecture* (1843) Pugin made a direct appeal for the revival of ecclesiastical textile-manufacture in England:

> "....why should not many of the looms which have so long laboured to supply the changing demand of worldly fashion, be again employed in clothing the spouse of Christ - the Church - in her ancient glorious garb........ York and Canterbury will furnish far better patterns than either Paris or Protestant Berlin"[29]

Generally speaking, and in the interests of economy and speed of production, Pugin used machine-produced braids and appliqués in the manufacture of vestments. The production of suitable threads and dyestuffs, and the working of designs by hand, were in any case highly specialised skills which had to be re-learned, and Pugin readily admitted that this would take time[30]. By the 1870s, however, the silk mills and embroiderers of Leek were set to take this particular art-form beyond anything that Pugin had been able to achieve, and even to match the original *opus anglicanum* of the Middle Ages. The key figures were silk-manufacturer Thomas Wardle[31], whose mills produced and dyed the fine tussore silk threads and fabrics, and his wife Elizabeth who formed the Needlework School. They did exactly as Pugin had urged back in the 1840s, studying the ancient authorities such as illuminated manuscripts, stained glass, memorial brasses and surviving examples of original work. At the same time they joined forces with contemporary architects and designers such as Shaw, Horsley, and William Morris, to produce new work primarily for the Leek churches. The success of their venture meant that by the 1890s "Leek Embroidery"

137. Opus Anglicanum *revived: hand-worked altar-frontal designed by R. N. Shaw (All Saints', Leek).*

was making a great impact in exhibitions at home and abroad[32]. All of the Leek churches have splendid collections of this work, the most extensive being at All Saints' and S. Edward's, which have full sets of altar-frontals in all the liturgical colours, vestments, and many smaller items **(137)**. Along with the ceramic products of Herbert Minton's factory, and the revival of alabaster-carving, the work of the Leek Embroidery Society highlights the very special role of North Staffordshire in the history of the Gothic Revival.

The key influence at work in this "Anglican dimension" - even with those who were reluctant to admit it - was undoubtedly Pugin. Though he had only one pupil in the formal sense of the word, and employed no clerks in his office, his influence on later generations of architects and artists was profound. He laid foundations of Gothic workmanship on which later generations were able to build to greater perfection. His rood-screen at Cheadle is splendid, but Bodley's at Hoar Cross **(Col. Plate 10)** is exquisite, and Pugin would have rejoiced to see it, for, as he himself once said, "Any man who possesses the true spirit of Christian art, so far from desiring to occupy an unrivalled position, is delighted when he is equalled, and overjoyed when he is surpassed"[33]. The re-integration of the arts with architecture as demonstrated by Norman Shaw at All Saints', Leek, would also have delighted him. While following Pugin's principles, later architects were able to fulfil his ideals in ways that were impossible in his lifetime, and to adapt and develop Gothic in ways that he was reluctant to do. The tradition continued locally well into the twentieth century. Basil Champneys' church at Slindon, near Stafford (1894) successfully combines both derivative and innovative elements, and Gerald Horsley's church of S. Chad, Longsdon (1905) was directly inspired by All Saints', Leek. In 1910 Bodley's successor, Cecil Hare, added a huge chancel, wholly in the style of Hoar Cross, to the medieval church of S. John at Ashley, near Newcastle-under-Lyme. Though outside the boundaries of "Pugin-land", Bernard Miller's rebuilding of S. Michael's, Tettenhall, Wolverhampton (1950) deserves mention because of his handling of the "pointed" style in a way that is unmedieval yet still recognisably Gothic. Finally, George Pace (1915-1975), whose work in this area is represented by Keele University Chapel (1964-5), was steeped in the tradition of Pugin and other architects of the Gothic Revival, yet his buildings, furnishings and fittings reflect his own personal and vigorous distillation of the Gothic spirit. Pace, no less than Pugin, regretted the demise of the organic culture of the Middle Ages which had embraced the architect,

138. Keele University Chapel, by George Pace, 1964-5. (Postcard View)

artist and craftsman, and expressed its faith, and like Pugin he asked fundamental questions about the principles and function of church architecture. The Keele chapel may not be overtly Gothic **(138)**, but it is an "honest" building constructed of local materials, with an open timber-framed roof, and it makes no concessions to secularism by attempting to conceal its function. It is, moreover, designed by an architect who was himself a committed Christian. The very notion of Roman-Catholics, Anglicans and Protestants sharing the same building would have been inconceivable to the mind of Pugin, but he would have recognised one of his own "true principles of Christian architecture" in George Pace's fundamental belief that

> "Worship is deemed to be pre-eminent, and architecture and the related arts to be its handmaidens..... for worship appears in its functions as the inspirer and consumer of architecture"[34].

171

CONCLUSION

In 1952 the centenary of the deaths of A.W.N. Pugin and his patron the sixteenth Earl of Shrewsbury were marked - coincidentally no doubt - by the gutting of the once-magnificent interiors of Alton Towers, in an asset-stripping exercise undertaken by the Towers' post-war owners. Thus perished what, outside the Palace of Westminster, were arguably Pugin's greatest achievements in the field of domestic interior design, along with the work of several other noted architects and designers. When Pevsner surveyed the building some twenty years later for the Staffordshire volume of *The Buildings of England,* he found Pugin's great banqueting hall to be "in a sad state, totally given up and only reached along a tunnel and across rubble". The loss was felt particularly keenly amongst the villagers of Alton and Farley for whom the Towers had, since 1839, been as much a part of their lives as it had been for "Good Earl John" who had first encouraged them to look upon the house and gardens as almost a common heritage. The sight of lorries piled high with timber, metalwork and other spoils, trundling daily through the village on their way to a scrap-yard in Uttoxeter is still remembered with great sadness by older generations of Alton residents, and the perpetrators have never been forgiven.

The 1950s and 1960s were lean years for Gothic Revival buildings generally, and Pugin's achievements as an architect and designer were seriously underrated. The absence of any major commemoration or exhibition to mark his centenary in 1952 is comment in itself. Then there were the changing liturgical fashions which affected the internal appearance of many of Pugin's churches following the Second Vatican Council; also the whims and fancies of individual clergy whose enthusiasm for modernity ran beyond the mere shifting of altars and the removal of rood-screens to obliterating stencilled wall-decorations, demolishing reredoses, and disposing of tiles, statuary and metalwork. Not even the church which Pugin paid for himself and where he lies buried - S. Augustine's, Ramsgate - was safe from the ravages of those who pulled down his rood-screen and removed his altar-fittings. The Anglican Church was not slow to follow, and although Faculty jurisdiction and Diocesan Advisory Committees exist to prevent ill-considered and precipitate action, "re-ordering" has left some Victorian churches looking - as Pugin would have it - "like an aisle sacked by the Calvinists".

The situation is now rather different. The post-war re-appraisal of Pugin as the key figure of the Gothic Revival may be said to have begun with the publication in 1971 of Phoebe Stanton's *Pugin,* and this was followed by Alexandra Wedgwood's meticulous cataloguing of the Pugin papers and drawings at the Royal Institute of British Architects and the Victoria and Albert Museum. Then in 1994 there occurred that memorable watershed, *Pugin: A Gothic Passion,* a major exhibition at the V & A (followed by another at the Bard Institute in New York) which drew together as never before in one place the many strands of his prolifically-creative genius. Pugin at last received the public recognition which he had long deserved, and which in the opinion of many he had been unjustly denied. More than that, the exhibition encouraged those who visited it to look again, or even for the first time, at Pugin buildings in their own localities, to help make them better known, and where appropriate to press the case for conservation. The Pugin Society, founded as a direct result of the V & A Exhibition, is an international organisation which seeks to promote public interest in the life and work of A.W.N. Pugin and other members of the Pugin family. As a consequence of all this, Gothic Revival architecture and art in general, and the work of A.W.N. Pugin in particular, is better understood than was the case a generation ago, and the legacy of his buildings is better appreciated and cared for.

This is especially true of Staffordshire's "Pugin-Land". Pearson PLC, who sponsored the Pugin Exhibition in 1994, were at that time the owners of Alton Towers, and to coincide with the exhibition they undertook the restoration of the roof in the Towers Chapel. Other parts of the building have since been restored, and a systematic conservation programme may soon be in place. Meanwhile the future of Alton Castle has been secured, and extensive restoration work has been carried out there and in the other Pugin buildings associated with S. John's. This has included complete re-pointing and repair of the exterior stonework of the castle, and renovation of the roofs, notably the renewal of the coloured tiles on the roof of the chapel. Sensitively adapted for use by the Catholic Youth Association as a residential centre for young people (139), the buildings are officially reopened in June 2002. The Pugin churches of the area, notably S. Giles', Cheadle, show that modern liturgical needs can be met without destroying the whole character of a building as originally conceived by its architect. Thus the 150th anniversaries of Pugin and Lord Shrewsbury are the occasion for some rejoicing. This book came to be written because a ten-year-old schoolboy was enthralled by what he saw on his first visit to Pugin-Land many years ago. Now more young people than ever before are being brought into contact with this unique heritage, and thus with the minds of Pugin and Lord Shrewsbury. Who can deny that these buildings are capable of speaking powerfully to present and future generations of a spirit which believes that beauty is preferable to ugliness, that order is better than chaos, that worship should be uplifting, and that art and architecture have a spiritual as well as an aesthetic role? Gothic forever!

139. Youth Group at Alton Castle (photo courtesy of Alton Castle).

NOTES TO CHAPTERS

Abbreviations

ATGW	M.J. Fisher, *Alton Towers: A Gothic Wonderland, Stafford: M.J.Fisher 1999*
BAA	*Birmingham Archdiocesan Archives,* S. Chad's Cathedral, Birmingham.
Belcher 2001	Margaret Belcher, *The Collected Letters of A. W. N. Pugin, vol. 1, 1830-1842,* Oxford:Oxford University Press, 2001
BOE	Nikolaus Pevsner, *The Buildings of England,* London, Penguin Books, 1951 -
Diary	Diaries of A.W.N. Pugin, *V&A L. 5156 - L.5170-1969,* printed in WW 1985
Ferrey	Benjamin Ferrey, *Recollections of A.N. Welby Pugin, and his Father, Augustus Pugin,* London: Edward Stanford, 1861
Glossary	A.W.N. Pugin, *Glossary of Ecclesiastical Ornament and Costume,* London, 1844
GP	Paul Atterbury & Clive Wainwright (eds.), *Pugin: A Gothic Passion,* Newhaven: Yale University Press, 1994
Gwynn	Dennis Gwynn, *Pugin, Lord Shrewsbury, and the Catholic Revival,* London: Hollis & Carter, 1946
HLRO	House of Lords Records Office
LOJ	*London & Dublin Orthodox Journal*
Phillipps	E.S. Purcell, ed., *Life and Letters of Ambrose Phillipps de Lisle,* 2 vols., London, Macmillan, 1900
Present State	A.W.N. Pugin, *The Present State of Ecclesiastical Architecture in England,* London: Dolman, 1843
SCRO	Staffordshire County Record Office
Sequel	Bernard Ward, *Sequel to Catholic Emancipation,* 2 vols., London, Longmans, 1915
Stanton	Phoebe Stanton, *"Welby Pugin and the Gothic Revival";* unpublished Ph.D. thesis, University of London, 1950
True Principles	A.W.N. Pugin, *The True Principles of Pointed or Christian Architecture,* London: Henry Bohn, 1841
V&A	Victoria and Albert Museum
VCH	*The Victoria History of the Counties of England,* London: Oxford University Press, 1899 -
WW 1985	Alexandra Wedgwood (ed.), *Catalogues of Architectural Drawings in the Victoria & Albert Museum: The Pugin Family,* London: Victoria & Albert Museum, 1985

1. The Landscape

1   BOE: *Staffordshire* (1974) p.97

2   See below, p. 29.

3   Simon Jenkins, *England's Thousand Best Churches,* 1999

4   This tour is described in detail in two letters sent by Pugin to his friends William Osmond of Salisbury, one dated 27 October 1833, and the other of 30 January 1834, both in private collections; printed in Ferrey pp. 76-89.

5   Ferrey saw fit to omit this incident from his transcript of the letter. The full text is given in Belcher 2001, pp. 22-3

6   See Rosemary Hill, "Reformation to Millennium; Pugin's *Contrasts* in the history of English Thought", *Journal of the Society of Architectural Historians 58: 1*, March 1999. See also below pp. 44-45.

7   For discussion of the date and circumstances of Pugin's introduction to Lord Shrewsbury see below, p. 33.

8   Pugin referred to it as the "Priory" (Diary, 19 August 1837), perhaps confusing it with the Augustinian priory of S. Thomas on the east side of Stafford. A Catholic chapel had been maintained here until the 1730s.

9   William Howard was one of the 136 English and Welsh martyrs beatified in 1929.

10   A number of the bones of S. Chad had survived the pillage of his shrine at the cathedral, and some had passed into the hands of the Fitzherberts, a noted Catholic family who lived variously at Norbury and Swynnerton, and who also owned Boscobel for a time. See M.W.Greenslade, *Saint Chad of Lichfield and Birmingham,* Archdiocese of Birmingham Historical Commission, 1996.

11   Pugin to Lord Shrewsbury, 4 July 1843, V&A MS L. 525-1965/14, WW 1985, no. 30

12   The letter, from Pugin to Minton, turned up at a Collectors' Fair in Australia, and is now in a private collection at Chatswood, New South Wales. It is postmarked Birmingham, 19 September 1840, and in it Pugin requests Minton to send the tiles to Birmingham. I am most grateful to Mr Willem Irik, a friend of the owner, for informing me of this, and for supplying me with a photocopy.

13   Pugin to Lord Shrewsbury, 28 November 1841, MS University of Notre Dame, Indiana; Belcher 2001 p. 290: "Is not the west end a compleat revival of that simple old church with the high and narrow Lancet windows". Pugin mis-spelt Croxden as Croxton, which is the name of a Premonstratensian abbey in Leicestershire, of which nothing survives.

14   See Dom Bede Camm, *Forgotten Shrines,* London 1910.

15   ATGW p. 115, and see below, p. 59.

16   See below, p. 137-8.

17   In 1815 Michael Bick, Lord Shrewsbury's agent at Alton, submitted claims for expenses for "going to Prayers at Cresswell 12 Sundays there being no priest at the Abbey". *Shrewsbury Papers* SCRO D240/E/F/2/19.

18   Ferrey p. 262.

19   A Gazetteer of the Catholic chapels in Staffordshire appeared in the *Catholic Magazine and Review*, V & VI, 1834 & 1835. It is reprinted in *Staffordshire Catholic History no.14,* 1974.

20   *BOE: Staffordshire,* p. 268

21   S. Gregory's was, regrettably, demolished in 1970

22   A.W.N.Pugin, *Some Remarks on the Articles which have recently appeared in the 'Rambler',* 1850, and quoted by Trappes-Lomax, *Pugin,* 1932, p. 321-2.

23   Lord Shrewsbury to Pugin, 1846, HLRO 339/110

2 Prest d'Accomplir - John Talbot, Sixteenth Earl of Shrewsbury

1   Extract from a verse based on the family motto, and painted over a doorway in the Octagon at Alton Towers. The verse was, apparently, written in the reign of Elizabeth I (William Adam, *The Gem of the Peak,* 1851, p. 252)

2　In the mid-1850s both Daniel Rock and Henry Winter were helping to gather information for an intended Life of Lord Shrewsbury to be written, so it would seem, by Henry Wilberforce to whom Dr Rock sent a collection of letters, and other information about the earl: BAA R825 (Revd. H. Campbell to Dr. Winter, 5th January 1854), and R833 (Rock to Wilberforce, 27th February 1856)

3　This particular fantasy may have its roots in the fact that the estranged wife of the twentieth Earl (of the Chetwynd-Talbot line) lived alone at Alton Towers between 1896 and 1923.

4　The reredos at Grafton was of embroidered tapestry. It is no longer extant, but the drawings are in the V&A Drawing Collection: D. 1065-1908, & D.1134-1908, WW 1985, nos. 307-8.

5　S. Edmund's College, Ware, Hertfordshire, also known as Old Hall, was established in 1793, and it traces its ancestry back to the English College at Douai.

6　Printed by J.B.G. Vogel, London 1809

7　J. Chetwode Eustace, *A Tour through Italy, exhibiting a View of its Scenery, Antiquities, and Monuments, particularly as they are objects of Classical Interest, with an Account of the Present State of its Cities and Towns, and occasional Observations on the Recent Spoliations of the French*, 2 vols., London 1813. Several revisions and enlargements between 1815 and 1841 earned Eustace a sudden and extended reputation. "His acquaintance was sought by almost all persons in this country, distinguished by rank and talents" - Gillow, *Bibliographical Dictionary of the English Catholics*, vol II, P. 185. Eustace was criticised by Bishop Milner for associating with Protestant clergy, and for the liberal tone of the Classical Tour.

8　Memoir of the late Earl of Shrewsbury by the Revd. Edward Price, *Catholic Directory*, 1854, pp. 141-161, from which much of the information about the early life of the earl has been taken. See also J. Gillow, *Bibliographical Dictionary of the English Catholics*, vol. V, p. 503

9　See below, p. 153.

10　*Annual Register*, 1827, p. 241

11　ATGWpp. 15-48

12　LOJ vol. XI, 1840, pp. 110-12; see also ATGW pp. 77-8.

13　*Staffordshire Advertiser,* 11th November 1843; J.A. Walsh, *Relation du Voyage de Henri de France en Ecosse et en Angleterre*, Paris 1844, p. 175-228; see also ATGW pp. 92-95

14　Gustav Waagen catalogued and commented on the collection in 1838; *Art and Artists in England,* vol. 3; Alton Towers Sale Catalogue, 1857; W. Adam, *The Gem of the Peak*, 1851, pp. 246-251.

15　In 1857 the Communion of S. Jerome was removed to All Saints' Church, Glossop, Derbyshire, and the Transfiguration to the new church of S. Charles Borromeo at Hadfield, a few miles away. Both churches were endowed/built by the Howard family, and the paintings were among the properties willed to Lord Edmund Howard by Bertram, 17th Earl of Shrewsbury. The paintings were removed/destroyed in the early 1960s, but two smaller paintings from the Towers Chapel survive at All Saints'. Information supplied by Mr. C. Sharples.

16.　Both Lord Shrewsbury and Ambrose Phillipps had a particular devotion to S. Elizabeth of Hungary (d.1231), and Phillipps wrote a Life of S. Elizabeth which he intended to be presented to Queen Victoria,

17　Adam, *The Gem of the Peak*, 1851, p. 257

18　The album was recently offered for sale by Hugh Pagan (catalogue 38) at £11, 500

19　ATGW p. 74. The 1857 Sale Catalogue lists over 300 items of arms and armour

20　W. Adam, *op. cit.*, p. 258

21　Times, 8th July 1857, contains a lengthy description of Alton Towers on the eve of the great Sale.

22　*ibid.*

23　Shrewsbury Papers SCRO D240/E/F/2/24

24   A. Zeloni, *Vie de la Princess Borghese*, Paris, 1843, p. 51

25   Denis Gwynn, *Lord Shrewsbury, Pugin, and the Catholic Revival*, London, 1946, pp. xxx-xxxi.

26   Memoir of the late Earl of Shrewsbury, *Catholic Directory*, 1854, p. 146

27   Central to the Catholic understanding of the Mass, the doctrine of Transubstantiation teaches that Eucharistic bread and wine become the Body and Blood of Christ. Though the outward appearance remains the same, the inner substance is changed.

28   *Sequel*, II, pp. 34-5.

29   Letter from Lord Shrewsbury to Ambrose Phillipps, 1st July 1834; Phillipps I, pp. 64-65

30   The *Almanac de Gotha* shows that Prince Frederick was still alive, and it seems unmarried, in 1857. One difficulty is hinted at in Lord Shrewsbury's letter to Phillipps: "We are perfectly satisfied on the score of religion". The House of Saxony was generally Lutheran, and there may have been a subsequent breakdown over this issue.

31   Catholic Magazine, III, 1839, p. 353

32   LOJ II, 1839, p. 76

33   Several letters from Pugin to Lord Shrewsbury contain references to the building of the Doria Rooms; HLRO 339/8, /60, /83.

34   See above, n. 24

35   Zeloni, *op. cit.*, p. 231

36   Bertram was son of Charles T. Talbot (d. 1838), a nephew of the 14th Earl, and his wife Julia (née Tichbourne). In 1839 Julia married Captain John Washington Hibbert of Bilton Grange, Warwickshire.

37   Lord Shrewsbury writes to Pugin in January 1851, "Bertram is going on extremely well .... all he wants is warmth to put his blood into good circulation"; HLRO 339/100

38   Abbé Vandrival, *Pèlerinages en Angleterre*, unpublished MS in the possession of the Squire de Lisle, pp. 121-125.

39   A former Anglican priest, George Spencer (1799-1864) was a major benefactor of Oscott College, and became better known as Father Ignatius. Pugin built the church of Our Lady and S. Thomas of Canterbury for him at Dudley.

40   Gwynn, *op. cit.*, p. 147, and Phillipps, I, pp. 103-114

41   The stigmata are the marks of the Crucifixion which have manifested themselves enigmatically, on the living bodies of several holy men and women. *The Letter Descriptive of the Estatica...* has an Appendix on the doctrine of the Mass and the Anglican position. So extensive was the Earl's historical and theological knowledge that doubts were expressed as to whether he was in fact the real author. In the Preface to the second edition of *Estatica*, he takes pains to refute these allegations.

42   For a description of Pugin's first visit to Ambrose Phillipps' chapel at Grace Dieu in 1837, see Phillipps, II, p. 288

43   B. Ferrey, *Recollections of A.W.N. Pugin*, 1861, p. 117

44   ATGW p. 103-4

45   Winifrede M. Wyse, Personal Recollections of Augustus Welby Pugin, MS HLRO 339/348. She quotes a letter written by her uncle "about 1832" telling her of the incident, and of his own introduction to Pugin.

46   Dr. Rock to Pugin, 19th August 1836, Ferrey, *op. cit.*, pp. 122-124.

47   See J.A.Hilton, *Daniel Rock; Goth and Cisalpine*, Wigan, the Lingard Fund, 1999; and J.A.Hilton (ed.), *Daniel Rock; The Church of Our Fathers - A Selection*, North West Catholic History Society, 1992.

48   Lord Shrewsbury to Pugin, March 1840, HLRO 339/101

49   Lord Shrewsbury to Dr Rock, 1st November 1841 & 25th September 1852, BAA R801 & R824

50   As above, n. 48.

51   e.g. J. Gillow, *Bibliographical Dictionary of the English Catholics*, V, p. 304, states that the Earl's gifts to the Church and to charitable causes is "said to have considerably exceeded to sum of half a million pounds". This statement appears to have been based on the estimate given by the Revd. Edward Price in his Memoir of Lord Shrewsbury, *Catholic Directory*, 1854, pp. 141-161. Trappes-Lomax (1932) attributed the entire half-million to churchbuilding projects, to the tune of £20,000 per year, and wrote that "the list can be prolonged almost indefinitely of ecclesiastical buildings which were largely or entirely erected at Lord Shrewsbury's expense" (M. Trappes-Lomax, *Pugin: A Medieval Victorian*, London, 1932, pp. 100-101). So the legend grew.

52   Quoted in VCH *Cheshire* II, 1980, p. 93

53   Lord Shrewsbury to Pugin HLRO 339.104, undated, but since it refers to the start of the scheme for S. Mary's, Ducie Street, Manchester, it must be no later than 1837 (see V&A cat. 573 for correspondence and drawings for this - eventually abandoned - project)

54   The lectern was removed to Oscott, and then sold in 1967 to the Metropolitan Museum in New York. Clive Wainwright, GP, p. 101

55   For the altar-cross see below, p. 61-2.

56   The Bridgettine Convent at Syon was one of the monastic restorations carried out during the reign of Mary I (1553-1558). Lord Shrewsbury also had the silver bell given by Mary to the nuns, the Deed of Restoration, a variety of crosses and seals, and a large crucifix which he gave to Ambrose Phillipps and which is still in the possession of the de Lisles. See W.Adam, *The Gem of the Peak*, p. 261; also J.R. Fletcher, *The Story of the English Brigettines of Syon Abbey,* 1933.

57   The Antiphonal described in an account of the sale of Lord Shrewsbury's books, *Staffordshire Advertiser*, 11th July 1857: "A very large and fine MS on vellum, written about the middle of the 15th century, with richly illuminated borders and initial letters .... knocked down to Mr Toovey for £40". The report also says that as a whole, the library "was scarcely worthy of so princely a residence". It needs to be remembered, however, that the sixteenth earl had to create a library almost from scratch, following the fire at Heythrop in 1831, based around what his uncle had taken to Alton between about 1810 and 1827. There were just over 4,000 individual volumes and sets. See ATGW. pp. 75-6

58   See R. O'Donnell, "The Pugins in Ireland", *A.W.N. Pugin: Master of Gothic Revival*, Yale 1995, pp. 137-60

59   Pugin to Lord Shrewsbury, 15th April 1846; HLRO 339/3. Mary Amherst was sister to Francis Kerril Amherst, later Bishop of Northampton, and their mother was a cousin of Lord Shrewsbury.

60   Belcher 2001, p. 309, note to letter from Pugin in which he congratulates the earl on his appointment to the Commission, 24th December 1841 (HLRO 339/17)

61   Pugin to Lord Shrewsbury ?2nd October 1845 HLRO 339/33

62   Pugin to Lord Shrewsbury, 1st May 1847, Ferrey, *op. cit.*, p. 226

63   Pugin to Lord Shrewsbury, 1840, MS V&A L.525.1965/6, cat. 19. He was later horrified to find that someone had bought the "horrid figures" and cast-iron brackets he had removed from the Towers Chapel and given them to the new church he had built in Manchester (S. Wilfrid's, Hulme). "They pursue me like the flying Dutchman". Pugin to Lord Shrewsbury, November 1847, HLRO 339/79.

64   Pugin to Ambrose Phillipps, 1st December 1839, Phillipps, II, p. 222; "For this he has been censured!!!" adds the outraged Pugin, reacting to a letter from Propaganda denouncing Gothic vestments.

65   Lord Shrewsbury to Ambrose Phillipps, 16th April 1839, Phillipps, I, p. 106

66   Lord Shrewsbury's Library contained some key works on Anglican theology and ecelesiology,

including Richard Hooker (c.1554-1600), *The Laws of Ecclesiastical Polity*, the classic defence of the Elizabethan Settlement of 1559; works by Pusey, and issues of *The Ecclesiologist.*

67   Appendix to Letter to *Ambrose Phillipps .... descriptive of the Estatica*, etc..., 1842, p. 143

68   Anon., *The Life of Cornelia Connelly*, 1809-1879, London 1924, from which much of the ensuing information is taken. There is also a large collection of letters and other material relating to Pierce and Cornelia Connelly in BAA R246-332

69   Enquiries from Robert Berkeley Snr. to Lord Shrewsbury about Connelly's suitability are in BAA 328-330; also notes by the boy himself about his journeys with Connelly.

70   Vandrival, *op. cit.* (see n.38 above), pp. 154-156

71   Wiseman to Lord Shrewsbury, 8th January 1849, *Cornelia Connelly*, p. 95

72   C.S. Dessain (ed.), *The Life and Letters of J.H.Newman*, vol. xiii, p. 460

73   The demonstrations reached their peak on Guy Fawkes' Night 1850. In Exeter there was a move to burn an effigy of the Tractarian Bishop Philpotts along with those of Pope Pius IV and Cardinal Wiseman.

74   Lord Shrewsbury to Pugin, 28th November 1850, HLRO 339/106

75   *Letter to the Rt. Hon. the Lord Russell*, London, Dolman, 1851

76   Lord Shrewsbury to Pugin, 13th September 1841, Phillipps, I, p. 80

77   Denis Gwynn, *op. cit.*, p. 41

78   Memoir of the late Earl of Shrewsbury, *Catholic Directory*, 1854

79   See above, n. 74

80   It was based on the French *Oeuvre pour la Propagation de la Foi* established in 1822.

81   Pugin to Lord Shrewsbury, 30th January 1851, HLRO 339/100

82   Lord Shrewsbury to Jane Pugin, 3rd March 1852, HLRO 339/111

83   BAA R824

84   See below, p145. *Catholic Magazine*, 1854, pp. 141-161; ATGW, p. 154.

85   *A Funeral Discourse, delivered in the domestic chapel of Alton Towers, after the Solemn Requiem Mass, celebrated for John, Earl of Shrewsbury,... ",* London, Dolman, 1852.

86   *Sequel*, II, pp. 198-9

87   Denis Gwynn, *op. cit.*, p. xxxvi, part of the Introduction written by Fr. S.J. Gosling, parish priest at Alton from 1923 to 1950, and who would have doubtless have heard of this from elderly parishioners who had taken part in the earl's funeral procession. also *Illustrated London News*, 25th December 1852;

3. S. Mary's, Uttoxeter

1   LOJ, IX, 1839, p. 33

2   P.F. Wilson, *S. Mary's R.C. Church, Balance Street, Uttoxeter, 1839-1989*, p. 7 BAA holds very little documentation on Uttoxeter for the early years.

3   Present State, p. 95

4   *ibid.*, pp. 5-6

5   Pugin to Ambrose Phillipps, 1st December 1839, Phillipps II, p. 224

6.   LOJ, IX, 1839, p. 36

7   According to the Census returns, Denny came originally from Swainsthorpe, Norfolk, and his wife, Jane, was born in Croydon. The 1841 Census gives his age as 30; i.e. he was just a year or

so older than Pugin, and only 28 when he undertook the work at Uttoxeter. Pugin's Diary for 1st July 1839 states simply "At Uttoxeter. Deny (sic) arrived". Payments to Denny from the Alton Estate Accounts begin in July 1839 (SCRO D240/E/F/9/2). For his subsequent career in Australia, where he emigrated in 1856, see Brian Andrews, "Pugin in Austalia", *GP*, p. 257. Denny's Australian churches were greatly influenced by the ones on which he had worked in Staffordshire.

8   Mr E. Bailey informs me that in 1987 an aunt living in Alton sold through Sotheby's a quantity of nineteenth-century drawings that had been held in the family. Sotheby's Sale Catalogue, *Early English and Victorian Watercolours, Architectural Drawings and Watercolours,* 30th April 1987, show that these were sold in several lots. Lots 514-518 consisted of pre-Pugin drawings for Alton Towers, and Lot 521 comprised eight drawings for Uttoxeter, four signed by Pugin with his initials in monogram, and dated 1838 and 1839. They include plans, elevations and sections of the church and presbytery, with details of windows, doorways, and a fireplace. The side-elevations of the church do not show a separate chancel. Most of the Alton drawings were bought by Alton Towers where they are currently displayed, and the Uttoxeter drawings were bought by the Getty Center for the History of Art and Humanities, Santa Monica, California. See Belcher 2001, pp. 108-9.

9   Pugin generally preferred the medieval spelling "Marie" for dedications to the Blessed Virgin Mary, but this does not affect the pronunciation.

10   LOJ, IX, 1839, p. 36.

11   *ibid.*, p. 34.

12   *ibid.*, p. 35, and see below, p. 112 (Cheadle) for an explanation of these features which Pugin believed were absolutely essential for the correct performance of the Sarum Rite.

13   The tower tabernacle is no longer in use, but it is kept in storage at S. Mary's.

14   Later reprinted in Present State, 1843, plate XV.

15   Metalwork Day Book, 16th August 1839, Hardman Archive, Brimingham Public Reference Library.

16   As above, n. 10.

17   Ambrose Phillipps wrote an Address on the subject of Gregorian Chant (*Phillipps*, II, pp. 186-1998) and in 1850 Pugin published, *An Earnest Appeal for the Revival of the Ancientr Plain Song*.

18   e.g. the 13th-century Clare Chasuble, now in the V&A Museum, was severely cut down from a very full vestment to one which barely covered the shoulders. The Syon Cope - also at the V&A and once owned by Lord Shrewsbury - is an example of a chasuble which has been converted into a cope: an indication of the voluminous nature of a fourteenth-century chasuble (See col. pl.1)

19   Pugin to Dr. Rock, 9th May 1839, Southwark Archdiocesan Archives; Belcher 2001, p. 115. The "Pugin" chasubles had been in use at Oscott since 1838, but this was probably the first instance in which they were used in a parish church. Surviving examples of these vestments show that they were generally rather less full than the medieval type. It has been suggested that Pugin may have misinterpreted their shape from his studies of figures on medieval brasses and manuscripts. This is very unlikely given what he actually writes about the chasuble in the *Glossary* and elsewhere. A more convincing explanation is that he modified the design somewhat on the grounds of practicality and to forestall criticism that the full medieval chasuble was so radically different as to be tantamount to an innovation. Bishop Wiseman appears to have suggested such a compromise: "As a coat may have different dimensions and form, yet still remain indisputably a coat, so may a chasuble; but if the change is so great as to make the coat look like some other garment, e.g. a cloak, or that of a chasuble like a cope or other garment, the change of the latter is not justifiable" (quoted by Bishop Baines in a letter to Dr Walsh, 26th May 1841, Sequel II, p. 14). In the discussions in Rome in 1839 a width of three feet six inches was talked about, which both Pugin and Baines knew was considerably less than the full width.

20   Pugin to Dr Rock, 1st December 1839, Southwark Archdiocesan Archives; Belcher 2001, p.

128. On the same day he wrote to Phillipps in similar vein; Phillipps II, pp. 222-5

21   Phillipps to Lord Shrewsbury, 7th December 1839, Phillipps II, pp 219-222

22   *Staffordshire Examiner*, August 1839, printed in P.F. Wilson, op. cit.

23   LOJ, IX, 1839, p. 336

24   *ibid.*, p. 36

25   Letter from Pugin to Editor of LOJ, IX (31st August 1839) pp. 150-154.

26   Letter signed "a looker-on", LOJ, IX, 1839, pp. 198-199

27   Denis Gwynn, *The Second Spring, London*, 1944, p. 133

28   William of Wykeham (1324-1404) was Bishop of Winchester and Chancellor to Edward III. He founded New College, Oxford, Winchester College, and restored Winchester cathedral.

29   Pugin to Walsh, 25th December 1841; Birmingham Archdiocesan Archives R870b; Belcher 2001, p. 311.

30   Pugin to J.R. Bloxam, 24th October 1840; MS Magdalen College, Oxford 528/12; Belcher 2001, p.153.

31   Information on later additions to S. Mary's taken from P.F. Wilson, *op. cit.*

32   Stanton, *Pugin*, 1970, p. 41

33   Pugin's first Oscott lecture, given in 1837, published in *Catholic Magazine*, II, 1838, pp. 193-213; Trappes-Lomax, Pugin, 1932, p. 153

4 Alton Castle & the Hospital of S. John

1   Phillipps I, p. 69.

2   On the 3rd October 1836 Pugin wrote in his diary, "Sent answer to Lord Shrewsbury". One would love to know details of this correspondence. The earl's domestic chaplain, Dr. Daniel Rock, was in touch with Pugin during August of that year.

3   Present State, 1843, p. 95

4   *ibid.*

5   Pugin remarked in 1843: "The ruins of this castle, as engraved in Buck's work, appear to have been very considerable in his time, but they have been sadly demolished during the last century, huge masses being frequently hurled down for the purpose of mending the roads. The ravages were stopped by the late earl; and these interesting remains are now preserved with the greatest care". Present State, 1843, p. 95

6   e.g. the Alton Abbey accounts record payments to stonemason Thomas Bailey for "underbuilding the ruins at the old castle to prevent their falling" (Shrewsbury Papers, SCRO D240/E/F/2/22 p. 9 (1824)

7   Present State, 1843, p. 95. The text originally appeared in the *Dublin Review* in February 1842.

8   The True Principles.... 1841, p. 51

9   He describes them in a letter to Lord Shrewsbury, December 24th 1841; HLRO 339/17 Belcher 2001, p. 307.The seating in S. John's has since been altered, with many of the finely-carved benches made originally for the chapel proper, i.e. the present chancel, relocated in the nave.

10   Letter from Pugin to Lord Shrewsbury, 13th February 1842; V&A WW 1985, no. 24, Belcher 2001, p. 320

11   Letter from Pugin to Lord Shrewsbury, see n. 9 above.

12   For the significance of the Counslow quarry see below, p. 96.

13   Present State, p. 93, contains a brief excursus on the use of alabaster, and Pugin's hopes for its revival.

14   Letter from Pugin to Lord Shrewsbury, December 1841, see above n. 9

15   Letter from Pugin to Lord Shrewsbury dated 31st March 1841, Stanton, Appendix VIII, p. 4., Belcher 2001, p. 227

16   Letter from Lord Shrewsbury to Pugin, Stanton, Appendix VIII, pp. 6-7 (December 1841)., Belcher 2001, p. 298

17   Letter from Pugin to Lord Shrewsbury, 23rd February 1842, HLRO 339/93, Belcher 2001, p. 325

18   Letter from Pugin to Lord Shrewsbury, 29th September 1841, V&A WW 1985 no. 23., Belcher 2001, p. 276

19   The building itself was not consecrated as a parish church until 1930, nor was it licensed for Catholic marriages which, until 1854, took place in the Towers chapel.

20   Present State, p. 93

21   A Chronological List of the Principal works in Stained Glass etc., designed and executed by Thomas Willement of London F.S.A. from the year 1812 to 1865. British Library Add. MSS 54413, and 34871 nos. 142 & 143.

22   See above, n. 10.

23   See above, n. 17

24   For the significance of the Easter sepulchre, and the ceremonies connected with it, see the chapter on S. Giles' Cheadle, below, p.112.

25   Letter from Pugin to Lord Shrewsbury, Stanton, Appendix VIII p. 15. The 1851 Census returns for Alton describe Kearns as a "Master painter employing 7 men" including his eldest son, also named Thomas, serving a painter's apprenticeship.

26   Present State, p. 94, and letters from Pugin to Lord Shrewsbury, V&A WW.1985nos. 15 & 19

27   In a private collection of drawings done by Pugin for Hardman, deposited in the Birmingham Museum

28   Letter from Pugin to Lord Shrewsbury, 5th December 1841, Stanton, Appendix VIII. pp. 6 & 7., Belcher 2001, p. 298 There was difficulty in finding a sacristan for S. John's, but an excellent one was found for S. Giles', Cheadle. Pugin told him to go occasionally to S. John's to look after the candlesticks and cross. HLRO 339/2

29   V&A WW 1985 no. 25

30   Present State, p. 19

31   Abbé Vandrival, Pêlerinage en Angleterre, 1847, p. 217. Unpublished manuscript in the possession of the Squire de Lisle.

32   Pugin to Lord Shrewsbury, HLRO 339/17, Belcher 2001, p. 306

33   Pugin to Lord Shrewsbury, 29th March 1846, Stanton, Appendix VIII, p 18

34   See above, n. 32

35   This was the time when Alton Towers was fortified against possible attacks by the Chartists, see below p. 85-6

36   According to Sister Mary Rose, one of the Sisters of Mercy at Alton, Higham & Carson, Pugin's Churches of the Second Spring, 1997, p. 16

37   Pugin to Lord Shrewsbury, 24th June 1843, HLRO 339/31

38   Pugin's Apology for the Revival of Christian Architecture in England (1843) was dedicated to Lord Shrewsbury, but his most severe criticisms of "mock" castles are in The True Principles (1841).

39   Pugin to Lord Shrewsbury, V&A WW 1985 no.95.

40   See below, p. 98

41   Shrewsbury Papers, SCRO D/240/E/F/2/24 p. 139; William Bick's Cash account with the Earl of Shrewsbury.

42   Pugin to Lord Shrewsbury, HLRO 339/34, and Stanton, Appendix VIII, p. 14

43   Lord Shrewsbury had an interest in Mary, Queen of Scots, who had been held prisoner in several Shrewsbury properties.

44   Pugin to Lord Shrewsbury, 30th July 1847, V&A WW 1985 no 52

45   For an examination of the influence of the buildings on Normandy on the young Pugin see T. Brittain-Catlin, "A.W.N. Pugin and Nodier's Normandy", *True Principles*, vol. 2 no. 3, Winter 2001, pp. 3-6.

46   Pugin to Lord Shrewsbury, 28th September 1848 V&A WW 1985, no. 59. Externally, the east end of the chapel is strikingly similar to that of the Convent of Our Lady, Bermondsly which Pugin designed in 1838. It is illustrated in the *Catholic Directory*, 1839; see also LOJ, IX (1839) p. 100.

47   Pugin to Lord Shrewsbury, "I think the look out turret will look very picturesque. The arrangement of the caps on the jambs are from Brown's hospital and are very knowing". Stanton, Appendix VIII, p. 26

48   Pugin's father had produced illustrations for John Britton (1771-1857), the compiler of very detailed illustrated books on English architecture, including a fourteen-volume series on the cathedrals of England. Pugin's diary records his visit to Southwell in September 1842, but he had also been there in March 1840 on his way to visit the East Anglian churches which he used as sources for S. Giles' Cheadle. Drawings of the Minster are included in the sketchbook which he took on this tour, V&A WW 1985 no. 1000.

49   Pugin to Lord Shrewsbury, Stanton Appendix VIII p. 26

50   Pugin to Lord Shrewsbury, November 1848, V&A WW 1985, no. 60

51   Lord Shrewsbury to Pugin, 1st March 1852, HLRO 339/112

52   It was suggested in the letter of March 1st; then two days later the earl wrote to Jane Pugin urging her to arrange for her husband to go to Palermo immediately and to stay through the Spring and Summer; details of trains and steamers are included. HLRO 339/111

53   Drawings in the Pugin collection at the V&A Museum, WW 1985, no. 176

54   Pugin to Lord Shrewsbury, 24th December 1841, HLRO 339/17

55   This was the view expressed by Pevsner, BOE Staffordshire, 1974 p. 60

56   Pugin to Lord Shrewsbury, HLRO 339/90

57   Brunel's father, Marc Isambard Brunel, like Pugin's, had come to England from France during the Revolution. They became friends, and worked together on designs for Kensal Green Cemetery. I.K. Brunel, like A.W.N. Pugin, was a visionary who believed passionately in what he was doing, and they were both enthusiastic for the Great Exhibition, but tantalisingly - there is no record of their having met.

58   Pugin to Lord Shrewsbury V&A WW 1985 no. 51, undated but believed to be 1846.

59   Pugin to Lord Shrewsbury, 5th October 1847, HLRO 339/89

60   Pugin to Lord Shrewsbury, 2nd October 1849, V&A WW 1985 no. 66

61   Pugin to Lord Shrewsbury, 10th June 1849, V&A WW 1985, no. 65

62   From the point of view of style, Alton Station has much in common with the Italianate estate lodges on the Farley Road ("Pink Lodge") and Red Road ("Ramblers' Retreat"). These were by Thomas Fradgley (1801-1883) whom Pugin displaced as architect at the Towers.

63   Pugin to Lord Shrewsbury, 1848, HLRO 339/153. "..Lodge is a modern word savouring of the Regent's Park, and Jackson is a plebeian name. All the entrances should be called gate, and gate houses, after the manner of the ancients".

64   Pugin to Lord Shrewsbury, 30th June 1841, Stanton, Appendix VI, pp. 3-4.

65   Pugin to Lord Shrewsbury, 24th December 1841, see above, n. 32

66   Pugin to Jane Pugin, 12th October 1849, HLRO 339/274

67   According to his obituary in the *Staffordshire Advertiser*, 7th February 1857.

68   Vandrival, *Pèlerinages en Angleterre*, p. 125, see above, n.31.

69   R. Speake (ed.), A History of Alton and Farley, University of Keele, 1990, p. 184.

5 Alton Towers

1   In 1997 this author was commissioned by the owners, Tussauds Ltd., to undertake detailed
        structural and historical survey of the Towers buildings, and to submit a report and recommendations
        for future conservation/restoration. This survey formed the basis of the published history of
        the building, *Alton Towers: A Gothic Wonderland* (1999).

2   Pugin to Phillipps 6th June 1851 HLRO 339/119

3   William Adam, *The Gem of the Peak*, 5th edn., London 1851, p.267

4   Several of Pugin's letters refer to "the Octagon job", alterations to the column, and the
        Willement glass. See ATGW pp 108-114

5   William Adam, *op. cit.*, p. 266

6   The celebrated Eglinton Tournament took place in August 1839 at the Ayrshire home of the
        Earl of Eglinton. It was a medieval-style jousting tournament reputedly attended by 80,000
        people many of whom turned up in medieval costume.

7   *True Principles*, p.49

8   Pugin to Lord Shrewsbury, 26th July 1842, Stanton p. 285, Belcher 2001 p. 368

9   e.g. A. Zeloni, *Vie de la Princesse Borghese*, Paris 1843, p. 32.

10   LOJ vol XI, 1840, p. 112 states "Around the sanctuary are arranged the panels formerly
        belonging to Magdalen College, Oxford". Magdalen Chapel was restored 1829-34 by L.N.
        Cottingham, so the panels were probably removed then.

11   For a full account of Pugin's work in the chapel, and references, see ATGW pp 143-156

12   *Catholic Magazine and Review*, vol 5, 1834, p. 662; see also LOJ vol. XI, 1840, pp 110-112.

13   Watercolour of chapel interior by J.A.Lynch, 1854, currently at Alton Towers, and reproduced
        in ATGW

14   e.g. William Adam, *op. cit.*, pp. 259-261

15   *Catholic Magazine and Review*, no. xxx, July 1839, pp.498-9

16   A large number of vessels and ornaments for a chapel is included in an entry to Lord Shrewsbury
        dated 20th June 1842 in the Hardman Archive (Metalwork Daybook). It includes two sets of
        candlesticks, a monstrance, a thurible, sacring bell, and a holy water vat. It is possible that these
        were intended for the Towers Chapel. In a letter to Dr Rock dated 9th May 1839 Pugin refers
        to the making of candlesticks for the altar in the Towers Chapel (Southwark Archdiocesan
        Archives; Belcher 2001 p, 115). Presumably they are the ones shown on Joseph Lynch's
        painting of 1854 and now at S. Peter's, Bromsgrove.

17   True Principles, pp 50-51.

18   Pugin to Lord Shrewsbury, 30th July 1847, V&A WW 1985 no. 52

19   The drawing is referred to in a letter from Pugin to Lord Shrewsbury, HLRO 339/50, undated but
        clearly of 1849, cf. Pugin to Lord Shrewsbury, 16th December 1848, I am preparing an interior
        view of the new Dining Hall at Alton for next year's exhibition at the Royal Academy.." V&A

WW 1985 no.63. The drawing is now missing.

20 These drawings are in a private collection on deposit in the Birmingham Museum.

21 See above, note 20. The plate is also described in the 1857 Alton Towers Sale Catalogue which lists fourteen sideboard dishes by Hardman. The sideboard itself is not listed in the Sale Catalogue, but it appears on an illustration of the Medieval Court at the Great Exhibition along with a detailed description (*Illustrated London News*, 20th September 1851). There is an identical sideboard, complete with brass candle-sconces, at Abney Hall, Cheshire, for which Pugin designed furnishings and interior decorations.

22 Pugin's manuscript account of estimates and expenses, 1845-52, p. 109; V&A MS L.50/31982, WW 1985 no.96.

23 Report from the Select Committee on Fine Arts, House of Commons, 18th June 1841.

24 e.g. Alexandra Wedgwood in a review of ATGW in Society of Architectural Historians of Great Britain: *Newsletter* No. 69, Spring 2000, p.20.

25 Pugin to Lord Shrewsbury, ?1845, Stanton, 1950, Appendix VIII p. 17

6 S. Giles', Cheadle

1 "Commissioners' Gothic" is the derogatory term applied to the unscholarly Gothic style used (along with Classical designs) by the Commissioners for Building New Churches under an Act of Parliament of 1818, and it was imitated by other architects. Most churches in this style were utilitarian preaching-houses with a thin veneer of ornament.

2 Pugin to Lord Shrewsbury, 23 February 1842, HLRO 339/93, Belcher 2001, p. 325

3 Pugin to Lord Shrewsbury, January 1841, Stanton App. VI, p. 1. Belcher 2001, p. 194

4 *Catholic Magazine and Review*, vol. 5, 1834, p.664.

5 Pugin to J.R.Bloxam, 13 September 1840. MS Magdalen College Oxford 528/8, Belcher 2001 p. 146; Diary March 2-8 1840

6 Pugin to Lord Shrewsbury, 24th December 1840, V&A WW 1985 no. 21, Belcher 2001, p. 178

7 Pugin to J.R.Bloxam, 10 January 1841, MS Magdalen College Oxford, Belcher 2001 P. 191

8 Pugin to Lord Shrewsbury, 5 January 1841, V&A WW 1985 no. 22, Belcher 2001, p. 187

9 Pugin to Lord Shrewsbury, 23 February 1842, HLRO 339/93, Belcher 2001, p. 325

10 Pugin to Lord Shrewsbury, 24 December 1841, HLRO 339/17, Belcher 2001, p. 306

11 Work on the Counslow Lodge is documented in various letters from Pugin to Lord Shrewsbury, e.g. V&A MS L.525-1965/6, WW 1985 no. 22 (January 1841); Stanton App. VI pp. 3-4; VIII pp 2-4, Blecher 2001, p. 187,249. The work appears to have been done in the summer of 1841.

12 Pugin to Lord Shrewsbury, 30 June 1841 Stanton App. VI & VIII, Belcher 2001 p. 250.

13 Pugin to Lord Shrewsbury, 28 August 1841, HLRO 339/71, Belcher 2001, p. 269

14 Pugin to Lord Shrewsbury 31st March 1841, Stanton App. VI, pp 3-4, Belcher 2001, p. 226

15 As above, n.13. Pugin later abandoned Wailes and set up his own stained-glass manufactory with Hardman. In February 1846 he wrote to Lord Shrewsbury, "...I have quite succeeded in establishing my new manufactory for stained glass at Birmingham. I shall be able to make very fine windows with old thick glass etc..." (HLRO 339/15)

16 V&A Drawings Collection, D.1064/1067/1068-1908 WW 1985nos. 248-50

17 Lord Shrewsbury to Pugin, undated but appears to be winter of 1845-46, HLRO 339/110

18 Pugin to Lord Shrewsbury 28 July 1843, HLRO 339/83

19 Pugin to Lord Shrewsbury 24 December 1841, see above, n. 10

20   Pugin to Lord Shrewsbury, 9 March 1842, HLRO 339/38, Belcher 2001, p. 328

21   Pugin to Lord Shrewsbury, 15 April 1846, HLRO 339/3

22   *ibid.*

23   As above, n.20

24   Pugin to Lord Shrewsbury, June 1841, Stanton App. VIII, pp.2-4, Belcher 2001, p. 250

25   As above, n. 13

26   As above, n. 20

27   As above, n. 13

28   As above, n.20. Jonathan Martin was a notorious arsonist who, on the night of 1-2 February
      1842, set fire to York Minster, causing extensive damage.

29   As above, n. 24.

30   Pugin to Lord Shrewsbury, HLRO 339/81

31   Pugin to Lord Shrewsbury, 17 November 1845, HLRO 339/84

32   As above, n. 13

33   Pugin to Lord Shrewsbury, 22 or 23 February 1844, HLRO 339/78

34   So Pugin told Lord Shrewsbury in 1841. Letter in MS University of Notre Dame, Indiana; 28
      November 1841, Belcher 2001 p.290

35   Pugin's 3rd lecture on ecclesiastical architecture to students at Oscott, *Catholic Magazine* vol
      III no. xxv (February 1839) p.93

36   Present State, p.27. Letter from Pugin to Ambrose Phillipps, Phillipps 1, p.223.

37   Pugin to Lord Shrewsbury, 17 August 1841, HLRO 339/18, Belcher 2001, p. 262

38   Pugin to Lord Shrewsbury, 9 March 1842, HLRO 339/38, Belcher 2001, p. 329

39   Present State, p.75

40   Pugin to Lord Shrewsbury, 25 April 1844; V&A MS L. 525-1965/22, cat 38; of Diary 22-
27   April 1844.

41   Diary 3-6 July 1845, & V&A MS L.5190-1969, WW 1985, cat.1007

42   Undated, but internal references suggest late March 1844, HLRO 339/47

43   Castle Acre, Norfolk, which Pugin visited on his East Anglian tours. In Present State he says
      that the lower parts of the Cheadle screen will have "Images of the apostles and martyrs,
      painted in the severe style of Christian art" (p.79)

44   As above, n. 40

45   *Glossary* p. 84

46   *Staffordshire Advertiser*, 5 September 1846; Illustrated London News, 9 January 1847

47   The genealogy of Jesus was a favourite subject for medieval artists in stained glass, sculpture and
      embroidery. It was usually in the form of the winding trunk of a vine springing from the
      recumbent body of the patriarch Jesse. The various stems carried representations of his
      descendants, and at the top was the Virgin and Child. Pugin includes a description of such
      windows in the *Glossary*. Lord Shrewsbury paid for a similar window for S. George's, Southwark.

48   So he told Lord Shrewsbury; letter of 28 July 1843, HLRO 339/38. Minton was also producing
      large quantities of tiles of various patterns for the chancel of S. Mary's, Stafford, and which were
      in place by December 1844.

49   Lord Shrewsbury to Pugin, undated, but internal evidence suggests the winter of 1845-46; HLRO
      339/110

50   The Blessed Sacrament was still reserved from the Maundy Thursday Mass, but only for the
      Mass of the Presanctified on Good Friday.

51   Phillipps II, pp. 187-88.

52   The addition of the Blessed Sacrament Chapel had been agreed by the middle of August 1841; letter from Pugin to Lord Shrewsbury, 17 August 1841, HLRO 339/18, Belcher 2001, p. 262

53   Quoted by Stanton, *Pugin*, 1971, p.108.

54   Pugin to Lord Shrewsbury, 29 March 1846, HLRO 339/96

55   Pugin to Lord Shrewsbury, 22 May 1846, HLRO 339/5.

56   Pugin to Lord Shrewsbury, 13 February 1846, HLRO 339/15. In the same letter Pugin mentions the installation on the font, and the completion of the brass railing for the Blessed Sacrament chapel, which he describes as "really an extraordinary piece of work".

57   *Staffordshire Advertiser*, 5 July 1846

58   For example, at Shepshed (Leics.) Pugin built a small aisled church with screens, stained glass, and even a crypt, for £700; and at Southport he built S. Mary's for £1,500 "with every requisite for a parish church" (Gwynn, p.xii)

59   Day Books and correspondence, Birmingham Public Reference Library; GP p.182. The £1400 spent by Lord Shrewsbury on metalwork between 1845 and 1848 could have included items for elsewhere. Higham and Carson, *Pugin's Churches of the Second Spring* (1997) put the figure at £1280.

60   Pugin to Lord Shrewsbury, 5 December 1841, Stanton App. VI, pp.6-7, Belcher 2001, pp.298-99

61   Pugin to Lord Shrewsbury 25 April 1846, HLRO 339/2; and 22 May 1846, HLRO 339/5. Pugin suggested that Mr Wheelwright could also go up to S. John's, Alton, from time to time and look after the metalwork there.

62   Not to be confused with the Shrewsbury Arms (now the Wild Duck) in Alton village, the hotel at Farley was run by the Orrell family and a known originally as Orrell's Hotel. Now a private home, the building stands next to the main public entrance to Alton Towers.

63   Brian Andrews, "Pugin in Australia" GP, pp.246-257

64   *Some Remarks which Have Recently Appeared in the 'Rambler'*, 1851, p.9

65   Trappes-Lomax, *Pugin*, p.118

66   Lord Shrewsbury to Pugin, see above, n.49.

67   For the significance of Scott's restoration of S. Mary's, Stafford, see below, pp. 158-60

68   Diary 18-23 May 1844; letter from Pugin to Lord Shrewsbury 30 May 1844, V&A WW 1985 cat. 39: "The restoration of the Sainte Chapelle at Paris is worthy of the days of St. Louis".

69   Pugin to Lord Shrewsbury, Summer 1843, V&A WW 1985 no.31. Because most of the original decorations in S. Barnabas' Cathedral, Nottingham, have been obliterated, it is often forgotten that this church - to which Lord Shrewsbury contributed generously - was coloured almost as intensely as S. Giles'. Thomas Kearns, who worked at S. Giles' and at Alton, carried out the stencilling which survives only in the Blessed Sacrament Chapel.

70   Pugin to Lord Shrewsbury, 29 March 1846, HLRO 339/ Pugin speaks of the schools as having been "a large job & taken a good many men, & are not yet finished". "The schools look exceedingly well".

71   Higham and Carson, Pugin's *Churches of the Second Spring*, pp.39-40

72   W.G. Short, *Pugin's Gem*, p.9

73   Pugin to Edward James Willson, 16 August 1835, MS Johns Hopkins University, Baltimore, 11; Belcher 2001, p. 50. Pugin was referring to his early days as an acolyte at the Catholic church in Salisbury, but it could well apply to other occasions.

7 S. Wilfrid's, Cotton

1   Pugin to Lord Shrewsbury, 28th August 1841 HLRO 339/71. Mrs Sophia Winter is recorded in the 1841 Census as wife of George Winter, organist at the Towers Chapel. They may well have been related to the earl's chaplain. In those pre-ecumenical days, clergymen of the Anglican Church who attended Catholic worship could find themselves compromised. Pugin's friend, J.R.Bloxam, was once spotted on the tribune of the Towers Chapel during Mass, and was reported to the Bishop of Oxford by none other than J.H. Newman, then still an Anglican (See Belcher 2001, p.141)

2   Pugin to Lord Shrewsbury, 17th March 1841 HLRO 339/7, Blehcer 2001, p. 219

3   Phillipps, I, pp.275-6

4   Letter from Faber to Michael Watts Russell, 5th October 1846, R.Chapman, *Father Faber*, London, 1961, p. 156.

5   Lord Shrewsbury to Ambrose Phillipps, 16th April 1839, Phillipps, 1, p.106

6   Chapman, *op. cit.*, p. 167

7   Vandrival, p. 152

8   Faber to Newman, 18th March 1847, Chapman, *op. cit.*, pp. 166-7

9   Chapman, *op. cit.*, p. 168

10   *ibid.*

11   Gwynn p. 111

12   Present State, pp.65-66

13   S. Marie's, Newcastle (opened in 1844) has nave and chancel under one roof. It needs to be remembered that Cotton was both a parish church and a conventual one. Provision would have had to be made for the Brethren to sing their offices in choir, which would account for the intended position of the screen between the fourth and fifth bays, i.e. to create sufficient space for choir-stalls to the east of it.

14   Faber to Newman, Chapman, *op. cit.*, pp. 183-5. The letter is dated 28th May 1848. Pugin's diary shows that he was staying at Alton between May 5th and 10th, so the incident must have taken place sometime then, although there is no specific mention of S. Wilfrid's until June 25th when he was once again at Alton for a few days.

15   M. Trappes-Lomax, *Pugin,* London, 1932, p. 226

16   Newman to Ambrose Phillipps, 15th June 1848, Phillipps, II, pp.205-8

17   A.W. Pugin to Jane Pugin, 24th August 1851, V&A WW 1985 cat. 92

18   V&A Museum, Drawings Collection, E77(23) - 1970, WW 1985 no.280

19   Higham & Carson, *Pugin's Churches of the Second Spring*, Cheadle 1997, p.63

20.   So Faber called it in a letter to the Italian Marchese Leopoldo Bartolommei, Chapman, *op. cit.*, p. 153. S. Wilfrid's is now (2001) under the aegis of S. Giles', Cheadle. Because of a procedural fault, the Faber School was mistakenly taken under Local Authority control in 1944, but it retained - uniquely - its Catholic ethos and head teachers. In 1999 it reverted to voluntary-aided status within the Birmingham Archdiocese (Tim Cockin, *The Staffordshire Encyclopaedia*, Stoke-on-Trent, 2000, p.160)

8 S. Mary's, Brewood

1.   M.W.Greenslade and D.G. Stuart, *A History of Staffordshire*, 1998, p. 64

2.   Among the tombs at Albrighton is that of Sir John Talbot of Albrighton (d. 1555) from whom the Second Line of the Talbot Earls of Shrewsbury (1630-1856) was descended. Not only that; through his second marriage he was also the forebear of the Third Line, the Chetwynd Talbots, who succeeded to the titles after the Peerage Case following the death of the seventeenth earl, Bertram, in 1856. (See fig. 2, p. 22)

3.   The Giffards had a chapel at Chillington until the late 1780s when it was demolished during alterations to the hall. A chapel was then built at Black Ladies and was open by 1791. The Chillington chapel had an impressive array of altar-plate including a gold chalice and silver candlesticks, a silver crucifix and a silver ciborium (V. C. H. Staffs,. vol. 5, p. 44).

4   Virtually nothing remains above ground of the nunnery itself. The chapel was built at the side of the house. It was partly timber-framed. Two illustrations of it are reproduced in David Horovitz, *Brewood*, Horovitz, 1988.

5   Boscobel was at this time tenanted by the Catholic Penderel family. The present "royal oak" is said to have been grown from an acorn from the original tree which appears to have perished in the 18th century. See O.J. Weaver, *Boscobel House and White Ladies Priory*, English Heritage, London, 1987.

6   The Fitzherberts' principal residence was at Swynnerton, Staffordshire. They inherited the barony of Stafford on the extinction of the Jerningham family in 1913.

7   James Hicks Smith, *Brewood - A Resumé Historical and Topographical*, Wolverhampton 1867, p. 28: "Since the marriage of Thomas, nineteenth Lord of Chillington, the Giffard family have ceased to be all Roman Catholics, but the late Mr (Thomas) Giffard on his death-bed received the rites of the Church according to the Roman formula, and the same were celebrated over his body before it left Chillington".

8   Richmond was Vice-President at Oscott, under Henry Weedall, when Pugin delivered the first of his definitive lectures on ecclesiastical art and architecture in November 1837. Two subsequent lectures given in 1838 formed the basis of The True Principles of Christian Architecture published in 1841. For details of Pugin's career at Oscott see R. O'Donnell, "Pugin at Oscott" in Judith F. Champ (ed.), *Oscott College, 1838-1988*, Oscott 1988

9   HLRO 339/26. In another letter to Lord Shrewsbury dated June 1843 (V&A Museum WW no. 29), Pugin states his intention of going to Brewood.

10   HLRO 339.26

11   P.J. Doyle, *The Giffards of Chillington: A Catholic Landed Family 1642-1861*, unpublished University of Durham M.A. thesis, 1968, p. 244 (copy in William Salt Library, Stafford)

12   Robert Richmond to George Richmond, 20th January 1844, BAA P99/8/45

13   Letter from Pugin to Lord Shrewsbury, 28th July 1843, HLRO 339/83

14   P.J. Doyle, *op. cit.*, p. 244

15   *ibid.*, p. 250

16   BOE: Staffordshire, p. 79.

17   Patricia Spencer-Silver, *Pugin's Builder: The Life and Work of George Myers*, University of Hull Press, 1993, p. 251. *The Tablet*, 24th June 1844, gives the cost of the church alone as £1,345.

18   *The Tablet*, 24th June 1844, quoted by James Hicks Smith, Brewood, 1867

19   Pugin had to fight Lord Shrewsbury's proposal to introduce a similar seating arrangement at S. Giles', Cheadle (see above, p. 100). The Religious Census of 1851 records that S. Mary's was always filled to its capacity of c.400 at the 10 a.m. Mass, and usually about two-thirds full at the

afternoon service that S. Mary's was always filled to its capacity of c.400 at the 10 a.m. Mass, and usually about two-thirds full at the afternoon service

20   P.J. Doyle, *op. cit.*, p. 251

21   James Hicks Smith, *op, cit.*, p. 21. A collection of documents in BAA (P99/14-20) concerns investigations into the age of the statue, and sampling of the substance exuding from it. Fr. Grady, parish priest of Brewood, sought permission from Archbishop Dwyer to re-establish devotions to Our Lady of Brewood, but was advised against it.

22   William Richmond to George Richmond, 18th June 1845, BAA P99/8/51

9 Unfinished Business

1   An account of the funeral was published in *Illustrated London News*, 25 December 1852. See above, p. 41, and also ATGW pp. 154-5,

2   *Staffordshire Advertiser*, 23 August 1856.

3   Earl Bertram to E.W. Pugin, 8 November 1851, HLRO 339/114.

4   Lord Shrewsbury to A.W, Pugin 1 March 1852, HLRO 339/112..

5   Birmingham Museum, private collection, L.25.83.

6   The painting is currently at Shrewsbury cathedral. It is shown in GP p.264.

7   Shrewsbury papers, SCRO D/240/E/F/9/25.

8   It was photographed by National Monuments Record in 1951, and the photograph is reproduced in ATGW, 141 p.135.

9   VCH Staffs., vol. VIII, p.273.

10   This is the opinion of Dr. R. O'Donnell, who has also kindly supplied references to S. Gregory's in *Building News*- 1868, pp. 152 & 351 , and *The Builder*, 1868, pp. 200 & 498. Pugin appears to have incorporated some of his unexecuted ideas for S. Austin's, Stafford, notably the high chancel and gabled apse (see below, n. 14)

11   See above, p. 18

12   The others were at S. Mary's, Nottingham, and S. Chad's, Birmingham; *Dublin Review* May 1841, reprinted in *Present State* (p.27). The font no longer exists.

13   James Joll, "A Pugin Commission", The Decorative Arts Society, Journal, no. 24 (2000) pp. 6-18.

14   A set of six large drawings for S. Austin's, signed by E.W. Pugin, are in the Birmingham Archdiocesan archive., (BAA APD/P255/1-6). They include elevations, sections, and alternative schemes for the west front. A southeast prospect of the proposed church was produced for a Mission Book (BAA P255/5/1) which is the one shown in pl. 116.

15   See below, p. 160

16   For a history and description of the church, see M.W. Greenslade, *Saint Austin's, Stafford*, Archdiocese of Birmingham Historical Commission, 1998

17   SCRO D(W)1734/3/,1/109

18   SCRO D/71 8/5/11, dated 19 October 1841. It is a certificate in respect of work done by George Myers at S. Augustine's, Kenilworth, and addressed to Mr Hemhurst (*recte* Amherst) at Oscott. Amherst must have later passed it on to Francis Whitgreave, and it is now amongst a small collection of Whitgreave papers held at SCRO. The collection does not, unfortunately, contain anything relating to the building of Burton Manor.

19   Mary Francis Roskell, *Memoirs of Francis Kerril Amherst, D.D.*, London 1903, p. 157. The month is given as July. but Pugin's Diary makes it clear that they sailed on June 1st

20   The contract - in Arabic - for the hire of five carriers and dromedaries for the journey from Cairo to Ramlet is amongst the Whitgreave papers, SCRO D/718/5/4-5. There was a third member of the expedition, François Baudry.

21   Pugin to Lord Shrewsbury, 1847. HLRO 339/49 "Francis Whitgreave sailed from Marseilles some weeks ago & the vessel has not been heard of since".

22   A.W. Pugin to Jane Pugin, October 1849, George Whitgreave was actually 63 at the time but the point is academic.

23   William White, *Directory of Staffordshire*, 1851, p.455.

24   C. Calvert, *History of Stafford*, 1886, p.,44. A lozenge-shaped stone plaque with a floriated cross was built into the foundations on the north side of the house where it was photographed before being obscured by the extensions built in 1930. According to some, this was the Greyfriars' cross (Information supplied by Mr B. Astbury, Bursar, Stafford Grammar School).

25   Information supplied by Mr. R.E.L. Button. No plans of Burton Manor appear to have survived; title deeds held by the school go back no further than 1913 when the Whitgreave family relinquished the Manor., and enquiries amongst present-day descendants of the Whitgreaves for early documentation have so far proved fruitless

26   *Staffordshire Advertiser* 10 January 1857.

27   A list of articles from Alton Towers is annexed to the will of Minna, Duchess of Norfolk, and mother of Lord Edmund Howard, dated 10 December 1873. There were some forty items in all, and many of these can be identified as having been in the chapel corridor at Alton from William Adam's detailed description of what was there in 1851, *Gem of the Peak*, 1851, p.261. A few of the items are still at Arundel Castle. I am grateful to Miss A.P. Taylor, Archivist at Arundel, for supplying me with a copy of the list, and for other useful information. Over fifty maps, plans and surveys of the Alton estate 17th - 19th century are currently in the Arundel Archives.

28   e.g. *The Times*, 8 July 1857; *Staffordshire Advertiser*, 11 July, 18 July, and 1August 1857. See also ATGW p. 159. The sale was conducted by Christie & Manson. The contents of the libraries were auctioned separately in London by Sotheby's, 22 June - 3 July 1857.

29   *Mary Howitt – An Autobiography*, London 1889, vol. II pp. 127-9.

30   "The eves of all wait upon thee, O Lord" - Psalm 145.

31   *Rambler*, NS VII, 1857, pp 318-323. Reference supplied by Dr. R. O'Donnell.

32   Phillipps and Scott Murray' were promised £40,000 each. In the end Phillipps received only £11,000. He set out the facts in a letter written to his son Everard in January 1853, Phillipps, II, pp.339-40. The greater part of the unsettled estate passed to Lord Edmund Howard whose name was then changed to Lord Edmund Talbot. The legal battle did not end until 1867. Hope-Scott and Serjeant Bellasis made a further appeal, and they recovered, on behalf of Lord Edmund, a considerable part of the unentailed estate (including Grafton Manor) which Earl Talbot had been awarded in the first place. Edward Bellasis, *Memorials of Mr. Serjeant Bellasis*, London. 1893. pp. 15-16

33   *Staffordshire Advertiser*, 4 July 1927

10 The Anglican Dimension

1   *Present State*, p.56

2   *Ecclesiologist*, January 1846. For an examination of the relationship between Pugin and the Camden Society, see R. O'Donnell, "Blink by [him] in silence"? Webster & Elliott (eds.), *"A Church as it should be"*, *The Cambridge Camden Society and its Influence*, 2002, pp. 98-120

3   Pugin to William Osmond, 3rd January 1834, original in a private collection; Belcher 2001, p.

23. The pupil of "the wretch" was Joseph Potter who preceded Pugin as architect at Oscott.

4   George Gilbert Scott, *Personal and Professional Recollections*, 1879, p. 97

5   Jesse Watts Russell had already rebuilt Ilam Hall (near Ashbourne) in Gothic style, and added an octagonal chapel to Ilam church. He had obviously come under the influence of the Ecclesiological Movement, and his second son, Michael, was one of the "Oxford Men" who followed Newman into the Roman Catholic Church.

6   Phillipps to Lord Shrewsbury, undated but probably 1841, Phillipps, I, pp. 79-80

7   *Staffordshire Advertiser*, 21st December 1844 : "...The Church is now one of which not only the Town but the County of Stafford may well be proud - the highest authority perhaps, on such a subject, Mr Pugin, the celebrated Ecclesiastical Architect and Author (who has, we believe, seen it more than once), having pronounced it the best restoration which has been effected in modern times",

8   John Masfen, *Views of the Church of St Mary at Stafford*, London, 1852

9   Pugin to J.R. Bloxam, 13 April 1841, MS University of St. Andrew's, Ward Papers V, 15; Belcher 2001 pp.231-2. It was the *Tracts for the Times*, written by Newman and others which gave the name Tractarian to the Movement which sought to emphasise the continuity of the Church of England with the Medieval Church. Tract XC caused a great furore by maintaining that even the most protestant of the Thirty-Nine Articles of Religion (1562) could be interpreted in a wholly Catholic manner. For Bagot's role in this controversy see Owen Chadwick, *The Victorian Church*, vol. I (London 1971), pp. 186-7, 194-5.

10 Information kindly supplied by Lady Bagot from the nineteenth-century diaries of Mary and Ann Bagot.

11 A.W.N. Pugin, Diary,, 3 October 1845.

12 BOE: Staffordshire, p. 174

13 Kenneth Beaulah and Hans van Lemmen, *Church Tiles of the Nineteenth Century*, 1987, p. 15. Stanton (Pugin, 1971, p. 203) refers to a drawing by Pugin of the chancel floor at Leigh, and a remark in a letter that he designed the tiles.

14 Pugin's Diary records visits to Blithfield on 17 January and 6-7 June 1851. Payments, in respect of "windows Blithfield" and "Bagot" are noted in the front end-papers. Stanton op. cit, credits Pugin with the glass of the east window, but she must have meant the east window of the clerestory. The chancel east window was re-glazed in 1856 as a memorial to Bishop Bagot who died in 1854. It was replaced in 1965.

15 The watercolour by Charlotte Sneyd, is dated 1852, but clearly shows the interior of the church as it was prior to the restoration of the chancel. There is heraldic glass in the east window (SCRO D4752/3). See also Pevsner, *Staffordshire*, p. 72, and Stanton, *op. cit.*, p. 205. The stone pulpit, has been attributed to Pugin, but, as Pevsner says, "It does not look it".

16 Pugin to Lord Shrewsbury, 13th May 1847, HLR0 339/130

17 The principal entrance to Alton Towers in those days was not the present visitor entrance on the Alton-Farley road, but the Quixhill Gate at Denstone. The Classical gateway remains, but it no longer belongs to Alton Towers.

18 A.J. Beresford Hope, "the Nestor of Ecclesiology" was the wealthy patron of the living who in 1853 gave the remote Moorland living of Sheen to fellow-ecclesiologist and Secretary of the Camden Society, Benjamin Webb, who engaged William Butterfield to complete the rebuilding of the church. A choir school was planned, and a parish library and reading room were provided. The *Ecclesiologist* commented, "the general effect is that of an ecclesiastical colony in the wilds of Australia"; V.C.H Staffs, vol. VII, p. 248

19 The early history of Denstone, including details of services and preachers in the 1860s and '70s is meticulously recorded in a contemporary hand-written volume currently held at the vicarage.

20 Quoted by David Verey, "George Frederick Bodley", J. Fawcett (ed.), *Seven Victorian Architects*,

1976, p. 89

21 Halifax was one of the leading figures in the attempt to secure formal recognition by Rome of the validity of Anglican Orders upon which no pronouncement bad been made since the Reformation. Notwithstanding the eventual condemnation of Anglican Orders by Pope Leo XIII in 1896, Lord Halifax continued discussions, notably with Cardinal Mercier in the Malines Conversations of the 1920s. See J.G. Lockhart, *Charles Lindley Wood, Viscount Halifax*, 1935.

22 Lockhart, *op, cit.*, p. 218

23 Shaw made this comment in a conversation with the builder, James Heath, 21st September 1887, and it is recorded in Heath's very detailed diaries for 1885-7 which contain a day-by-day account of how All Saints' was built (private collection).

24 Andrew Saint, *Richard Norman Shaw*, Yale, 1976, p. 308

25 James Heath of Endon and Leek. He used pink sandstones from Ladderedge, and gritstones from nearby Kniveden, and the Roaches. See above, note 23

26 Apology, p. 21

27 R.N. Shaw writing to Mrs Foster, the patron of the church he was building at Richard's Castle, Shropshire, GP, p. 21.

28 In 1828 Lord Shrewsbury, had subscribed £130 towards £700 needed to build a Catholic chapel in Leek. Like most of the other North Staffordshire missions, it was ripe for replacement by the 1840s. A scheme was in place by 1841, and Pugin would undoubtedly have been the architect, but the sudden increase in the size and cost, of S. Barnabas', Nottingham resulted in the shelving of the plan. "I fear we shall be obliged to defer Leek," he wrote to Walsh in November 1841 (BAA B606; Belcher 2001 p.294-5)

29 *Present State*, p. 83

30 *ibid*, "We cannot yet hope to revive the expression and finish of the old work, but we may readily restore its general character...... We may have made great improvements in steam-engines, but not in frontals and orphreys"

31 Thomas Wardle (1831-1909) was churchwarden of S. Edward's church at Cheddleton, near Leek, and a friend of William Morris. In 1863 he brought in Gilbert Scott Jun. to restore the chancel at Cheddleton, which was furnished with a screen and a reredos made from a fifteenth-century Flemish carving of the Deposition to which Morris added side panels to make a triptych. These, together with sonic fine Morris glass, and items of Leek embroidery, make this an important building in the context of the Gothic Revival.

32 The fascinating history of the Leek Embroidery Society and the Wardle family is told in detail by Ann Jacques, *The Wardle Story*, Leek, 1996.

33 Quoted by Ferrey p. 260, who refers to it as a quote printed in *The Tablet*, 15th September 1852.

34 *Worship and Architecture*, an unpublished book written by George Pace between 1963 and 1975, and quoted by P. Pace, *The Architecture of George Pace*, London, 1990, p. 47

SELECT BIBLIOGRAPHY

Archival material

Birmingham Archdiocesan Archives, S. Chad's Cathedral, Birmingham.

Brimingham City Archives, Birmingham Museum.

House of Lords Record Office: Pugin Family MSS in a Private Collection (MSS PC Franklin), Historical Collection 339.

Staffordshire County Record Office. The Shrewsbury Papers, D240.

Victoria & Albert Museum, London: Pugin diaries, letters, correspondence between Pugin and Lord Shrewsbury; some drawings of items for Alton Towers chapel etc., Crace Archive.

Unpublished Research

Doyle, P.J., *The Giffards of Chillington: A Catholic Landed Family 1642-1861*, University of Durham M.A.thesis, 1968

Stanton, Phoebe, *Welby Pugin and the Gothic Revival*, University of London Ph.D. thesis, 1950

Printed Sources

Adam, William, *The Gem of the Peak*, London, J.& C. Mozley, various editions, 1838-1857. The 5th edition (1851) is the one most frequently referred to in this book.

Anon *The Life of Cornelia Connelly*, 1809-1879, London: Longmans 1924

Atterbury, Paul, and Clive Wainwright (ed.), *Pugin: A Gothic Passion*. New Haven; London: Yale University Press, 1994

The Bard Graduate Centre for Studies in the Decorative Arts, New York, *A. W.N. Pugin, Master of Gothic Revival*, New Haven and London: Yale University Press, 1995

Belcher, M., *A.W.N. Pugin: An Annotated Critical Biography*, London: Mansell, 1987

- - *The Collected Letters of A.W.N. Pugin*, Vol. I, 1830-1842, Oxford: Oxford University Press, 2001

Champ, J. (ed.), *Oscott College, 1838-1988*, Oscott, 1988

Chapman, R., *Father Faber*, London: Burns & Oates, 1961

Cockin, T., *The Staffordshire Encyclopaedia*, Barlaston: Malthouse Press, 2000

Ferrey, Benjamin, *Recollections of Pugin and his father Augustus Pugin*, 1861; Reprint; Introduction and index by Clive and Jane Wainwright, London: Scholar Press, 1978

Fisher, Michael J., *Alton Towers: A Gothic Wonderland*, Stafford: M.J. Fisher, 1999

Fisher, Michael J., *A Vision of Splendour*, Stafford: M.J. Fisher, 1995

Gillow, J., *A Literary and Biographical History, or Bibliographical Dictionary, of the English Catholics; from the Breach with Rome in 1534 to the Present Time*: 5 vols., London and New York, 1885-1903.

Greenslade, M., *Saint Austin's, Stafford,* Birmingham: Archdiocese of Birmingham Historical Commission, 1998

Gwynn, Denis, *Lord Shrewsbury, Pugin, and the Catholic Revival*, London: Hollis & Carter 1946

- - *The Second Spring*, 1818-1852, London: The Catholic Book Club, 1944

Higham D. & Carson P., *Pugin's Churches of the Second Spring*, Cheadle, 1997

Pevsner, Nikolaus, *The Buildings of England: Staffordshire*, Harmondsworth, Penguin Books Ltd., 1974

Pugin, Augustus Welby Northmore, *An Apology for the Revival of Christian Architecture in England*, London: John Weale, 1843

- - *Contrasts, or a Parallel between the Noble Edifices of the Middle Ages and Corresponding Buildings Shewing the Present Decay of Taste*, 2nd edition, London: Dolman, 1841

- - *Glossary of Ecclesiastical Ornament and Costume*, London: Henry Bohn, 1844

- - *Gothic Furniture in the Style of the 15th Century*, London: Ackerman, 1835

- - *The True Principles of Pointed or Christian Architecture*, 1841. Reprint, Oxford: St. Barnabas Press, 1969.

- - *The Present State of Ecclesiastical Architecture in England*, London: Dolman, 1843

Purcell. E.S., *Life and Letters of Ambrose Phillipps de Lisle*, 2 vols, London: Macmillan, 1900

Redfern, Francis, *History and Antiquities of the Town and Neighbourhood of Uttoxeter*, 2nd edn., 1886

Rock, Daniel, *Hierurgia*; or, *The Holy Sacrifice of the Mass*, 2 vols., London, Joseph Booker, 1833 (vol. I dedicated to John, 16th Earl of Shrewsbury).

- - *The Church of Our Fathers*, 3 vols., London: Dolman, 1849-54

Short, W.G., *Pugin's Gem*, Cheadle, 1981

Speake, Robert, (ed.), *A History of Alton and Farley*, Keele: Centre for Adult Education, Keele University, 1996

Spencer-Silver, Patricia, *Pugin's Builder: The Life and Work of George Myers*, Hull: Hull University Press, 1993

Stanton, Phoebe, *Pugin*, London: Thames & Hudson, 1971

- - "Some Comments on the Life and Work of A.W.N. Pugin", RIBA Journal, 3rd Series, 60 (December 1952)

Trappes-Lomax, Michael, *Pugin. A Medieval Victorian*, London: Sheed & Ward, 1932

Ward, Bernard, *The Sequel to Catholic Emancipation*, London & New York: Longmans, Green & Co., 1915

Webster, C. & Elloitt J., *"A Church as it should be": The Cambridge Camden Society and its influence*, Stamford, Shaun Tyas, 2000

Wedgwood, A., *Catalogue of the Drawings Collection of the Royal Institute of British Architects, The Pugin Family*, Farnborough: Gregg International, 1977

- - *Catalogue of the Architectural Drawings in the Victoria & Albert Museum: A. W. N. Pugin and the Pugin Family*, London: Victoria & Albert Museum, 1985.

Zeloni, A., *Vie de la Princesse Borghese*, Paris, 1843

GLOSSARY OF ECCLESIASTICAL TERMS

AGNUS DEI Literally "Lamb of God", it is a an artistic representation of Christ shown as a Lamb bearing a flag with a Cross upon it. Agnus Dei is also a devotion said during Mass.

ALTAR The most important item in a church. Made of stone or wood, it is the place where the Holy Sacrifice of the Eucharist is offered. On the surface of the altar (the mensa) five crosses are incised, representing the Five Wounds of Christ. The principal altar is known as the High Altar.

AUMBRY A small cupboard set in the wall close to the altar, used for the keeping of sacred vessels. In medieval times, and currently in many Anglican churches, an aumbry is used for the Reservation of the Blessed Sacrament.

BAPTISTERY The area of the church - normally at the west end - where the font is situated, and sometimes defined by structural screenwork.

BENEDICTION A service of devotion to the Presence of Christ in the Blessed Sacrament. A blessing is given by the priest, using the Sacrament enclosed in a vessel known as a monstrance (q.v.).

BENEDICTION ALTAR An altar and reredos (q.v.) with a large central niche above the tabernacle (q.v.) on which the monstrance is placed for Benediction.

CHALICE A cup made of precious metal used to contain the wine at Mass

CHASUBLE The principal priestly vestment worn at Mass. It is found in two main styles; "Gothic" which is very full, and "Latin" which has the sides cut away for ease of movement.

COPE A semi-circular full-length cloak, often elaborately embroidered, worn in processions and at Benediction. It is fastened across the chest with a clasp known as a morse.

CRUETS Jug-shaped vessels used to contain the unconsecrated wine and water used in the Mass

DE PROFUNDIS "Out of the deep....... the opening words of Psalm 130 which is often used in prayer for the Departed.

DOOM A representation of the Last Judgement showing Christ in glory surrounded by angels and saints, welcoming the Blessed and condemning the wicked. In medieval times the Doom was painted over the chancel arch

HERSE A frame covered with cloth and ornamented with banners and lights, set up over the coffin in funeral ceremonies.

HOST A large wafer of unleavened bread which is consecrated in the Mass.
The word derives from the Latin hostia (victim), signifying the Body of Christ.

MASS The name given to the Church's principal act of worship in which the Last Supper is recalled, and in which bread and wine are consecrated to be the Body and Blood of Christ. It is also known at the Eucharist ("Thanksgiving") and Holy Communion. The word "Mass" (Missa) is derived from the concluding words of dismissal in the Latin Rite, *Ite, missa est.* "High" Mass is celebrated with music, incense, and elaborate ceremonial. "Low" Mass is said rather than sung, and the priest is usually attended by only one server (assistant).

MISSAL	The book containing the texts of the Mass, used by the priest at the altar.
MONSTRANCE	An ornate vessel, often of precious metal, for the exposition of the Host (q.v.) for veneration and the rite of Benediction
PATEN	The plate, usually of precious metal, on which the Host is placed.
PYX	A metal container for the reservation of the Host, and for carrying the Reserved Sacrament to the sick and dying.
REREDOS	A picture, sculpture, or hanging placed behind the altar.
ROOD	A large crucifix, often flanked by figures of Our Lady and S. John, and carried on a beam or rood-screen spanning the chancel arch.
SACRISTY	The place in a church where the sacred vessels and vestments are kept.
SACRARIUM	recess in the wall close to an altar, with a shelf for the cruets (q.v.), and a stone basin (piscina) for washing the vessels and the priest's hands.
SANCTUARY LAMP	A hanging lamp suspended before an altar. A lamp showing a clear white light signifies that the Blessed Sacrament is reserved nearby. Blue is used at altars dedicated to Our Lady, and red elsewhere.
SEDILIUM(A)	The seat, or seats of the Sacred Ministers (Priest, Deacon, Subdeacon) at Mass; normally on the south side of the sanctuary.
STOLE	A priestly vestment resembling a narrow scarf, often embroidered.
STOUP	A vessel placed near the door of church, containing holy water used to make the sign of the cross by those entering, as a reminder of their baptism.
TABERNACLE	A small safe fixed centrally at the altar, and used for the Reservation of the Blessed Sacrament
TRIPTYCH	A carved or painted panel, often a reredos (q.v.) which has two folding panels enabling it to be closed up.
VESTMENT	The collective name used of any garments worn by the priest at Mass

INDEX
(Numbers of illustrations printed in italics)